HENRY SLOANE COFFIN

HENRY SLOANE COFFIN

HENRY SLOANE COFFIN

THE MAN AND HIS MINISTRY

by

Morgan Phelps Noyes

CHARLES SCRIBNER'S SONS

New York

CONTENTS

FOREWORD

"THERE was no more vivid and brilliant personality in the Christian Church of his time," wrote John Baillie of Edinburgh when he received the news of Henry Sloane Coffin's death. "It takes the colour out of things," he added, quoting a remark made to him by David Cairns at the time of William Temple's passing. "Henry had lent so much colour and life and grace to the whole scene in which we all moved for a very long period— and for me ever since I first heard him preach in St. George's and the High Church of Edinburgh when I was only eighteen or twenty years of age." It is with the hope that younger generations may take courage and hope for their tasks from the story of this man and his ministry that this book has been written.

It would be impossible to name all the persons who have helped generously in the gathering together of the materials which have gone into these pages. The author's greatest debt of gratitude is to Mrs. Henry Sloane Coffin who made available her husband's letters and papers with the single request that his critics as well as his admirers should be heard. Dr. Henry Pitney Van Dusen, while President of Union Theological Seminary, furnished material from the seminary. Both Mrs. Van Dusen and he read the manuscript and made helpful suggestions. Mr. Reuben A. Holden, Secretary of Yale University, gave the writer access to files from his office. Dr. and Mrs. James M. Howard had in their possession notes written by Dr. Coffin about his pastorate in the Madison Avenue Presbyterian Church and an unpublished manuscript of their own dealing with that period. These they permitted the writer to use. Dr. Harry Emerson Fosdick kindly gave his consent to the publication of an important letter which he had written to Dr. Coffin. Others too numerous to mention cooperated in the production of this record and to them all the author expresses his heartfelt thanks.

MORGAN PHELPS NOYES

HENRY SLOANE COFFIN

EARLY YEARS

THE life and ministry of Henry Sloane Coffin constitutes one of the most significant chapters in the story of the Christian Church in the United States during the first half of the twentieth century. As minister of the Madison Avenue Presbyterian Church in New York City, he was for twenty years a preacher and pastor who combined intellectual brilliance, profound Christian conviction, warm interest in all sorts of people and social concern in a balance which led many of his contemporaries to regard his pastorate as a demonstration of the Christian ministry at its best.

His ministry coincided with a period of theological discussion when the scientific theories of the late nineteenth century were puzzling many people in the Christian churches. Dr. Coffin through his theological writing and preaching made the basic Christian convictions persuasive to many who would otherwise have felt out of place in the churches.

It was a time of awakening social conscience, when problems produced by a rapidly growing industrial society were becoming acute. In bringing the Christian ethic to bear upon these problems of a perplexed society, he was a fearless and constructive interpreter.

Deeply committed to the Church as the body of Christ in which he was called to serve his generation, he gave distinguished leadership to his own denomination while he labored effectively to bring about cooperation among the various communions and the eventual unity of the whole Church. As President of Union Theological Seminary in New York City, which Dr. William Temple, Archbishop of Canterbury, called "the greatest theological college in the world," Dr. Coffin set high standards for the training of ministers of all denominations from 1926 to 1945, and was widely recognized as the foremost theological educator of the time. Behind these varied activities was the man himself, indescribable to those who never knew him, unforgettable to everyone who had even a fleeting contact with him. Endowed with a keen and vigorous mind, profoundly and honestly religious, one of the most fascinating of conversationalists, delighting in the friendship of all sorts and conditions of men, gay and overflowing with high spirits and yet deadly in earnest about the things in which he believed, he was one of the rare people who are the center of any group in which they appear. Yet he never claimed the center but sought to bring out leadership in other people around him.

He was born on January 5, 1877, at his family home, 13 West 57th Street, New York City. He was baptized by the Reverend John Hall, D.D., at the Fifth Avenue Presbyterian Church, a few blocks south of the Coffin home, on April 8, 1877. The neighborhood was in the heart of the mid-town residential district, and in the "brown stone fronts" of the streets which Henry Coffin walked as a boy lived families who were leaders in the life of the city. A few doors from the Coffin home, at 5 West 57th Street, lived the Roosevelts, whose son Theodore brought his bride home to live with his family for a brief time in 1880. It is not likely that Henry Coffin took any personal interest in that event, but from his earliest years he was among people to whom civic leadership and public service were regarded as obligations to be prepared for and accepted. An old family notebook records the fact that early summers were spent at Long Branch and Elberon, New Jersey, before Southampton, Long Island, became the scene of summer holidays for the Coffin family. The same notebook has records of brief visits to Saratoga, New York, and to Manchester, Vermont, while Henry was still a young child. These were all places frequented by people from New York City. Although he was to become to a marked degree a citizen of the world, Henry Coffin never ceased to be a New Yorker through and through in a sense never duplicated among those transplanted to the city from elsewhere. He had a deep love for the city of his birth to which he often referred in Biblical language as "a city set upon a hill" and as "no mean city." He was proud of the city's achievements, felt a personal obligation to serve its highest interests, and grieved over its civic sins. His entire ministry was to be spent in the city where he was born, a record for which there are few parallels in an era of rapidly shifting populations.

People who like to trace out the influences in his background which revealed themselves in his character and life point out that he had both the New England tradition and the Scottish inheritance in his make-up. He himself sometimes jokingly referred to the Yankee and the Scot in his ancestry, and if industry, profound respect for intellect, hard-headed shrewdness coupled with idealism and a deeply religious nature be the marks of those traditions, he was the product and heir of them both.

His father, Edmund Coffin, was born at 20 University Place in New York City on November 8, 1844, and spent his life as an attorney-at-law in the city. Henry's grandfather, also an Edmund Coffin, was born at Saco, Maine, whither his family had migrated from Newbury, Massachusetts. He went to live in New York City in 1832 or thereabouts. In the City Directory of 1841–1842 his name appears as a Merchant at 41 Exchange Place with a house at One Park Place. Later he moved to an outlying section. When Henry Coffin discussed the changes which transform New York City neighborhoods he was fond of referring to the fact that his grandfather had a farm on what had since become 69th Street.

He had in mind a lease of land between Bloomingdale Road and the River on which his grandfather had a large house and grounds, a stable, a well, cows, horses, wagons, etc. The grandfather subsequently had a place at Irvington, New York, on the Hudson River. There Henry Coffin's family spent some of their summers with him. Mrs. William Sloane, Henry's maternal grandmother, accompanied them and the combined families enjoyed a congenial comradeship. Henry Coffin did not talk as much about his New England ancestry as he did about his Scottish forbears, but through his father's family New England was an important element in his background.

The Scottish influence, in which he took great delight, came through his mother's family, the Sloanes. His grandfather, William Sloane, came to the United States from Edinburgh in 1834, crossing the ocean on the Brig *Atlantic*, the voyage taking something over sixty days. After nine years of employment in a carpet house in which his brother-in-law, William Douglas, was a partner, he founded a carpet business of his own and in 1852 admitted his brother John to partnership, the firm taking the name "W. and J. Sloane." He was an active churchman, at one time serving as Treasurer of the Fifth Avenue Presbyterian Church. In Scotland he had married Euphemia Douglas of Dunfermline who followed him to America. They had four sons, John, William, Thomas and Henry. Their daughter Euphemia married Edmund Coffin. Euphemia Douglas Sloane exerted a profound influence upon her grandson Henry Coffin in his early years. The house at 13 West 57th Street was her home, and the Coffin family lived with her all through Henry Coffin's boyhood. She carried him as an infant in her arms while she talked to him in the broad Scottish accent which she never lost. She taught him the Shorter Catechism when he was a young boy, and communicated to him the deep respect for the ministry as the highest of callings which was characteristic of the Scotland of her day. At her death the house came into the Coffins' possession. Her influence on her grandson continued throughout his life. He was drawn naturally to Scotland for theological study after his undergraduate course at Yale and with a minimum of adjustment found himself thoroughly at home in Scottish friendships which he made easily and lastingly. Later on as a pastor he would delight his parishioners of Scottish origin by talking with them in the Scottish dialect which was an echo of his grandmother's tones so accurately reproduced that his hearers found it difficult to believe that he had not himself grown up among the heather. He took special delight in Scottish humor and loved to repeat quaint remarks of canny or cautious Scots whom he had known. But it was something deeper than this that he owed to his Scottish background—an unsentimental but strong piety, a devout sense of reverence and awe before the majesty of God, a basic conviction that he was responsible to God for the use of the talents entrusted to him.

While a student in Edinburgh in 1898, he was invited to preach in the Queen Anne Street United Free Church of Dunfermline in which his grandmother had been baptized. In commenting on his sermon, the local newspaper in Dunfermline made this interesting report:

"The Reverend Henry Sloane Coffin, M.A., of New York, who preached for the Reverend R. Alexander in the church of his grandparents and great-grandparents afforded most pleasing evidence of the Dunfermline impress in spite of long separation. His accent and utterance were much more Dunfermline than American. They were characteristic of the speech of educated Dunfermline people familiar from their youth not only with the Scriptures but with the manner in which they are read in our pulpits."

Through the Sloane heritage, the tradition of Scottish Presbyterianism became one of the dominant factors in Henry Coffin's thought and work.

Edmund Coffin, Henry's father, was graduated from Yale in 1866. As a lawyer he numbered distinguished citizens and corpo-

rations among his clients, but he spent much time with his two
sons, Henry and William. He personally supervised their study
during their earlier years. Henry Coffin in his mature years attributed his ability to get work done on schedule to his father's
training. The father would give the boys a definitely allotted
period in which to learn a lesson. If they failed to learn the
lesson in the appointed time, no further study of that particular
material was permitted. There was nothing for it but to go to
school unprepared, the father contending that if they could not
learn it in the time he had allowed them for the task, they deserved to fail. By this Spartan discipline he developed in his sons
a capacity for meeting a deadline in getting work done which
was the admiration and envy of many who worked with them in
later years.

Edmund Coffin was a man of strong convictions, steadfast principles from which he did not swerve, undemonstrative but deep
in his affections and loyalties. Of scrupulously honest mind, he
was one of a generation which had difficulty in reconciling the
knowledge science had opened up in the late nineteenth century
with some of the creedal formulations of the Churches. He therefore never became a church member, although he was a regular
church attendant and in his later years was a Trustee of the Brick
Presbyterian Church in New York City where his younger son,
William Sloane Coffin, was an elder and a Church School Superintendent. As attorney for the Phelps Dodge Corporation he was
associated in various matters with Mr. Cleveland H. Dodge who
was one of the principal financial supporters of Dwight L. Moody.
When Mr. Moody held his evangelistic meetings in New York
City, Edmund Coffin was called upon to act as treasurer of the
campaign. In that capacity he developed a profound admiration
for the evangelist, not only as a religious leader but also as a man
beyond criticism in all his financial dealings. Through his relationship with Mr. D. Willis James, Edmund Coffin also became
the attorney for the Union Theological Seminary of New York
City. In 1893 a Union Seminary professor, Charles Augustus

Briggs, was tried for heresy by the Presbyterian Church in the U.S.A. In the heated atmosphere which the trial engendered, some misinformed and unfounded statements were made about the Seminary's alleged dishonesty in its financial relationships with the Presbyterian denomination. In the Seminary's interest, Edmund Coffin sat through the hearings as the institution's legal representative. By his side sat his elder son, Henry, then sixteen years of age, getting his initiation into a theological controversy in which thirty years later he was to be a leader and a healing force. When it became apparent that it would be to Union Seminary's advantage to move from its location at the corner of Seventieth Street and Park Avenue to a site farther uptown and nearer other educational centers, as the representative of Mr. D. Willis James, Edmund Coffin was active in purchasing lots and in assembling the real estate on which the Seminary's Quadrangle now stands, between Broadway and Claremont Avenue, extending from 120th Street to 122nd Street. Henry Coffin's later devotion to Union Seminary was therefore in a sense an hereditary interest.

Edmund Coffin lived to be eighty-five years of age and died in 1929. Those who knew him in his latter years remember him as a gentleman of the old school, erect, dignified, courteous and kindly. There was a vein of iron and no nonsense in him. He was proud of his minister son and rejoiced in his usefulness but he never hesitated to differ from him on questions on which they took divergent positions. He gave to his sons' wives the tenderness and warm affection which he would have given his daughters had there been any. When he was over eighty he was invited to be one of the guests of honor at a dinner to which former Yale oarsmen were invited. He went with alacrity but returned home somewhat disappointed. "They only asked me to stand up and be exhibited as an example of longevity," he reported when asked how the evening had gone. "If they had asked me to speak, I could have told them some very interesting things."

The relationship between Henry Coffin and his mother was very close. She was very conscientious in her attitude toward life, and communicated to both her sons a keen sense of responsibility for the right and generous use of their privileges. She was very strict in the ordering of the home, and in her expectations of her sons. In later years Henry Coffin told class after class of theological students how as a boy he would be playing out-of-doors when he would hear a rapping on an upstairs window-pane of his home. There would stand his mother beckoning. He knew that the hour for piano practice had arrived, and instantly dropping whatever he was doing he would run into the house and take up his task. (His point to the students was that it takes hard work and discipline as well as native gifts to do the work of the ministry as it does in any art.) She was deeply religious, devoted to her Church and to the ways of a Christian home. Family prayers were held daily, and Christianity was a subject of daily interest and conversation as well as practice. She was a woman of dignity and charm, regal in appearance, hospitable and generous. As her sons grew up she entertained their friends in her home. Even when Henry was studying abroad, his friends found her table and her guest rooms welcoming them. While her sons were at Yale she was a frequent visitor to New Haven when there were events of special interest. Several times she was invited to serve as one of the patronesses at University social functions and she always accepted and enjoyed the parties. After Henry had returned from Edinburgh she sometimes entertained his Scottish theological friends when they were lecturing in this country. He was completely devoted to her. He wrote to her every day while he was away from home at college and seminary. Her happiness in his choice of the ministry as his vocation doubled his own joy in it. She was not, however, a possessive mother in the sense in which that term is used nowadays. Nor was he a dependent son. They were two strong personalities who loved and respected each other, strengthening one another rather than draining strength from each other.

For the most part she had the social outlook of the people among whom she had been reared. In contrast, her son was thoroughly at home with all kinds of people and was eager to see artificial barriers of class and race and condition forgotten. He and his mother held differing opinions on this as well as on some other matters, but they were always one in heart.

The home in which Henry Coffin grew up was one in which the advantages and opportunities which ample means can provide were taken for granted. It was also a home where duties and responsibilities were never taken for granted but were taken seriously. When he was old enough to go to school he was sent to the Cutler School, a private school for boys, which he attended until he went to college. When the family were at the seashore in the summers he was fond of sailing and swimming. A hereditary difficulty with one eyelid handicapped him for tennis, baseball and games requiring quick and accurate vision. He could play them but he could not excel in them, and he did not enjoy sports in which he did not excel. As soon as he was old enough to benefit by foreign travel, his parents took him to Europe for a summer, and thereafter it was a rare season which did not see the Coffin family crossing the Atlantic for at least part of the boys' vacation from school. His brother William Sloane Coffin was two years his junior. The bond between the two brothers was close and affectionate, not altogether without the healthy rivalry which usually obtains when there are two brothers sufficiently near each other in age to encourage a competitive spirit. Even when he was in college and theological seminary, Henry in his letters home invariably referred to his younger brother as "the kid." It was a happy home which demanded a great deal of the two sons who grew up beneath its roof and gave them a great deal for which they never ceased to be grateful.

The Coffin family had a pew in the Fifth Avenue Presbyterian Church. It was the custom in New York City churches at the time to rent or sell outright the title to designated pews, reserving a

more or less limited number for the use of strangers who might
drop in for particular services. When he became a minister himself, Henry Coffin thought that this custom was undemocratic,
and he persuaded the Madison Avenue Presbyterian Church,
when he was its pastor, to adopt the system under which all pews
are free and unassigned. In that later day, however, his own
mother and father tried to dissuade him from the advocacy of
free pews, not because they regarded the ownership of a pew as
a special privilege to be cherished but because they honestly felt
that a family pew promoted family religion. They liked to feel that
they had a place in their church where they belonged as a family,
just as they had a house on 57th Street which was their family
home. They believed that the family pew had been an enriching
element in their own home.

Henry attended Sunday School in the Fifth Avenue Presbyterian Church. One of his teachers was the mother of Maitland
Alexander who in his manhood became minister of the First
Presbyterian Church of Pittsburgh and a leader in the conservative wing of the Presbyterian denomination when Henry Coffin
was a leader among the liberals. At the age of fourteen Henry
was received into the full membership of the church by Dr. Hall.
In due time he became active in the Young People's Association,
which, aside from the preaching services, seems to have been the
aspect of the church life which had the greatest influence upon
him. His cousin, William Sloane, who was a little older than he,
was president of the society, and the two cousins worked together
in its program. Sunday evening meetings were held for the discussion of religious topics and were led by the young people
themselves. They engaged in various forms of social service. They
studied and supported the work of Christian missions. On occasion they would go as a group to the docks to bid Godspeed
to some newly appointed missionary who was embarking for his
journey to the field. They would stand on the pier singing hymns
as the steamer left its moorings. In later life Henry Coffin remembered that at one such farewell he had seen a young man named

Robert E. Speer on the dock with another group of young people. When he was fifteen Henry helped his cousin and other members of the Society to found a Mission Sunday School on 63rd Street, a school which developed into the John Hall Memorial Presbyterian Church. Henry played the organ and taught a class in this new Sunday School. It was the heyday of such missions, and groups of young people from privileged homes were glad to go over east of Third Avenue on Sunday afternoons to teach children who came from homes of more meager resources. When William Sloane went on to college, Henry Coffin was chosen president of the Young People's Association, and threw himself enthusiastically into its work. Even after he went on to Yale he maintained his interest in the Society, corresponded with those who were guiding its activities, and sometimes came back to New York to help in its programs. It had a profound influence upon him.

The pastor of the Fifth Avenue Church all through Coffin's boyhood and young manhood was Dr. John Hall who had baptized him as an infant. Dr. Hall had come from the North of Ireland and was gifted with the eloquence which Americans associate with the best of the preachers from that staunchly Protestant region. He was conservative in his theological views, and as Coffin became familiar with the historical criticism of the Bible through sermons and studies at Yale and Edinburgh, he gradually adopted a theological position which differed from that of his pastor. While Coffin was a student at Edinburgh differences developed in the congregation, not over theological doctrines but over practical matters, and Dr. Hall resigned. At that time the Coffin family transferred their memberships to the Brick Presbyterian Church at Fifth Avenue and 37th Street, where Dr. Henry van Dyke was pastor. Coffin always respected Dr. John Hall and received a great deal from him, but there is no indication that he was ever very close to him, or that Dr. Hall exercised any determining influence over his choice of the ministry as his own life work.

It is not easy in retrospect to single out the influences which were responsible for that important choice. There seems never to have been a time after he first began to think about his future when he did not plan to be a minister. One of his childhood games was to play church on Sunday afternoons, gathering some of his Sloane cousins and neighborhood friends together for the purpose. He was always the minister, standing on a chair in an improvised gown and addressing the others who were allowed to serve as the congregation. Many other children of church-going families, however, have played church without any intention of devoting their lives to the ministry. Undoubtedly the deep feeling for the Church on the part of his grandmother, Mrs. William Sloane, was a contributing factor in turning his mind toward the ministry. His parents were delighted to have him become a minister but exerted no pressure in that direction. His father did caution him about the unwisdom of a premature decision with regard to his plans for the future. One of the letters which he preserved all his life was an undated note written to him by his father, evidently when he was in the early stages of his college course. Apparently on a visit home he had discussed his future with his mother, expressing disinclination for a mercantile business career. She had repeated the conversation to Edmund Coffin who wrote his son pointing out that there is detailed drudgery in each of the professions as well as in business and that each involves exposure to the seamier side of human nature. He pointed out, however, that there is interest and charm about the work of life in any field, and expressed the belief that a vigorous, honest, hard working man can enjoy his work in any place. He referred to the fact that his son would be graduating from college at the age at which many men are entering, and suggested that he had ample time in which to make up his mind. All the indications are, however, that Henry's mind was already pretty well made up, and that when he considered a legal or business career, it was only to return with greater conviction to his purpose to make the ministry his future work. His activities in the Young People's Association of the Fifth Avenue Presbyterian Church had given him a taste of religious leadership and an assurance that he had the gifts and capabilities for it. The decisive factor seems to have been his own sincere commitment to the Christian cause, made articulate at an early age, and a compelling desire to devote the abilities which he knew he possessed to that cause. To him this constituted the call of God. By the time he was ready for college it was with a fairly clear intention to prepare himself to become a Christian minister.

CHAPTER TWO

FOUR YEARS AT YALE

ON September 27, 1893, Henry Coffin, sixteen years of age, arrived in New Haven to begin his Freshman year at Yale College. Having lived at home in New York City while he prepared for college at the Cutler School, he had never been away from his family for any extended period of time. Four years later he himself was to smile as he remembered the unsophisticated picture he must have made arriving "from Southampton with my jar of coral bugs and my two tin pails of fish," prepared to keep up his interest in an aquarium which was a lifelong hobby with him. By family connections, however, he was better prepared than most Freshmen for what he would find at Yale. His father and several of his uncles on both the Coffin and the Sloane sides were Yale graduates. He found a portrait of his uncle, Thomas C. Sloane, hanging in Alumni Hall among those of other benefactors of the University. His cousin William Sloane was in the Junior Class ahead of him. He dropped in at Henry Coffin's room at 248 York Street the day Coffin arrived in New Haven, took him down town and helped him buy the furniture that he needed. Coffin's entrance into the student body marked the beginning of a personal association with Yale which made a profound impression upon him, became a source of endless satisfaction to him, and eventually constituted one of his major fields of distinguished service.

14

If he was not a complete stranger to the ways of Yale, he was far from prepared for the rough and ready methods by which Freshmen were introduced into the life of the college in 1893. He described that introduction in a letter of rare candor which he wrote to his mother on his second day as a student at Yale. It was his first letter home:

"I ought to have written you sooner but yesterday was no day for calm, collected thought so I have waited until today to tell you the chapter of horrors that have occurred to your little lamb.

"When I arrived here yesterday at twelve o'clock I found my room as barren as it could possibly be. Three boxes were piled up in one corner, the rug all untouched was at one end and piled in the center were a bed, bureau, table and three chairs. . . . So far the lot of your lamb was all right but no sooner had I got in the room when I was scared out of my wits to see Emory Harvis appear through the doorway. However he had come with most kindly intention and asked if he could help me in any way. I unrolled the rug and Mrs. Smith's sister who has charge of this house came and admired its beauties and also told me of the dreadful things which had occurred to the unfortunate freshes.

"After supper W. S. and numerous other Juniors marched all through the streets and assembled all the '97 (class) together. We were marched down to the grammar school where all the rushes used to take place. Here we found all the Sophs assembled, and under the direction of the Seniors wrestling contests were held between '97 and '96.

"After this Edgar Auchincloss took me under his protecting wing and we went down to a saloon where the hazing was going on. The Sophs had caught half a dozen freshes whom they had stood on tables and were making them drink beer and milk mixed together and shampoo one another with the same concoction.

"About ten o'clock I went home and found my trunk had arrived. I soon went to bed but I could not go to sleep because pandemonium reigned supreme in the streets. Carle and Bosworth were taken out and their trousers rolled up to their knees and their coats turned inside out. They were made to walk down the middle of Chapel Street singing and dancing and every large store they came to they had to go in and 'holler' out. 'I'm a G.D. little fresh.' About one o'clock they gathered outside of our house and broke in with a crow bar as they could not break the door. They took out all the freshes on the first floor and then about two they came back and took those on the second. At exactly three-thirty, they ascended to my abode. But I had carefully locked up everything so that after they had knocked and cried out 'Ho, Fresh, come out of your hole' several times they departed for which your humble servant was so overcome with joy that he never got to sleep.

"This morning I have had a sick headache from packing and excitement. . . .

Your affec

Son"

Soon, however, he was swinging enthusiastically and happily into the life of the college, and the major interests which were to dominate his four years at Yale became apparent. He went at his studies with zest and enthusiasm. At the end of his first term he awaited the announcement of grades with trepidation like any other Freshman, but with a name beginning with one of the initial letters of the alphabet, his was the first name to be read out in the First Division.

On his first Sunday at Yale he went to Chapel and listened to what he described as "a lengthy and not over edifying discourse from Prexy Dwight." After Chapel he attended a Class Prayer Meeting in Dwight Hall, where 110 Freshmen came together for an informal meeting led by one of their number. The next day he received a visit from Anson Phelps Stokes who was in the class ahead of him. Stokes was chairman of a committee in charge of the Grand Avenue Mission, a type of work in which he was in-experienced. He thought that Coffin's experience in mission work on New York City's East Side would be helpful in the New Haven enterprise. Coffin promised to help out to a limited extent but told his friend that he could not bind himself to any regular responsibilities. His studies had priority in the budgeting of his time. That first Monday in New Haven, William Sloane took him for a long drive out to and up East Rock, the conspicuous brown cliff which is the landmark on the eastern side of the city. Sloane's horse, named Eli, was, in Coffin's opinion, "a good goer" and he enjoyed the speed of a brisk drive timed to get them back to the campus for Coffin's class in German. Coffin was hardly settled in New Haven before he set out to make arrangements to take lessons on the organ. At first he had some difficulty in arranging for a teacher, but he eventually worked it out. His family came up from New York to see him almost as soon as he was well settled, and in the evening after they had gone he invited thirteen of his friends in to eat the cake which they had brought with them. He sent a message of thanks to the family cook and asked his mother to assure her that they had done "ample justice to her culinary skill." Before many weeks had passed he was writing home that he had secured a large black sign with gilt letters reading "Office." "I had some difficulty in swiping it but with the assistance of deacon Fincke it has been safely gotten." So he quickly found himself living a busy, happy, normal life as a Freshman at Yale.

His contemporaries remember him as a strikingly handsome man in his youth as he was throughout his life. There was never a time when in any group he did not command attention by his mere presence. He was outgoing and friendly, making friends easily and holding them. In conversation his face lighted up, he talked with animation and charm, and brought into play the resources of a vigorous, retentive mind. Though he came from a home where every advantage had been provided for him as a matter of course, he welcomed the opportunity to extend the range of his friendships which Yale afforded. There was perhaps a vein of intellectual arrogance which made it necessary for him to learn to be patient with people with sluggish or mediocre minds. He was always impatient with lazy minds and never concealed his scorn for intellectual indolence. He was brimming over with fun, and his keen humor played through his conversation and his letters. Deeply and naturally religious, he carried into his college life a profound concern for human need, a concern which had gripped him in New York before he went to college and never left him. Though free from snobbishness, he was honestly and frankly ambitious for college honors which could only be won by his own effort and ability, though he wore those honors modestly when they came to him. As a leader in student affairs he was confident and sure of himself, somewhat imperious in holding others up to the high standards which he set for himself, but always determined to keep the standards high.

There was never any doubt in his mind as to why he had come to college. He had come to study. All other activities were secondary to his primary purpose of securing intellectual preparation for the Christian ministry to which he looked forward. In his Freshman year pressure was put upon him to attend a Student Volunteer Movement Convention in Detroit as a representative of Yale. He wanted to go but after careful consideration he declined on the ground that the journey would take time he could not afford to spare from his studies. Incidentally he remarked that he could imagine his father saying that he had not sent his son to college to go off on excursions. His course of studies was a broad one. It included both Latin and Greek. He enjoyed both and developed a love for the classics which never left him. To the end of his life they were a source of pleasure and enrichment to him. He also studied physics and mechanics and did well in them, although his bent was not predominantly scientific. He studied German but did not think highly of the way it was taught at Yale. He was enthusiastic about the expansion of the courses in literature, modern as well as ancient. William Lyon Phelps as a young instructor was giving courses in the modern novel and drama. He was looked on with suspicion by older members of the faculty, who thought his innovations a lowering of academic standards. The students hailed him for bringing fresh air and reality into the curriculum, Coffin among them. After working on his essay in the competition for the Townsend Prize in his Senior year he wrote: "I am delighted to find what I never knew before, that I am really very fond of literature and especially poetry and that I thoroughly enjoyed even the labyrinthine mazes of Shelley. I think all my reading of plays with Dr. Phelps this year has helped me." Apparently Dr. Phelps approved of his work also for he suggested to Coffin that he go on after graduation with the necessary work in literature to receive the degree of Master of Arts. This Coffin did later on while at the same time carrying on his theological studies. It was characteristic of him as an undergraduate that when his family wrote him asking what he wanted them to give him at Christmas, he replied, "Books." College was for him an intellectual adventure and he rejoiced in the expansion of horizons which it made possible.

The Yale of 1893–1897 was of course very different from the University of today. Outwardly it was still in transition from the college of colonial days to the nondescript collection of buildings familiar to those who studied at Yale in the early twentieth century. North Middle, the last building of the Old Brick Row to disappear, was razed in the summer of 1894. The Old Chapel, which had been replaced for religious services by Battell Chapel in 1876 but had been preserved for use as a place for assemblies of various kinds, was torn down in the summer of 1896. Phelps Hall, through whose archway commencement processions today enter the Old Campus from College Street, was completed in 1896. Vanderbilt Hall, at the Chapel Street end of the Old Campus, had been opened the preceding year, and Coffin had a room in it in his Junior and Senior years. White Hall and Berkeley were completed in the same year, constituting part of Berkeley

Oval which was later torn down to make way for Berkeley College in 1933. When Coffin entered Yale College he was one of 318 entering Freshmen, of whom 279 survived to receive the degree of Bachelor of Arts in 1897.

In the light of the strenuous debates over the curriculum in which Coffin was in later years to participate as a member of the Yale Corporation, it is interesting to look back in detail at the course of study which he pursued as an undergraduate. With minor exceptions, all students in Yale College took the same prescribed courses in Freshman and Sophomore years. In Junior and Senior years there was a little wider choice, but the emphasis was heavily upon philosophy, history, political science, and languages. The records in the Dean's Office at Yale indicate that in his first year Coffin studied Greek, Latin, mathematics and English. In his Sophomore year he took Greek, Latin, physics and English. (In the English Literature course he studied Shakespeare, Spencer, Milton, Pope, Addison, Gray, Goldsmith and Johnson.) In his Junior year everyone was required to take Philosophy I, an elementary course in Logic, Psychology and Ethics under Professors Ladd, Duncan and Sneath. In addition Coffin took a general course in Economics under Professor Arthur T. Hadley and Professor Irving Fisher, a course in the History of Europe from the Reformation to the French Revolution, and a course in American Constitutional History. He studied Classical Lyric and Elegiac Poetry under Professors H. P. Wright and Morris, English Poets under Professors Beers and Lewis, and Biblical Literature under Professor Sanders. Philosophy was still a required subject in Senior year and Coffin studied the History of Continental Philosophy under Professor Duncan, Popular Discussions in Philosophy, also under Professor Duncan, and a course designated Philosophy and Literature, given by Professor Sneath. The most popular course for Seniors was Professor William Graham Sumner's The Science of Society, and Coffin was among those who sat at Sumner's feet. He also studied Mediaeval History with Professor George B. Adams, The History of Europe Since 1789 with Professor Arthur M. Wheeler, American Political History with C. H. Smith, and Elizabethan Drama with William Lyon Phelps.

An ingenious member of Coffin's class tabulated the total number of hours spent by the members of the class in the various disciplines. The results show clearly where the main stress was laid in American education near the turn of the century. "Of the 623,733 hours spent in the classroom, 143,418 have been devoted to the classics; 92,565 to European languages; 72,105 to political science; 65,406 to history; 65,010 to mathematics; 59,928 to philosophy; 59,367 to English; 52,635 to science; 9,702 to Biblical Literature; 1,782 to art; 1,320 to music; 264 to physical culture; 231 to military science. We have also spent 134,400 hours in Chapel." Apparently the Yale students of that era were satisfied with the intellectual fare which was selected for them. On a ballot taken at the end of their Senior year, hardly more than half the class voted one way or another on the proposition that the elective system should be extended to the first two years of the college course. 142 voted against such extension and only 30 favored it. Perhaps the prevailing impression that the elective system was a Harvard specialty colored the viewpoint of the men at Yale.

Coffin ranked 16th in his class among the 279 men who graduated. His marks averaged 333 on a scale of 400, which would be between 86 and 87 on a scale of 100.

Coffin identified himself with the organized religious life of the college as naturally as he had made himself a leader in the young people's activities in the Fifth Avenue Presbyterian Church in New York City. On Sundays there was a service at eleven o'clock in Battell Chapel. Distinguished preachers came to New Haven to conduct the services. Attendance was compulsory on the part of the students of Yale College, although a certain number of absences each term were permitted. On week-days there was a fifteen minute service conducted by some member of the faculty. Attendance at these services also was compulsory. Coffin entered into these services with spirit, enjoyed them and while critical of certain aspects of the chapel system found it on the whole congenial. His Sunday letters to his family frequently contained some reference to the preacher of the morning and some comment, favorable or otherwise, on the sermon. In March 1895 his friend Anson Phelps Stokes, later the notable Secretary of the University and a distinguished Episcopal clergyman, came out with what Coffin characterized as "a very violent and radical attack upon the college authorities for the 'unattractive lifelessness of the Chapel services both daily and Sunday'" and stated that "sermons by extremely *good* but fossilized theological professors are exasperating in the last degree." Coffin expressed sympathy for the particular theological professor who had preached in Battell Chapel on the preceding Sunday and feared that his friend was "going too rapidly, necessary as the reform is." He was glad to accept some responsibility for the Sunday services when in his Sophomore year he was elected a deacon in the Church of Christ in Yale University.

The voluntary religious activities of the campus centered in the Yale Christian Association, popularly known as Dwight Hall from the name of the building which had been erected to house its work. A general meeting was held each Sunday evening, frequently addressed by the minister who had preached in Battell Chapel in the morning. After church every Sunday morning each of the four classes held a class prayer meeting in a room specially designated for its use on the first floor of Dwight Hall. These prayer meetings were led and participated in by students only. One-third of the members of his class spoke at one time or another in these meetings. There were also mid-week Bible classes led by members of the faculty and smaller Bible Study groups led by students. Altruistic humanitarianism found expression through boys' clubs conducted by students for the less privileged youth of New Haven. Coffin found himself thoroughly at home in

Dwight Hall and rapidly became a leader in its work. In March of his Freshman year he was elected secretary of the student organization of Dwight Hall when his cousin, William Sloane, a Junior, was elected president. In his Sophomore year he became active in the leadership of a Bible Class made up of men from his own class of 1897, studying "The Parables and Miracles of Our Lord." He also helped Anson Stokes in the organization of a Bible Class for Freshmen. Later on he became the leader of a Bible Class for Freshmen, and felt that things were going well when he could report an attendance of fifty-seven one evening. In his Senior year, in cooperation with E. T. Ware, Coffin led a group of his classmates in a study of "The Life of Paul." At one time he conducted a class for Negro men who were employed by the University as sweepers and cleaners in the students' dormitories. This he finally had to give up when the load became too heavy. He put in a great deal of time in getting ready for each meeting of these classes and refused to make other engagements which would interfere with the preparation which he considered necessary for them. Men who were in these groups never forgot the indelible impression which he made upon them. A distinguished physician in New York City wrote after Coffin's death: "I have loved Henry Coffin just sixty years, since I joined his Bible Class in Dwight Hall in our Freshman year in '94."

Always in the back of his mind was a sense of social obligation, and a concern for the needs of city-dwellers who lived in tenements rather than in such homes as his own. He wanted to know their problems at first hand. When a member of the East Street Mission Committee asked him to help canvass one of the more dilapidated neighborhoods of the city in order to find out how many children there were who could be enrolled in a Sunday School if one were started, he accepted and spent a discouraging Saturday afternoon finding few candidates. "I had never been really in such tenements before and was glad to have a chance to see for myself cases such as the City Mission Monthly reports," he wrote. His experience in the Young People's Association of the Fifth Avenue Presbyterian Church had introduced him to the debate between those who believed that the Church should confine itself to social service in its dealing with underprivileged neighborhoods and those who believed that a distinctively religious approach should parallel the humanitarian efforts. He was enthusiastic about an address which he heard given in the North Church by Miss Julia Bradford from Whittier House in Jersey City. He was impressed by her interpretation of the work of her settlement as based on the spirit of Isaiah 58:6–10 and on James 1:27, but as being non-religious in the sense that the program included no Sunday School or devotional meetings. He thought her address and that of a worker from the University Settlement in New York City admirable, but felt that they would do better to make "more prayer go with the potatoes of humanization and civilization and all their other 'zations.'" The type of ministry which Coffin was to carry on so magnificently in later years was foreshadowed by this burning interest in the Church's obligation to meet the needs of all kinds of people in a wide variety of ways. This concern was never far from his mind even in the most carefree days of his youth.

During his college years he was a regular and an enthusiastic member of the Yale delegations to the Student Conferences held each June at Northfield, Massachusetts. In his Sophomore year he was put in charge of the Yale group. The conferences brought together students from the Eastern colleges and from Canada for a week on the grounds of the Northfield Seminary, which had been founded by Mr. Dwight L. Moody. There were daily addresses by religious leaders who had special gifts for meeting students' problems, Bible classes, out-door Vesper Services on Round Top looking off up the Connecticut River valley, and intimate meetings of the Yale delegation at the end of the day. Coffin was himself, after his student days, one of the most helpful speakers at these student conferences for many years, all the more helpful because he had in his younger days been one of the student leaders at the conferences. One of the opportunities which the Northfield Conferences opened up for him was an intimate friendship with Mr. Dwight L. Moody. Mr. Moody was always one of the speakers at the conferences, and although not a college graduate, his humanity, his breadth of experience, deep understanding of human need and genuine religious reality made him an appealing speaker to students as he was to all sorts of people. He took a particular interest in Coffin who stood out head and shoulders above his fellow students in personal attractiveness and in religious leadership. Mr. Moody lived in the old Moody home on the grounds of the school, and was a familiar sight driving his horse and buggy around the campus and in the nearby countryside. During the student conferences a frequent companion in the buggy was Henry Coffin. They had long talks which Coffin never forgot, although in later years he used to say laughingly that Mr. Moody's avoirdupois in his old age made the buggy-seat very crowded so that the rides were more conducive to spiritual stimulus than to physical comfort.

In the winter of his Freshman year, a week of religious addresses was given at Yale by Dr. Alexander McKenzie, a Congregational minister from Cambridge, Massachusetts. These met with an enthusiastic response on the part of the students, who not only came in great numbers to hear the addresses but also came in such numbers for personal talks with the speaker that he was asked by them to come back for another week, which he consented to do. In later life Coffin frequently referred to the McKenzie meetings as evidence of the fruitfulness of the right kind of approach to student groups. That he was not necessarily susceptible to the evangelistic appeal if couched in terms which did not appeal to his intellect and good taste as well as to his emotions was evidenced by the fact that he was completely unresponsive to addresses given in Dwight Hall by B. Fay Mills, a popular evangelist of the day whose message was of the more con-

ventional sort and whose theology was what later came to be
called "fundamentalism." In his Junior year the Lyman Beecher
Lectures on Preaching were delivered in the Divinity School by
John Watson, the Scottish clergyman who was widely known in
this country as "Ian MacLaren," author of *Beside the Bonnie
Briar Bush* and other Scottish tales. Coffin had read his stories
and enjoyed them. He made it a point to hear all of the lectures and was captivated by the speaker and his message. The
next year he was very much excited over the news that Dr.
Watson was to be tried for heresy. "If such a man cannot be a
minister," he wrote, "I am afraid every Yale graduate is forever
barred, for he is surely a good Christian man. It seems a shame
that any group of men could be so narrow minded." Thus he was
again made aware of theological controversy in the contemporary
Church, and of the doggedness with which differing definitions of
the essentials of the faith were held by different groups. In this
case the excitement was short lived and Dr. Watson retained his
standing in the Church.

Coffin's family were somewhat concerned lest he confine himself exclusively to Dwight Hall work. He defended himself on
the ground that he had made Phi Beta Kappa, had attended to
various tasks in the societies to which he belonged, and had been
getting a useful preparation for his future career in the work he
had done with his Bible class. "Besides," he added, "I like to take
some time for loafing and chinning with the fellows." He might
have added what his letters reveal, that along with his interest
in religious work he had many other healthy, human interests to
which he gave himself. At each stage of the rather peculiar
social system in vogue at Yale in those days he was elected to
the society which he wanted to join: the Sophomore Society of
Kappa Psi; the Junior Fraternity of Delta Kappa Epsilon; and
the Senior Society of Skull and Bones. He busied himself over
the details of a new building for D.K.E., going into such matters
as the selection of a lot, costs of building, and other unfamiliar

matters. His election to the Senior Society to which his father had belonged before him was the fulfilment of his boyhood dreams, and he made no attempt to conceal his elation in writing the news to his family when Tap Day was over. Nor did he disguise the fact that "The nervous strain has been terrible and I am pretty well broken up." He took no part in organized athletics, but he was fond of taking long walks and bicycle rides. One Monday he wrote home, "Saturday afternoon Bob Gilman and I rode over twenty-two miles down the Coast of the Sound. It was simply fine and coming back the sunset was gorgeous. Today I have ridden about twelve miles, so I take plenty of exercise." He was fond of sailing and bathing during his summer holidays. He enjoyed to the full his participation in college events. In the autumn of his Sophomore year he went with some classmates to the Fall Regatta on Lake Whitney after which he wrote home: "It has been such a lovely day that the races were a most delightful scene. Lake Whitney presented a fine sight lined with autumn foliage and Connecticut hills in the background. I could not help contrasting my own position today with that of a year ago. Then I footed it out and back glad to have a right to walk on the sidewalk; while today we chartered a carriage and decked it with flags and rode in state to be admired of the Freshmen and thinking ourselves lords of creation. 'Tempora mutantur et nos cum illis mutamus.' "

When cautioned not to overdo in the busy round of activities in which he was engaged, he wrote, "I find so many interesting things to do that it is hard to keep quiet long." Now it was seeing Joseph Jefferson play *The Rivals* "from the third row in the peanut" because orchestra seats cost five dollars. Again it was leading cheers for McKinley at a campaign meeting addressed by William Jennings Bryan. "I had rather an exciting day yesterday," he wrote his family, "as I led cheers for McKinley at the Bryan meeting and the cops tried to arrest me. Fortunately the fellows closed in and I crawled behind and escaped. Only one man was caught and we pulled him away by force. We certainly gave Bryan all he wanted." Many years later, when William Jennings Bryan and Henry Coffin were leading opposite sides in theological controversy in the General Assembly of the Presbyterian Church, he recalled this youthful exuberance. Frequently it was some social festivity in which he participated. The Coffins had friends in New Haven who invited him to dances which he greatly enjoyed. As a Freshman he went down to the Armory on the day before the Junior Promenade with William Sloane, who was a member of the "Prom. Committee" and was awed by the splendor of the decorations. That night he sat as a spectator with the other Freshmen in seats they had stood in line for hours to secure. In later years he entered enthusiastically into the parties, inviting girls from New York to be his guests, giving teas in his room, and going the rounds of festivity which culminated in the Promenade itself. Young women did not visit men's colleges in those days without chaperones, and his mother was glad to come to New Haven for the social events in that capacity. All through the four years at Yale his hard work for the classroom and for Dwight Hall had a background of social life in which he took pleasure and found relaxation. His religious activities were his dominant concern outside his classroom work, as was natural with a young man committed to entering the ministry, but they were far from being his exclusive interest.

Wherever he went, he enjoyed life to the full. After a Y.M.C.A. Conference in Danbury, Connecticut, which he attended with Anson Phelps Stokes when a Sophomore at Yale, he wrote characteristically: "The Convention yesterday was a most successful and helpful one in every way and I am very glad I attended it. I arrived at Danbury a little late and met Anson at the depot. We were seized by a small boy having a big Y.M.C.A. Convention Guide written on his hat and immediately escorted to the headquarters where we received the right hand of fellowship etc. We then went to the Congregational Church where the session was

being held and stayed through the exercises until one when all the
delegates were given a banquet in the Sunday School room of the
church. All of the ladies of Danbury had sent in most generous
contributions of food including turkeys and pies, cakes of all descriptions and preserves so we had a grand feast. We were waited
upon by the young ladies of Danbury who certainly are exceeding
fair. The young lady who presided over the tea table was so particularly beautiful that both Anson and I drank enormous quanti-
ties of that beverage. I had a very loquacious gent. opposite who
wanted to tell me what the hand of the Lord had done or failed
to do in Naugatuck but I fear that my eyes were so intent on
watching the damsels that I did not pay much attention to the
spiritual condition of that abandoned place of sin at Naugatuck."
He was called into conference with the Negro delegates on their
Bible Study program, and was glad to find among them the
brother of the "sweep" who took care of his room at Yale. He was
welcomed by the delegation from the Connecticut Agricultural
College at Storrs, which he had previously visited as a speaker.
Then: "We finished our work at four, so we hired a team of studs
and took a fine drive over to Bethel and back."

It was a foregone conclusion that he would be elected to serve
as president of Dwight Hall in his Senior year. When the election
took place, late in his Junior year, it seems to have occasioned no
surprise and little comment on his part. He took the position
very seriously, however, and gave powerful leadership to the
work. He was gratified by the enthusiasm of the response on the
part of his classmates which he thought exceeded anything that
he had seen in their four years at Yale. In his more mature years
he believed that ecclesiastical authority was most effective when
least in evidence but as president of Dwight Hall he seems to
have been a rather firm disciplinarian. A Bible class leader who
had been indiscreet offered him his resignation which he accepted
at once until the man expressed sorrow and repentance, when he
reinstated him. "Matters of this kind are always unpleasant," he

commented, "but the position of religious organizations must be consistent and the best element here has backed me up." In later life he was extraordinarily understanding of younger men's undeveloped capacities but as a Yale Senior he wrote, "I have also descended with a rod of iron on the Freshman Committee and asked two men to resign on account of neglect of duty but they pleaded for another chance so I have given them until April 1st." One of the Episcopal rectors of the city invited him to dinner and took issue with him because he had persuaded several Episcopalian Freshmen to attend Sunday services in Battell Chapel instead of in some local Episcopal church. Feeling that he could not argue with his host at his own table, he simply replied that he entirely disagreed with the rector and preferred not to discuss matters of this sort with him. When the rector sought another interview on the subject, he sent back word that he did not care to discuss the matter further with him. (Coffin was in later years to spend endless hours in conference and negotiation in endeavors to bring about a union between the Church to which he belonged and the Protestant Episcopal Church.) If, however, he was self-assured as a young man, he was a most effective leader in the Christian Association, partly because of his personal popularity and prestige but far more because of the sincerity of his Christian dedication and the depth of his desire to help his fellow students know the resources of the Christian faith.

At the beginning of his Sophomore year there began the close association between Coffin and Edward S. Harkness which continued throughout their lives and resulted in their cooperation in rendering magnificent service to Yale and to many other institutions in which they were both interested. Few friendships have been more fruitful. It began quite casually. One day in June, at the end of his Freshman year, Coffin wrote home: "Today a notice appeared in the News saying that no single rooms would be available for our class so a fellow named Harkness whom I know very well and who is very much thought of in our class came to me and said he had intended to room alone but in view of that notice he had given it up and asked me to go in with him; and as I had thought of him all winter I agreed. He is a New York fellow and goes to our church. His people sit on the side aisle behind General Hanes." Many years later, after the name of Edward Harkness was universally known as the generous benefactor of Yale, Harvard, Union Theological Seminary, St. Andrew's University, and educational institutions throughout the world, Coffin was asked by the *Yale Daily News* to describe Harkness as an undergraduate. Among other things he said of his one-time room-mate: "He was extremely shy. His father had died when he was thirteen; a brother and sister were considerably older than he, his widowed mother had lived most quietly, and Ed had almost no boyhood friends, none at all in college with him. He had gone to a large preparatory school, where he had been very homesick, and he was intimate with only one or two of his schoolmates who went on with him to Yale. As a freshman he roomed alone in an unattractive boarding-house on Elm Street, where to his discomfort his fellow lodgers were noisy and included a group whose idea of fun was to invade their neighbors' rooms and leave them in a mess. . . . Behind his reticence, those who came to know him discovered a warmly affectionate nature, hungry for companionship, a delightful sense of humor, and one of the most high-minded of men. There was a vague rumor that his father had been among the founders of the Standard Oil Company, but the few classmates who knew him never saw any indication of great wealth. One or two whom he took to his home at Willoughby, Ohio, found a comfortable but simple house, where life was lived very seriously."

Coffin and Edward Harkness roomed together for three years at Yale. It was a happy and congenial friendship from the start. They enjoyed together the boxes of food which occasionally came from their homes. They went together to Cambridge to watch

Harvard-Yale games. They bantered one another without fear of being misunderstood. "Tomorrow is the Day of Prayer," Coffin wrote home in 1895, "and instead of praying up here Ed has gone to New York where he says he can combine prayer and a theater tonight in a better way." When Harkness was going down to New York to make a party call he turned to his roommate for advice as to whether the call should be made in the afternoon or the evening, saying that in Cleveland where he had lived most of his life evening calls were the custom. His roommate informed him that in New York an afternoon call would be correct. When Harkness was planning his first trip to Europe for the summer of 1897 his anxiety over his arrangements seemed somewhat strange to his more widely traveled companion. When Tap Day came with its announcement of elections to the Senior Societies, Coffin felt that the greatest pleasure of all was to see Edward Harkness chosen for membership in one of them. Harkness had not been prominent in extra-curricular activities, and Coffin attributed his election to the fact that he was "such a perfectly smooth fellow." Out of their close association as Yale undergraduates grew a lifelong friendship based on mutual confidence and liking for each other. When in later years Edward Harkness became one of the princely benefactors of his generation, Coffin was one of those on whose judgment he not infrequently relied in his philanthropies.

As the four years at Yale began to approach their end, the question as to the next step in Coffin's education became insistent. That he would go on to a theological seminary was taken for granted. That had long been his intention. But where? He sought advice from older men and received different suggestions. The possibility of studying at New College in Edinburgh came naturally to the mind of one with such strong Scottish ties. Dr. McKenzie advised him to take a year at the Andover Theological Seminary and then finish his course at Edinburgh. In May Dr. McKenzie's church offered him a position on its staff to carry on a religious program for Harvard students at the church while he gave part of his time to theological study. This offer he declined. One day on the train from New York to New Haven he found himself sitting in the seat just in front of Dr. Henry van Dyke. He went back and asked him, "Which Seminary do you consider best?" Dr. van Dyke replied that Auburn and Yale were the two best and that of the two he preferred Auburn where he had recently given a week's lectures and had been delighted with everything that he found. When Dr. Charles Cuthbert Hall, the new President of Union Seminary in New York City, came to preach at Yale, Coffin's classmate Thatcher Brown, whose father was a benefactor and director at Union, took occasion to point out to him that Union was making great strides forward under its new leadership. In the end he decided to go to Edinburgh in the autumn after his graduation at Yale with the prospect of taking the final year of his theological course at an American seminary. One of the considerations which weighed heavily on the side of going at once to Scotland was his feeling that his training in writing had been deficient. At Edinburgh he would be able to take a course in rhetoric under Professor George Saintsbury which included the criticism of essays and themes. He looked forward eagerly to this training.

The informality of life at Yale in the nineties as well as Coffin's place in the college community is revealed in one of his letters home written in his Senior year: "I had just written the date of this letter when a knock was heard at the door and in came no less personages than President Dwight and Dean Phillips. Ed and I were in rather negligé costume and certainly startled to receive such guests. The Prex was on ecclesiastical business with me as a deacon in his church but after that was over he sat and told us some great tales."

The years at Yale were happy, busy, growing years. Like every Senior, when he had taken his last examination, he looked back and wondered how the time had passed so quickly. They were

years in which he had prepared himself for further study, the
need for which he expressed in later life by saying with characteristic self-depreciation, "I graduated from college an uneducated
man." They were also years in which he had already begun the
Christian ministry which was to be his life. He concluded the
article on religious life which he was asked to write for the 1897
Class Book by saying, "Among all the pleasant associations these
years have for our class, for some of us by no means the least
memorable are those found in the Student Christian Work. Of
the many ties that knit us together as classmates none unites us
more closely than

> *the tie that binds*
> *Our hearts in Christian love.*

We leave Yale feeling that if we have not known the truth we
have at least 'beheld her bright countenance in the quiet and
still air of delightful studies.'" As in most colleges, it was the
custom at Yale for the outgoing Senior Class to appraise its members in a Senior ballot. Coffin did not receive the largest number
of votes in any one category, but a number of his classmates
voted for him as Most Admired, Has Done Most for Yale, Most
Likely to Succeed, and Brightest. The man who was voted Most
Popular was to write of Henry Coffin more than fifty years later:
"I think of all those whom he has helped and all the honors he
has achieved, and then I find myself thinking back to the shy,
pink-cheeked boy I first met in our Freshman year at Yale, living
in an upper room in a boarding house on York Street with his
little parlor organ and a bowl of gold fish. And again I think of
him at graduation the most admired and most beloved of the
class."

CHAPTER THREE

THEOLOGY IN SCOTLAND

SEPTEMBER, 1897, found Henry Coffin at Edinburgh ready to begin his theological course at New College, the seminary of the United Free Church of Scotland. His family had crossed the Atlantic with him and they had traveled together on the Continent as was their annual summer custom. Then they had sailed back to New York and he had gone on alone to the old gray city where he was to spend the next two years. The theological college is on a height of land which leads up to the Castle. It looks down upon the National Gallery and the Princes Street Gardens with Princes Street, the city's main thoroughfare, beyond them. Coffin found a room reserved for him in the New College Residence at Two Mound Place on the college property. It was not yet time for the autumn term to begin when he reached Edinburgh. Only one other theological student was in residence when he arrived, but he quickly made friends with the assorted group who had rooms in the building during the summer. There were students of law, medicine, and economics, as well as a continual procession of ministers who came to Edinburgh for committee meetings and made their headquarters at The Residence. All of them he found interesting. After the middle of October the building was occupied only by theological students and the life of the Seminary was in full swing.

The manner of life was so different from that in the dormitories and dining halls at Yale that he described it in detail in his letters home: "The room faces the north and the wind howls like sixty around this building and the halls are very draughty. A buxom girl named Katie makes my fire every morning about 7:15 and blacks my boots. She is also very anxious to please and brings hot water whenever I want to shave. The meals are very plain and I believe healthy. Breakfast at 8:30 consists of porridge, tea, toast, marmalade and jam and one substantial dish either meat or ham or eggs. . . . Dinner at one consists of soup, meat and boiled potatoes and some form of dessert. Tea from 5 to 6 is very 'informal.' On the table is tea, bread and jam or marmalade and you help yourself. Supper at nine is exactly like tea except that milk is substituted for tea and cheese is added to marmalade and jam." As the days grew colder he was to find that the unheated classrooms necessitated his being as warmly dressed indoors as outdoors. But whatever discomforts there were in his new manner of life, they were more than compensated for by the satisfaction and excitement of being among theological scholars and students whom he found congenial and stimulating.

A glowing recommendation from Dean Henry P. Wright of Yale College had preceded him to Edinburgh, as had a personal letter from Dr. John Hall to Principal Rainy. Apparently he knew none of the members of the faculty or of the student body personally prior to entering New College. One of his fellow lodgers at The Residence on making his acquaintance at once wrote to Professor Marcus Dods about him. Professor Dods replied by sending a postal to Coffin making an appointment to see him. This marked the beginning of a friendship which was to be one of the richest and most rewarding in Coffin's life, although that was not apparent in their first interview. When they met, Professor Dods asked him, "Do you know anything about the Life of Paul?" Coffin named the books which he had read, inwardly giving thanks for the work he had done in preparation for the

Bible classes which he had led in the Yale Y.M.C.A. Professor Dods was satisfied that he could enter his third year class but gave him some bulky books containing a great deal of Greek to read before the beginning of the term. An invitation to dinner at an early date concluded the interview and Coffin went back to his room to write home that the professor had "impressed him very favorably" and "appeared to be a most genial old Scotchman." A few days later he met Alexander Martin, who began his long service as a Professor of Pastoral Theology at the opening of the term in which Coffin began his life as a student in Edinburgh. Between the older and the younger man a friendship developed which in later years found expression in a correspondence which continued without interruption all their lives. A. B. Davidson he met apparently in the classroom. "Rabbi Davidson" he was called by the students because of his Old Testament scholarship. He, too, recognized the brilliance and charm of the young American student and soon began to project plans for him to take the full three year course for the Bachelor of Divinity degree at Edinburgh with a term at Oxford University thrown in, a plan which as it eventuated was not carried out. Coffin recognized him as one of the theological giants of the day, respected and admired him as he sat in his lecture-room, and quickly won his warm friendship.

From the very beginning of his days in Edinburgh he enjoyed the friendship of ministers in the city whom he admired and at whose feet he sat eagerly. On his first Sunday evening in the city, while the regular ministers of the churches were still away on their holidays, he went to Free St. George's and heard a sermon by "a Dr. Black of Inverness," little supposing that subsequently he and Hugh Black would for many years be colleagues on the faculty of Union Theological Seminary in New York. Early in October he received a note from Mrs. Alexander Whyte, the wife of the minister at Free St. George's, inviting him to Sunday evening supper. This invitation he was unable to accept, but there were other opportunities later on to meet the great preacher whom crowds were thronging to hear, and a deep and lasting friendship developed between them. The first time he dined with the Whytes, he asked Dr. Whyte, who was famous for his lectures on John Bunyan, what was the best edition of Bunyan's complete works. The old Puritan, who was almost as much at home in *Pilgrim's Progress* as in Edinburgh, showed him his volume of what he considered the best edition, but said that unfortunately it was out of print and could only be secured at second-hand book stalls. A few days later a large parcel was delivered at Coffin's room. It contained a copy of the desired work, together with a note from Dr. Whyte saying that he had seen a good second-hand copy which he begged the younger man to accept as a token of his great interest in him. One of Coffin's early invitations was to the home of R. S. Simpson, the minister of the Free High Church. This was the beginning of a close association, and before long he was working with Mr. Simpson as a student assistant and finding him a splendid man with whom to work, ready to give younger colleagues freedom to work out their own plans but always ready to aid them with counsel and support when needed. From time to time he went to hear other preachers and was enthusiastic about the Edinburgh churches. "I do not expect ever in my life to be able to hear such good preaching as in this city or to enjoy going to church so much." Another minister, not yet famous, with whom Coffin soon established a firm friendship was John Kelman, minister of Free New North Church. Coffin was fond of going to the Kelman manse for a chat with the young minister who was not many years his senior whom he found most attractive and interesting. Their friendship ripened during the years when Kelman was Alexander Whyte's successor in Free St. George's and still later when Kelman became minister of the Fifth Avenue Presbyterian Church in New York City.

Hardly had the term begun before he was overflowing with enthusiasm over New College and his course of study. He had courses in Hebrew and in Old Testament with Professor A. B. Davidson, Apologetics with Professor Alexander Martin, and New Testament with Professor Marcus Dods. In addition he took two courses in Edinburgh University, one in English with Professor George Saintsbury, and one in Metaphysics with Professor James Seth. At the University his first impressions of the students were distinctly unfavorable. "It is an old custom here that the first lecture can be as disorderly as possible and the disorder increases in proportion to the unpopularity of the instructor. Professor Saintsbury is very unpopular and I never saw such a scene. . . . When Professor Saintsbury entered there was a howl of derision and for fully five minutes he was not allowed to utter a word. His lecture was a comparison of Dante and Wordsworth but he was constantly interrupted with shouts of 'Hear! Hear! —Splendid old chap! Gie us nae English but gude Scotch! My laddie.' Saintsbury is an Englishman and speaks with a very English tone and the men never lost a chance to twit him. He quoted a Latin sentence and the men bawled 'Graund tongue the Lā-tin' and a few lines of Italian were greeted with a chorus of cat calls. He tried to call for order several times and once stopped and refused to go on but it was all to no use." After the fiasco of the opening lecture, however, Coffin was delighted with Saintsbury's course and felt that it was just what he wanted. On the whole he found the atmosphere of both New College and the University intellectually stimulating. He was particularly impressed by the degree to which students were put on their own and were expected to follow out a course of study for themselves in a rather concentrated field. Before many days had gone by he was writing to his father that he could see that he would have to get right down and grind out his work in a way his undergraduate course at Yale had not demanded.

As at Yale, however, he was eager to be of Christian service while he was preparing for the ministry and even before his classes in Edinburgh began he went down and volunteered as a

worker at "The Pleasance," a social settlement with a religious
background carried on by New College in the slums of the city.
Each of the New College students who worked there was expected to visit in some of the homes of the neighborhood. Coffin
was assigned six families who lived in a "close" on St. John's hill
just off the Cowgate. Mr. Dawson, the missionary in charge of The
Pleasance, took him around and introduced him to the people
on whom he was expected to call at least once a month. He was
impressed by their cordiality, delighted in their broad Scottish
dialect which he had difficulty in understanding, and found himself a bit appalled at the dirt and the smells, to say nothing of the
cats and the dirty babies that tried to climb over him. Three
weeks later he conducted his first tenement meeting. It was held
in a room packed to the door with a congregation consisting of
"fifteen women, eight bairns, a cat and a canary." They sang
Moody and Sankey hymns, and Coffin gave a ten-minute talk. One
Sunday afternoon Professor Davidson preached to the members
of the Men's Club at The Pleasance. "There were only about
forty there but the old Rabbi gave one of the finest addresses I
ever heard," Coffin reported. Afterwards he went to a kitchen
meeting in a place called Rob's Entry. "From the name," Coffin
wrote home, "you can infer the character of our audience. Unfortunately I had to start all the tunes unaided and lead the singing which really progressed better than I had expected. The
audience were most of them suffering from the effects of Saturday
evening sprees and were too stupid to notice any slight musical
aberrations." All through his life Coffin had an extraordinary
capacity for being at home with people regardless of their status
or condition, and he was equally successful in making them feel
at home with him. His experiences in Rob's Entry and in the
neighborhood of The Pleasance no doubt combined with his
Christian concern for his fellowmen in developing this gift which
counted for so much in his later ministry.

Among the students in Edinburgh Coffin was with men to

whom argument was second nature. He enjoyed the arguments and took his part in them with spirit. A student organization called "The Theological Society" met once a week. One or two essays would be read, followed by a vigorous informal debate which sometimes lasted into the small hours of the morning, spilling over "into some one's room in The Residence after the regular meeting had adjourned." "The spirit of argument and the gift of the gab certainly prevails here and The Theological is the great outlet of the week," Coffin wrote to his family. Before the first year was over he had been elected to the Executive Committee in the Society and was one of its moving spirits. Student arguments, however, were rampant on all sorts of subjects and on all manner of occasions. At one time New College was in an uproar over a lecture by Mr. Simpson in which the Highland contingent among the students thought they detected ritualistic leanings. Because Coffin was helping in the church of which Mr. Simpson was pastor he was called upon to defend the professor against his critics. Even he thought that Mr. Simpson had gone a little far toward ritualism, although he agreed with him in his plea for dignity and carefully prepared services in the Free churches. "I cannot see that a man can hope to lead a congregation in prayer unless he thinks it out beforehand," he wrote, in describing the controversy. "The Highlanders think a minister should 'wrastle wie th' Almichty' in prayer and anything like a prearranged program dooms the wrestling to degenerate into mere 'trumpery and ritual.'" The argument lasted until a late hour, and Coffin enjoyed it. "The Scotch mind seems never to be satisfied unless an argument is engrossing its attention," he concluded. He never lost his liking for the Scottish mind.

He was deeply impressed by the cheerful good humor of his Scottish fellow students, and by the courage with which they put up with all manner of privations in order to secure the prized education which every Scottish family coveted for its sons. He was startled to find that many of them brought oat meal with them from their homes and that a surreptitious bowl of porridge in his room frequently had to do duty as a meal for many an impecunious student. One day he was making up a bundle of laundry to send out for washing when a student asked him what he was doing. He told him, and added, "Don't you ever have your underwear washed?" "Oh, no," replied the other. "I just hang it out o' the window and gie it a wee whisk o' the breeze!" Coffin adopted for himself a regime of self-imposed simplicity, although he never deceived himself into imagining that voluntary abstemiousness (with a family in the background able to meet any financial emergency that might arise) is identical with the self-denials for which there is no alternative and from which there is no relief even in time of urgent need. Nevertheless, he curtailed his expenditures to conform to the circumstances of his fellow students. His letters home contain no requests for more money, as students' letters frequently do, but instead assured his family that he had not used all the funds with which they had supplied him. When he finished his course and had paid for his passage home, he still had sixty pounds in the Bank of Scotland and a draft for two hundred pounds which he had never cashed.

Coffin went to Edinburgh just four years after the Presbyterian Church in the United States of America had gone through the excitement of its most famous heresy trial. Professor Charles Augustus Briggs, of Union Theological Seminary, had been suspended from its ministry because he accepted and taught the results of historical research into the documentary background of the Bible which were popularly designated by the term "higher criticism." The Coffin family had been sympathetic with Dr. Briggs. At the same time the Biblical views on which Coffin had been brought up at home and under Dr. John Hall in the Fifth Avenue Presbyterian Church were fairly conservative. He went through no intellectual upheaval at Edinburgh, but he found himself in a new atmosphere. "If I am not a deep dyed higher critic," he wrote home soon after his arrival in Edinburgh, "it will be no fault of New College for you get it everywhere in most attractive form and I must say whatever more conservative ideas I had have been rudely blown away. The criticism is not however of a negative character but a new view of the Bible and of theology is given in its place and the spiritual tone of all the teaching is very marked. The remarkable thing is that these advanced views are held not only by theological professors but by nearly all the ministers and by a large majority of the ordinary listeners. You have advanced theology from almost every pulpit and all Scotland with very few exceptions is in the same boat with Professor Briggs." A year later he wrote, "Sunday I went to the Free High both morning and evening and stayed to Mr. Simpson's class. He was speaking about the ideal man in the Old Testament and of course looked at it from the viewpoint of modern criticism. Twenty years ago the Free Church put Robertson Smith out on the same charges on which Briggs was tried. Today those ideas are not only preached from almost every pulpit but are so thoroughly accepted by the people that a minister in teaching a Bible class can take it for granted that his people are familiar with them." Referring to one of the Dunfermline cousins, he went on, "Even Maggie Bardner knows all about the P.J.E.D.[1] writers. So you see orthodoxy is progressive and I believe the United States will be of a different opinion some few years hence so that my Edinboro training will keep me abreast of the times." Evidently there was some concern in his family over the matter for some time in 1898 he wrote, "Do not worry about the heresy of New College. The Scotch Church seems to stand it and preach better sermons than the bluest Princetonians. It is not very bad anyway and I am now just in the unfortunate position where I have not enough knowledge to know just where I am at and so my best policy is to keep still and do a good deal of thinking and very little talking and see how I come out . . . I am getting plenty of good

[1] P., J., E., and D. are the letters used by Old Testament scholars to designate the documentary sources which lie behind the present text.

Calvinism and lots of the Confession of Faith only with a new interpretation." In later years when Biblical interpretation was the cause of bitter controversy in the Presbyterian Church in the United States, he often referred to the fact that in Scotland after the Robertson Smith case the Scottish Presbyterians had solved their problem by education without any such upheaval as that which shook the American Presbyterian Church to the foundations. As a student in Scotland he had a vivid sense of the wide gap between Scottish and American Presbyterians in matters of Biblical scholarship. "I realize more and more," he wrote in 1898, "that there is a wide difference between Scotch and American Presbyterianism and that it will be many years before our people as a whole get to the point where Scotland is today."

As an attractive and interesting young man, Coffin was showered with invitations to suppers, dinners, teas and social occasions of varied descriptions almost from the moment of his arrival in Edinburgh. Always a delightful conversationalist, he added zest and good humor to every occasion. Many of these invitations were to take tea or dinner in the homes of members of the faculty. He was a frequent guest in the home of Principal Rainy, of the Marcus Dods, the Simpsons, the Davidsons and others. For the most part it was to the homes of Free Church people that he was invited. At first he was a bit overwhelmed by the frequency with which guests were asked to exhibit their musical attainments at social functions even if these attainments were not very high. "An Edinboro custom that is a little odd is the constant amateur musical performance you are called on to listen to. At the R.'s one gentleman and two ladies who called during my stay of half an hour were called on to perform—two played the piano and one played and sang Scotch ditties. Last night Mrs. S. played and sang a German song and several others performed. When the player finishes no one applauds as that would break the solemn dignity that pervades all Edinboro drawing rooms but everyone very quietly and very gravely sighs as if deeply touched by the music and murmurs 'thank you.' " Coffin could not possibly accept all the invitations which he received and there were times when he was afraid that he was accepting too many. In commenting on one dinner invitation which he had declined, he said in a letter home, "I really am going to stop all this social racket or my studies will be simply a minus quantity." But he enjoyed his Scottish friends and they enjoyed him. He admired the simplicity with which they entertained, contrasting it with the magnificence of social functions with which he was familiar in New York. "And," he said, "the conversation is far more interesting than anything you ordinarily hear on our side. Of course I have never been to entertainments at home composed of professors, ministers and literary lights so comparisons are not fair but I must say I enjoy these here very much."

Only rarely did he leave Edinburgh to visit friends elsewhere, but when he felt that he could do so he found great enjoyment in the more intimate contacts with Scottish life. There were occasional visits to the relatives in Dunfermline, where "Cousin Maggie" hovered over him with embarrassing solicitude. He spent a stormy week-end with the Robert Barbours at their country place near Pitlochry where he took a walk and enjoyed the views of the mountains while most of the guests shot rabbits and pheasants. He shivered in the Pitlochry church on Sunday morning and was glad to discover that there was a fire in the Chapel where they went to the evening service, although he thought it very undemocratic that the landed gentry sat in special front pews while the rest of the people sat in back. He spent his first Christmas away from home with the Templetons at Knockderry Castle at Cove in Dunbartonshire. Christmas dinner was in the evening, and he was delighted when the gardener appeared in kilts and after the dessert marched round the long table playing the bagpipes. He spent his second Christmas in Scotland under the same hospitable roof. The New Year's week-end of 1899 he spent with the Nairns at Kirkcaldy. Again on this visit pheasant shooting was part of the program. Coffin followed the shooters for a while but it was sleeting and when he could do so politely he slipped back to the house and settled down by the fire with a book. That evening there was dancing. On Sunday the household went to church morning and afternoon, walking the two and a half miles home after the second service. On Sunday evening all gathered in the hall for hymn singing. Coffin conducted prayers for the establishment both Sunday morning and evening. At noon on New Year's Day the neighbors began to pour in for greetings and refreshments, and later in the afternoon Coffin started back to the more Spartan regime of New College.

Occasionally he went off for a week-end and preached in some rural church. This brought him in touch with Scottish life from a different angle from that which was available to him in Edinburgh. One Sunday, for instance, he preached in St. Abbs, a small village on the coast, inhabited almost entirely by fishermen. On Sunday morning, after spending Saturday night at the manse, he began a crowded day which he described in a letter to his mother: "About 10:30 I went to the vestry and the beadle helped me on with the cassock and gown. Next the chorister or precentor arrived who is quite a character. He reassured me by announcing, 'Ye ha selecktit very bonnie tunes the dae,' 'Ane's my favorite.' At the proper time preceded by the beadle I was ushered into a rather high pulpit and found about 150 people there—farmers and fishermen and their families—a typical Scotch crowd. You could imagine yourself a character in Watson's books.

"Directly under the pulpit sat Robert Nesbit the precentor. Facing him were four very red-cheeked lassies composing the choir and on my left was a small harmonium. I had four prayers to make and a sermon. I tried to go very slowly but I could feel that I was not carrying the crowd along very well. After the service I met the elders in the vestry. One old elder who rejoices in the name of 'Wullie' Dickson and who according to Mrs. A. is the great critic of the congregation, informed me that the matter of the sermon was very good and that he could name all the heads and was greatly interested, but that I had 'spokit so fast and ha jerkit out the worrds so shairp that he couldna follow very well.' This as you may imagine was hardly encouraging, as the service was about as hard work as I could do.

"At 2 p.m. I had to go and open the Sabbath School and superintend it. By this time it was blowing a perfect gale and both the Church and the Manse shook terribly. It rained very heavily about every hour.

"The evening service came at six and was somewhat larger than the morning in spite of the awful weather. We had a few over 200 out and the choir was augmented by two men and two lassies. Again I had four prayers and the same number of hymns, psalms, and readings. My sermon which I would ordinarily have gotten off in 25 minutes took me nearly forty and I used every gesture I ever learned from old Mack Bailey or the Pater. I could feel that I was getting the people when I wanted them so I felt greatly encouraged. Old Mr. Dickson told Mrs. A. to my great satisfaction at the conclusion: 'I likit him awfil weel the nicht.' It was very dark and stormy outside so two of the elders insisted on taking me home lest anything should happen en route.

"After supper I had family prayers again which made the eleventh prayer for that day so you can easily imagine that during the course of the day I gave thanks for about everything an ordinary man could remember and asked for all that could be reasonably demanded. Toward the end I had to resort to geography and go off to heathen lands.

"Monday was a perfect day. The sky was blue and the air soft and balmy so that you really felt warm. After another edition of prayers I took a long walk over St. Abbs Head and enjoyed the country air and scene immensely. After a small collation at 11:30 I started back to Coldingham on foot and thence by bus and rail to Edinboro where I arrived at 2:50."

The academic year at New College closed early in April in

order to give the students ample opportunity for summer work.
Hardly had Coffin matriculated in the autumn of 1897 before
some of his professors began to advise him to go to Oxford for
the Spring Term which would include the period between April
22 and June 18. R. S. Simpson in particular urged him to do so,
arguing that he would miss the chance of a lifetime if he did not
have at least one term in residence at Oxford. Accordingly he arrived in Oxford on April 15, 1898 and after much difficulty found
rooms in which he and another student from Edinburgh could
live during the term which was about to begin. A few days later,
however, he was on board the S. S. *Kaiser Wilhelm der Grosse*
en route to New York. Two circumstances were responsible for
his sudden change of plans. One was his disappointment with the
courses available to him. He discovered that the theological lectures for the term at Oxford University were expressly planned
for the purpose of preparing Anglican students for their diocesan
ordination examinations. A talk with Principal A. M. Fairbairn at
Mansfield College, the Congregational theological school, held
out little hope that he would fare much better there. The other
circumstance was his growing restlessness because of the Spanish-
American War. On February 19, 1898, he had written home that
the British papers were full of accounts of the sinking of the
Maine, and that the *Glasgow Herald* represented everybody in the
United States as shouting for war. "Of course I suppose the whole
business is a falsehood from first to last as the explosion seems to
have been due to an accident," he wrote. On March 30 he wrote,
"The newspapers here one day say that war is inevitable between
Spain and ourselves and the next say nothing will come of all the
Jingo war talk." On his way to Oxford in April he attended a
Y.M.C.A. Student Conference in Birmingham. One of the speak-
ers was Dr. John R. Mott, whom Coffin had known through his
Y.M.C.A. activities at Yale. After the address Coffin and Mott had
a talk in the latter's hotel room. "We both read over the account
of that disgraceful scene in the House of Representatives and be-

moaned the inevitableness of war. It seems sure now and we must hope that it will be short and accompanied by as little loss of life and property as possible." He had a few days in London before the Oxford term began and wrote from that city: "London is in great excitement over this war and extras are cried all day. I feel sort of restless and if I could see any good in it I should come home and enlist in some capacity. But I cannot feel any warlike enthusiasm and fighting is not in my line. . . . However if Oxford is not most satisfactory I may come home." When he found that the Oxford courses available to him were not what he had hoped, he decided to read quietly at his home in New York until the summer when, as will be seen, he expected to preach at Water Mill on Long Island.

In January he had written to his family that most of the men at New College were expected to do preaching during the summer. He recalled that a small white church or chapel had been put up at Water Mill near Southampton on Long Island. He did not know whether it belonged to any denomination, but he wondered if they could use a theologue during the summer. He thought that people from a nearby inn could be attracted and that possibly there would be a chance to do some good there. The suggestion bore fruit and Coffin spent two summers as temporary supply preacher at the little chapel. There was a struggling little congregation of people who lived all the year round in the neighborhood. Coffin's ministry there was something of a sensation. People from Southampton who knew him and his family crowded the pews and he preached to congregations which filled the church. No doubt some of them came at first because there was a certain novelty about the spectacle of a young man of his type, identified with the "summer people," in the pulpit of a country chapel. If so, all that was soon forgotten in the devout worship and stirring preaching to which they were exposed. Coffin went back to Edinburgh in the autumn of 1898 confirmed in the conviction that he had been called to be a preacher, humbly aware of the powers with which he had been endowed for the ministry of the Church. In the summer of 1899 he returned to supply the Water Mill church, and again the church was crowded Sunday after Sunday. He was gratified that many people from the countryside who had not previously been church attendants were drawn to the services.

On one of John R. Mott's visits to Edinburgh, Coffin suggested to him that he write to Dwight L. Moody proposing that George Adam Smith be invited to speak at a Northfield Student Conference. Smith was planning to visit the United States to deliver the Lyman Beecher Lectures on Preaching at the Yale Divinity School in the Spring of 1899. Coffin had been so deeply impressed with Smith as a preacher and particularly as a speaker to students that he was eager to have American young men hear him. Mott made the suggestion to Mr. Moody who extended the invitation which resulted in Smith's address at Northfield in 1899. Because George Adam Smith was widely known as a Higher Critic of the Bible, Mr. Moody received protests from zealous Biblical literalists who objected to Smith's appearance on the program at Northfield. As the story has been often told, the critics said to Mr. Moody, "Don't you know that George Adam Smith says that there were two Isaiahs?" to which Mr. Moody is said to have made the characteristic reply, "So long as there are so many people who do not know that there was one Isaiah, I shall not worry about a man who says there were two."

Coffin's admiration for George Adam Smith began with his reading a little book by him while the Coffin family were traveling in France during the summer prior to the opening of his first term at New College. He also read Smith's *Life of Henry Drummond* on the train going to and from Newton Stewart where he preached one Sunday. His personal friendship with Professor Smith began in February, 1898, when the latter was in Edinburgh speaking to the students in connection with a Day of Prayer. After the evening meeting Coffin and a few other students sat until midnight in R. S. Simpson's library listening to Smith as he talked about City

Mission work in Glasgow in which he was deeply interested. The conversation ranged over a wide field, including the Beecher Lectures which Smith had promised to deliver at Yale the following year. When Coffin later was in Glasgow, Smith invited him to his room to sit by the fire and talk about American student interests saying that he was terribly worried about his Yale lectures as he was having trouble getting them written as he would like to have them. He also had on his mind the promise which he had made to preach in Battell Chapel to the undergraduates at Yale and to speak three evenings at student meetings in Dwight Hall. A few weeks later, when Smith was in Edinburgh, he had another long talk with Coffin, this time about the possibility of his speaking at the Northfield Conference. Apparently Smith had been sounded out in the matter but had received no official invitation as yet. He was anxious to go and was eager to meet Mr. Moody, but he was afraid that his presence at Northfield might arouse controversy, particularly after his Yale Lectures in which he intended to speak on the subject, "Modern Criticism and the Preaching of the Old Testament." Coffin urged him to go and got him to agree to leave the dates open and to accept the invitation if it came to him from Mr. Moody personally, as it subsequently did.

While Coffin was studying at Edinburgh he was disturbed by reports which came from the United States that charges of heresy had been brought against Professor Arthur Cushman McGiffert by the Presbytery of Pittsburgh and that several resolutions of a similar tenor had been introduced in the Presbytery of New York. The criticisms were directed against Dr. McGiffert's book *The History of Christianity in the Apostolic Age.* Coffin read the book and while he disagreed with McGiffert's conclusions regarding the historical value of the Book of Acts and of the Pastoral Epistles he thought that the book as a whole was "not at all out of the way." He felt strenuously that there ought to be a place in the Presbyterian Church for men of widely differing views and he began to have serious doubts about trying to enter the Presbyterian ministry if men like McGiffert were put out. In this he reflected the atmosphere about him. He reported that the *British Weekly* was the only paper in Britain which regarded McGiffert as too advanced and quoted Professor A. B. Davidson as saying that it would be a crying shame if McGiffert were put out of the Presbyterian Church as he was one of the ablest young men in his field of study. Coffin thought McGiffert's statement of his loyalty to Presbyterian standards a model of courteous and conciliatory affirmation. The General Assembly of the Presbyterian Church took no action against McGiffert, but in 1898 it expressed "its emphatic disapproval of all utterances in the book called to its attention by the Presbytery of Pittsburgh, not in accordance with the Standards of the Church," and it issued a deliverance reaffirming the inerrancy of Scripture and other doctrines held to be essential by what later came to be called the Fundamentalist wing of the Church. Coffin was outraged by the action of the Assembly. "It is simply a disgrace to the Church," he wrote. "It seems almost incredible that a body of men possessed of education and common sense could frame such a deliverance. What is the use of study if all the results are fixed beforehand and you are told beforehand what your conclusions must be?" McGiffert ended the controversy insofar as he was concerned by simply withdrawing from the Presbyterian Church and becoming a Congregationalist. The episode made a deep impression upon the young student in Edinburgh, and coming as it did so soon after the Briggs controversy, it helped to lay in his mind the foundations of convictions concerning freedom of scholarship and honest scholarship in the service of religion for which he was to contend all through his strenuous life.

Before leaving Yale he had decided to fulfil the requirements for the Yale M.A. degree while taking his theological course. Correspondence with Dean Andrew Phillips of the Yale Graduate School brought him the information that a thesis would be required and a comparison of the philosophy of Tennyson with that of Carlyle was agreed upon as the subject on which he was to write. He fulfilled the requirements and received the degree in 1900.

His arduous academic life was relieved by long bicycle rides and by long walks through the country around Edinburgh, the two forms of recreation in which he took most pleasure. To a generation not accustomed to bicycling as a sport, the distances covered by these rides is surprising. There are not infrequent references in his letters to eighteen and twenty mile rides, and one description of a ride twenty-six miles and a half. On March 22, 1898, he wrote home: "We have had a spell of almost spring weather with warm sun and bright blue sky. Saturday our bike ride was most successful. The party consisted of five males and seven females and our ride was of 26½ miles. . . . These Scotch girls and some of the older ladies are very muscular and quite delight in scorching. We rode out past the Pentlands to Pennicuik and on to Auchterdenney to Nine Mile Burn where there is a famous inn of which Allan Ramsay wrote. Here we had a very good tea of scones and jam and tea. We came back by the High Road and had some splendid views. When we got to Edinboro it was about 7 o'clock and dark. Mr. and Mrs. Low insisted that Strachan, Cooley and myself should come and take dinner with them just as we were in our golf suits. This we did and a very good dinner went down easily after that ride." His enthusiasm for walking, which was one of his lifelong pleasures, was whetted by such expeditions as one which he took in December of his first year at Edinburgh: "Saturday last was a magnificent day and a party of seven of us went out to Colinton by train and walked all the way in across the Pentlands. The hills were covered with snow and the views were grand. We walked about eight miles chiefly up and down hill and at a good Scotch rate and your humble servant was very well prepared for bed by night. It was a great expedition and very pleasant."

While Coffin was in Edinburgh letters from America brought reports of difficulties in the Fifth Avenue Presbyterian Church in New York. Dr. John Hall, the minister, resigned, then withdrew his resignation, and finally requested the Presbytery to release him from his pastorate. Coffin received letters from Mr. John Sloane, his uncle, asking for information about men in Scotland whom the officers of the church thought might possibly be invited to succeed Dr. Hall, and he replied as best he could.

Running through Coffin's letters to his family during his second year at Edinburgh are occasional references to "the Californians." "Remember me to the Californians if they are with you." "I dare say the Californians are having the time of their lives." The Californians were friends and relatives from San Francisco who were visiting the Edmund Coffins in New York. One of them, Dorothy Eells, was destined to become the most important person in Henry Coffin's life.

When Coffin went to Edinburgh he was undecided as to whether to study there for three years and take the Bachelor of Divinity degree from New College, or to return to the United States and take his final year in an American seminary. He became so enthusiastic about his Scottish professors that there were times when he wanted very much to take the full course in Scotland. In the end, however, it seemed wiser, since he was determined to be a minister in his native land, to have his third year in an American theological school. Because of the controversies over Dr. Briggs and Dr. McGiffert, Union Seminary was not in good repute among the conservative leaders of the Presbyterian Church in the U.S.A., but after his Scottish training he knew that he would be in a more congenial atmosphere there than in any of the other American seminaries. He examined the Union course of studies and found that in his two years at Edinburgh he had covered more ground than would be required for entrance into the Senior class at Union. So he began to make his plans to leave Scotland in the Spring of 1899 and enter Union Seminary the following autumn.

He found it a painful business to say farewell to the friends he had made on the faculty and in the city as well as among the students. He had taken prizes in most of his courses, and had a distinguished scholastic record to leave behind him, but even more outstanding had been his success in winning the friendship of a people who are not popularly supposed to give their friendship easily. His last days in Edinburgh were a round of lunches, suppers and teas with families that wanted to have him at their tables once more before he departed. The Alexander Martins and R. S. Simpsons begged him to come and stay with them for a few days before he left Edinburgh, which he was unable to do. He had a last tea with the Marcus Dods and supper with the Alexander Whytes, and visits with many others. "I hate this saying good-bye and feel very blue at leaving some of the chaps here. They will be scattering to the ends of earth as is the way with the Scots and there is little likelihood of our meeting again." But the inevitable final day came and he was off for a term in Germany and then home.

CHAPTER FOUR

ON THE THRESHOLD

FROM April to June, 1899, after the year's work at New College in Edinburgh had been completed, Coffin studied in Germany at the University of Marburg. His primary purpose in doing so was to acquire a command of the language which would enable him to read German theological publications. He lived in German families and was soon able to converse freely with his friends as well as to take lectures in the classroom. Marcus Dods had given him a letter of introduction to Professor Herrmann, whose book *Communion with God* was widely known in English-speaking circles. Herrmann admitted him to a Seminar on the ethical teaching of Jesus which Coffin found very stimulating. He was curious about student customs in a German university, appalled by the scarred faces which told the story of inter-society duels, and welcomed the opportunity to walk and talk with groups of students whom he met. He was disturbed by the rift between the churches and the University circles and felt that in their rigid orthodoxy the churches were failing to establish contact with the intellectual groups.

George Ichn, the eldest son of the family with whom Coffin boarded during most of his stay, took upon himself special responsibility for their American boarder. He corrected the papers which Coffin wrote and carried on daily conversations with him in German. He impressed Coffin as "a decent chap," aside from his enthusiasm for some of the less attractive sides of German student life. Coffin remarked that "he belongs to the Westphalian Verbindung, has unlimited capacity for beer, and 'his chief end' seems to be to fight duels and mar himself forever. So far he has succeeded fairly well and his face is a sight to behold." Coffin was very much excited when George Ichn took him as a guest to a gathering of his society. "Let me tell you of the fearful adventures of H.S.C. and his method of spending a Sunday evening," he wrote home. "May 1 is a great day in Germany and for many years has been 'seen in' with appropriate ceremonies by German students. Last night Ichn had a fellow student in to supper and the two of them asked me to go with them to their society and see the ceremonies. It was Sunday evening and I debated with myself what I ought to do, but curiosity overcame piety and I also did not like to hurt the fellows' feelings. So I went and spent from 8:40 to 1 a.m. with them. Their Verbindung has a very handsome house at a short distance from the city limit, with a fine balcony overlooking the valley and right above the river *Lahn*. The hall was about the size of our library in New York and very handsomely decorated and filled with relics of duelling, trophies of the Franco-Prussian War and any number of steins, drinking horns, antlers, etc. There are 12 active members in the society and 6 sort of under members called Fuchs. A man is a Fuchs for a year and then becomes active for two more and after that is an 'alter Herr.' Last night all the Fuchs and active members were there and about six alter Herrs including a professor. A band hired from a neighboring village was playing and the members were all seated around a horseshoe-shaped table drinking beer and singing songs.

"I was brought in and everyone rose and I had to go the rounds and bow to each member. Then I was given a seat on the chairman's left while the professor sat on his right. A stein of beer was placed before me and each member proceeded to toast me and at each toast I was expected to bow and drink with the man.

I looked about the room and saw after a drink or two that at this rate half a dozen steins wouldn't last me around that crowd and if I was to spend the evening I thought the end of it would see me under and not above the board. So I made a lightning calculation and drank as little as I could at each sip.

"The singing was very good and I was furnished with a book so that I could take part. I managed to converse pretty well with different members who would take turns at coming up and chatting with the guests. It is needless to say that I learned a good deal of German. Two chaps had their heads all done up in slings and bandages and smelled of antiseptics—they had fought on the previous day with members of another Verein. Every member has to fight eight duels to get his sash—a band they wear with great pride—so you can imagine the faces of the company.

"About 10:45 the president made a speech and called on the professor who told some funny stories. I say funny because the crowd were highly amused, but I could not find the point owing to my poor grasp of German. Drinking and singing went on up to 12, by which time I had put two huge steins under my chest. At 12 we went out to the balcony. Fireworks were being set off in all directions and the hills were lit with bonfires. Each Verbindung had its hired band out playing and as the church clock struck the whole city led by the students sang 'Der Mai ist gekommen.'

"When the lied was over a huge drinking horn was filled with beer and carried about by a couple of Fuchs, out of which we were all to drink the 'Frühling' toast. It was filled and refilled several times and luckless I had also to empty a portion of its contents into my already well filled inner.

"By 1 I was awfully tired and broke for home much to Ichn's disappointment who stayed on until 4. This morning all the classes were very sparsely attended." . . .

Late in May, when the University closed for a week, Coffin took a bicycle trip through the Hartz Mountains. His companions were two friends who had gone to Marburg with him from Edinburgh, Herbert Gallaudet, whom he had previously known at Yale, and Paterson, a Scot.

The term at Marburg was over by the middle of June. Coffin sailed at once for the United States, his two years of European study behind him. They had been happy, fascinating years which left their mark indelibly upon him. He was still thoroughly American, and was conscious of no temptation to become an expatriate. In fact, when invited to remain in Scotland as assistant to the Reverend R. S. Simpson at the Free High Church, he declined at once on the ground that he had no intention of losing his identity as an American. He had, however, learned to understand how some aspects of American life appeared to Europeans, and all through his life he had an uncanny ability to view the American scene as an American and at the same time to see it through the eyes of his British and German friends. The promotion of better understanding between Europe and America, and especially the promotion of deeper friendship between Britain and America became one of the dominant ambitions of his life. In Scotland he had imbibed the Scottish respect for the dignity of the ministry, a high doctrine of the Church as the communion of Christian believers, an appreciation of the Reformed tradition of worship, an abiding conviction that religion and learning must go hand in hand, and a clear realization of the difference between the non-essentials of the Christian faith which the Higher Criticism of the Bible might subject to reinterpretation and the essential convictions which are more fundamental than interpretations. At Marburg he had become familiar with German scholarship, had been exposed to Ritschlian theology in its native haunts, had acquired a renewed concern for enlisting the highest intellect in the service of the Church, and had developed an affection for the German people which later made the First World War an acute torture for his spirit. All in all, they had been two rich years which had given him friendships and outlooks which he treasured all his days. He went back to the United States in June, 1899, well content with what the experience had given him and eager for the next stage in his preparation for the ministry. In September he entered Union Theological Seminary in New York City for his final year of work looking toward the B.D. degree.

Union Seminary was located at 700 Park Avenue between 69th and 70th Streets. Coffin studied there for one year and graduated *summa cum laude* in 1900. He did not live in the Seminary, but made his home with his family at 13 West 57th Street. Each day he walked up Fifth Avenue and across Madison Avenue to Park Avenue to attend his classes at the Seminary. The distance presented no problem, but living at home meant that he did not share in the student life with the same intimacy that he had enjoyed at Yale and in Edinburgh.

Less than a decade before Coffin entered Union Seminary, the institution had passed through a turbulent period which had tested the loyalty of its friends and its own loyalty to the principles of its founders. Because the feelings engendered by the Briggs case still ran high when Coffin was a student and because in later life he was concerned that the issues involved should be understood, it may be worth while to recall here the history of that controversy as he on many occasions described it.[1] In 1870, at the time of the reunion of the Old School and New School Presbyterian Assemblies, Dr. William Adams, a leader of the New School group, in the interests of harmony persuaded the directors of Union Seminary to allow the Presbyterian General Assembly the right to veto the choice of professors. Previously the Assembly had elected professors for the Presbyterian seminaries but had no control either positive or negative over the election of faculty members at Union. Princeton Seminary, an institution under the control of the denomination, wished to elect its own professors, according the General Assembly only the right to

[1] Sermon by Henry S. Coffin at Centennial of Union Theological Seminary, May 17, 1936.

veto. It was thought that if Union Seminary consented to a similar relationship it would make for the greater freedom of all the denominational seminaries and for goodwill in the Presbyterian Church. One of Union's directors, Mr. D. Willis James, warned that the proposed change "was a very serious mistake and calculated to produce great and unfortunate mischief," a prediction which subsequent events unfortunately proved to be accurate. In 1891 a new chair of Biblical Theology was created in Union Seminary and Charles Augustus Briggs, who had been teaching the Old Testament for many years in the Seminary, was transferred to this new position. The General Assembly of the Presbyterian Church vetoed the transfer. The directors of the Seminary held that inasmuch as a transfer and not an election was involved this action of the Assembly went beyond the power granted in 1870 and proceeded to inaugurate Dr. Briggs in the new professorship. On the basis of his inaugural address, charges of heresy were brought against Dr. Briggs in the Presbytery of New York. He was promptly acquitted, but the decision was appealed before the General Assembly. After a trial which consumed many days and attracted attention throughout the Christian world, Dr. Briggs was held to be heretical in that he had taught that there was "a three-fold fountain of divine authority: the Bible, the Church, and the Reason;" that Moses did not write the account of his death; that there were two Isaiahs; and that there was progressive sanctification after death. He was deposed from the Presbyterian ministry. The directors of Union Seminary were told by their legal counsel that their action in 1870 when they had voluntarily surrendered some of their power in the appointment of professors had been *extra vires* and that under their Charter they had no legal right to divest themselves of any share in this responsibility. They retained Dr. Briggs in his chair and resumed the complete independence which the Seminary had enjoyed prior to 1870.

Coffin entered Union Seminary when the memory of the Briggs

case was still fresh in the minds of many people. It was fresh in his own mind because his father had been legal counsel for the Seminary and in that capacity had been present when the General Assembly made its decision in 1893. As a boy of sixteen Coffin had accompanied his father to the Assembly and had witnessed the scene which left an indelible impression upon his mind. Coffin entered the Seminary fully convinced that Union Seminary had an important mission to perform in promoting Christian unity, honest, fearless scholarship and enlightened, loyal churchmanship. For many years the charge was bandied about by people unfamiliar with the facts that Union Seminary had diverted to other purposes funds given by Presbyterians to found and maintain a denominational institution. Coffin's family and personal background had furnished him with a thorough knowledge of the Seminary's history from which to refute the baseless charges, which he was always zealous to do.

While in Germany, Coffin had met some Union Seminary students who had seemed to him intolerant in their liberalism and somewhat arrogant in their pretensions to omniscience. He thought that they compared rather unfavorably with the students he had known in Edinburgh where "if you don't learn anything else you certainly learn a little caution and canniness." He hoped that he would not find all Union Seminary men like these particular students whom he happened to encounter in Germany who "are so fearfully proud of their heresies and so anxious to tell you that they are not as other men." His year as a student at Union allayed whatever anxieties he may have had on that score, however, and resulted in a lifelong devotion to the Seminary. He responded enthusiastically to the breadth of outlook at Union, where men from different denominations were being trained together, learning to appreciate one another's backgrounds and to work fraternally for the common goals cherished by their various communions. He found at Union an emphasis upon painstaking, careful scholarship which was congenial to him after his work in Scotland and Germany. Some of the members of the Union Seminary faculty had been trained in Germany. The so-called Higher Criticism of the Bible taught at Union and looked upon with suspicion by the more conservative circles in American Churches had been taken for granted in Scotland and Germany and presented no problem to Coffin. His year of study on Park Avenue set its mark upon his future and helped to make him an effective leader in the movement for the freedom and unity of the Christian Church.

The President of the Seminary when Coffin entered as a student was Charles Cuthbert Hall who in 1897 had come to Union from the pastorate of the First Presbyterian Church on Brooklyn Heights. Dr. Hall had taken one year of his theological training in England and was perhaps for that reason prepared to take a special interest in the young New Yorker who came fresh from the halls of Edinburgh. Whatever may have been the initial attraction the two men were drawn to each other at once, and a friendship developed which grew steadily in warmth and strength until Dr. Hall's untimely death in 1908. It was to Dr. Hall that Coffin turned with the request that he preach his ordination sermon when the time came for that sacred service. It was Dr. Hall who laid the cornerstone of the new church in Coffin's first pastorate. On the other hand it was to Coffin that Dr. Hall turned before the younger man had been four years out of the Seminary with the plea that he come on the faculty as a part time teacher of pastoral theology. He took Coffin with him to meetings of the General Assembly of the Presbyterian Church to help him in a variety of ways. In his absences from the Seminary he delegated heavy responsibilities to his young colleague. From the beginning of their relationship, the older man saw in the younger a companion whose comradeship he enjoyed and also a fellow worker who would carry forward the things in which he most deeply believed. With equal devotion the younger man looked up to his senior with loyalty and admiration.

Among the members of the faculty who made a profound impression upon Coffin as a student was George William Knox, Professor of the Philosophy and History of Religion.[2] Dr. Knox had been a missionary in Japan for sixteen years and had held the Chair of Philosophy and Ethics in the Imperial University of Tokyo. Coffin thought him a remarkable lecturer, had deep respect for his learning and found him fascinating in conversation. Even in his latter years, Coffin frequently recommended that theological students read Dr. Knox's *The Direct and Fundamental Proofs of the Christian Religion,* the chapters of which were delivered as the Taylor Lectures at Yale in 1903. He found congenial Dr. Knox's insistence that Christianity is not an attempt to go "through nature to God" but starts with God's finding men through Christ and then interprets nature in the light of the revelation given in Christ. One of Dr. Knox's most brilliant students has recalled that long before the reaction against a superficial interpretation of liberalism had set in Dr. Knox warned his students against identifying evolution with inevitable progress and against substituting faith in progress for faith in God. Coffin delighted in Dr. Knox's independence of prevailing trends of thought, and found him a stimulating and enriching teacher.

There were other professors at Union to whose lectures Coffin always looked back with gratitude and whose continuing friendship he cherished: Francis Brown, the Old Testament scholar and president-to-be whose encyclopaedic learning and devout spirit he revered; Arthur Cushman McGiffert whose comprehensive knowledge of the history of Christian thought and superb clarity as a lecturer Coffin greatly admired; Thomas C. Hall, the son of Coffin's boyhood pastor, a pioneer in the field of Christian social ethics; Charles P. Fagnani, a Hebrew and Old Testament scholar whose gift for teaching and audacious humor delighted Coffin; William Adams Brown, Roosevelt Professor of Systematic The-

[2] Henry S. Coffin, *A Half Century of Union Theological Seminary,* Scribners, 1954, pp. 42-45.

ology, just beginning his career as an irenic theologian striving to conserve the best in the traditional theology and to combine it with the newer insights of his own day; James Everett Frame whose thorough scholarship in New Testament studies and exacting academic conscience Coffin esteemed while he regretted Frame's reluctance to publish the results of his painstaking labors. In the classrooms of these and other able scholars and teachers, Coffin found an atmosphere of intellectual excitement which was congenial to him. He soon developed an ardent loyalty to Union Seminary which was to become one of the dominant factors in his life.

Among his classmates also he found men who shared his interests and ideals, and, although he was not a resident of the dormitory, he established firm friendships with men who remained his lifelong friends and admirers. William Raymond Jelliffe was later on to be his associate for nearly twenty years in the ministry of the Madison Avenue Presbyterian Church. Murray Shipley Howland, who had also been his classmate at Yale, as minister of Presbyterian churches in Buffalo and Binghamton, was to work side by side with him through stormy years in helping to maintain Presbyterian freedoms. Julius V. Moldenhawer, as minister of the First Presbyterian Church in New York City and a Director of Union Seminary, was to be a neighbor and colleague of Coffin's in the years when both men were at the height of their powers. Benjamin T. Marshall was to become a Congregational minister near the Dartmouth College campus in Hanover, New Hampshire, and subsequently President of Connecticut College for Women. These men and others of their kind resolved whatever doubts Coffin had harbored with regard to the quality of the Union Seminary student body.

In March he began to preach each Sunday at the services of a little mission which was meeting in a hall in the Bedford Park district in the Bronx. Bedford Park, while within the limits of New York City, was hardly more than a rather sparsely settled village on the outskirts of the city, near one of the entrances to the Bronx Botanical Gardens and the Zoo. There was only one Protestant Church in what was obviously going to be a thickly populated region, lying as it did in the path of the city's northward growth. That church had fallen into difficulties, and a small group who lived at some distance from it had withdrawn and begun to hold services in Winghart's Hall, at the corner of Webster Avenue and Suburban Street, now called 201st Street. At first it was called "The Union Church of Bedford Park," a name adopted on November 3, 1898. Early in 1899, however, it was decided to affiliate "our little but active society," as the church records describe it, with the Presbyterian denomination. The Presbyterian Committee on Sabbath School Work was interested in finding a location in the neighborhood in which to start work, and the struggling little Union Church with its handful of members needed the support of some larger body. On March 14 the congregation took the decisive vote and at the invitation of Dr. Henry van Dyke, the president of the Church Extension Committee of the Presbytery of New York, Coffin was asked to take charge of the work. Fifty years later he recalled that "the little group which founded the Church met in Winghart over a butcher shop. The pulpit was a former oyster counter in a fish shop attached to the butcher enterprise. Everything in the hall was primitive so that it was difficult to have orderly services, but the people were in earnest." There were forty-seven members. Coffin preached there regularly during the final three months of his Seminary course.

At the April meeting of the Presbytery of New York, Coffin was "licensed to preach," which in the Presbyterian system is the step immediately preceding ordination in the progress of a candidate for the ministry. During his days in Edinburgh as he had read of the action of the Presbytery of New York with regard to Dr. McGiffert, Coffin had sometimes wondered if the Presbytery would accept him as a candidate for the ministry, coming fresh from Scottish lecture halls where the Higher Criticism of the Bible was taken for granted. His fears proved to be exaggerated, however, as his examination in theology was sustained by the Presbytery and the vote to ordain passed without controversy. The Service of Ordination was held in the University Place Presbyterian Church on May 2, 1900. Dr. Charles Cuthbert Hall preached the ordination sermon. His text was Matthew 6:33, "Seek ye first the kingdom of God, and his righteousness; and all these things shall be added unto you." The Ordination Prayer was offered by Dr. Thomas Hastings, who had been Dr. Hall's predecessor in the presidency of Union Seminary. The charge to the newly ordained minister was delivered by Dr. George Alexander, the pastor of the church in which the service was held, a man to whom Coffin looked up with reverence and whose counsel he sought again and again through the years. The Moderator of the Presbytery who presided and propounded the constitutional questions was Dr. David G. Wylie. William Bennett Bebb was ordained in the same service, and the Minutes of the Presbytery of New York record in Presbyterian language that the two young men "were by prayer and with the laying on of the hands of the presbytery, according to the apostolic example, solemnly ordained to the holy office of the gospel ministry. These brethren took their seats as members of the presbytery."

A quarter of a century afterwards Coffin wrote an article for a national magazine under the title: "Why I Am A Presbyterian."[3] It contained some significant autobiographical references:

"I am a Presbyterian by inheritance. My forbears, on both my father's and mother's side of the family, belonged in this part of the Church of Christ, and I was thus 'foreordained.' My training in home and church was along Presbyterian lines. I was given a thorough education in the contents of the Bible, committing many chapters and verses to memory, and I grew up with a genuine relish for the things associated with religion. I early learned by

[3] *The Forum,* New York City, March, 1926.

heart the Shorter Catechism of the Westminster Divines, which is an excellent mental discipline in its logical reasoning and rhythmical English. Many of its formulations are obsolete, and I am not passing it on to another generation, but its purpose, to supply Christians with definite convictions and to make them think for themselves, is part of the inheritance worth striving to maintain.

"When I came to prepare for the ministry, the Church in this country had been troubled by a heresy trial in which the less educated and more intolerant elements had attacked and driven out Professor Briggs. Partly from the Scottish traditions of my family, I began my preparation in Edinburgh, where Scotch Presbyterianism was then, as it still is, much more open-minded and modern than most of the theology taught in this country. The findings of science both in evolution and in historical criticism were taken for granted. The views of the Bible, now labeled 'fundamentalist', were not held thirty years ago by any accredited leaders in the Scottish Kirk. . . . The Westminster Confession of Faith, which is a standard of the churches of Scotland, as well as of the Presbyterian Church of this country, was viewed as an historic expression of the beliefs of Christians in the Seventeenth Century, which modern ministers were expected to subscribe only in the sense that they accorded with its main convictions and stood in the same devout succession.

"I completed my course in Union Theological Seminary, which I found certainly not one whit less orthodox than the Scottish halls of divinity, and where a similar view of the Church and her creeds was inculcated. I presented myself for licensure in the Presbytery of New York, where the large majority impressed me as an open-minded and open-hearted company of Christian leaders, apparently sympathizing with the outlook on truth and life in which I had been trained.

"I remain a Presbyterian, not because I believe that the Presbyterian Church is better than any other, but because I owe to it whatever religious inspiration I possess, and because I believe that in it for the present I, with my ancestry, training, and temperament, can most usefully serve the Kingdom of God."

He concluded with a ringing affirmation of his faith in a coming organic union of the Protestant Churches: "So I may say that I am a Presbyterian only temporarily. The name carries many hallowed memories and associations, but it seems to me to belong to the past rather than to the present. . . . Once granted that no existing church is specially gifted with true doctrine or correct orders or the only valid mode of administering some sacrament, and that all have valuable historical heritages and large present contributions to make to the united Church of Christ, it ought not to be impossible to arrive at some form of organization which would combine liberty and unity, conserving the values in our differences and making possible the gains of united life and service. Already just across our northern border, Methodists, Congregationalists, and Presbyterians are consolidated in the United Church of Canada. The time is ripe for a similar and even more inclusive organic union among the churches of the United States. I hope to live to see it, and I am ready to do my utmost for its accomplishment. Meanwhile I remain a Presbyterian, resolved to seek to end any barriers in our communion which render it less comprehensive than the United Church of Christ should be." It was not given to him to live to see his faith fulfilled, but he passed it on to generations of students who cherished the dream and in many different communions strove to make it a reality.

As his year of study at Union Seminary drew near the end, the question of where to begin his ministry became insistent. There was no dearth of opportunities. He declined the successful, prosperous churches which, although he was a young man of twenty-three who had never held a pastorate, were ready to welcome him to their pulpits. The little mission which he was serving in Bedford Park showed signs of promise and offered opportunity for the kind of pioneer work which he wanted to do. On June 21,

1900, the congregation of forty-seven members voted to become an organized Presbyterian Church. A week later a special meeting was held with the Reverend Wilton Merle-Smith as Moderator and the Reverend Henry Sloane Coffin was elected as Stated Supply for one year at a salary of one thousand dollars for the year, one half of which was to be paid by the congregation. Presumably the other half was to be provided by the Church Extension Committee of the Presbytery of New York. Coffin eagerly accepted the call. He did not have to begin work, for he was already busily engaged in the activities of the little church, but when the Seminary year ended in May and he was a full-fledged Bachelor of Divinity, he turned with great enthusiasm and high spirits to give his full time to the work for which at Yale, Edinburgh, Marburg and Union he had been preparing himself.

Only twenty-three years of age when called to his first pastorate, Coffin had already reached a maturity of outlook which was the admiration of men who had enjoyed much longer experience in the ministry. As a matter of fact, he was always one of the rare men whose wisdom and vitality seem to bear no relation to their years. In his youth he displayed judgment and foresight which would ordinarily have been expected only in a much older man. To the close of his life there was a youthfulness of spirit and an uplifting buoyancy about him which made it impossible to think of him as a man in his seventies. And always there was a refreshing realism and candor in his utterances which made him trusted.[4] Toward the end of his initial pastorate he was to define the man needed in the ministry as one "who wishes above all to be a leader in the establishment of the Kingdom of God, but feels himself more or less out of sympathy with the teaching and the methods of the church as it at present exists"; who "cherishes the ideal of the ministry in his heart, but holds back because he finds it extremely difficult to speak out on religious topics"; who

[4] "The Men We Need in the Ministry Today," in *The New York Observer*, June 22, 1905.

"feels that his own religious experience is so limited, that he is so uncertain about many aspects of religious truth that he ought not to go into the ministry, although he would like to be a leader in the cause of Christ"; and "whose own modesty makes him shrink from entering the ministry although he feels an impulse toward it." Surely there was a large element of autobiography in that description.

CHAPTER FIVE

BEDFORD PARK

IN 1900 the Bedford Park district in the Bronx was a pleasant, rather sparsely settled neighborhood some six miles from the heart of New York City. Survivors of that era, who see it through the nostalgic mists of memory, remember it as a delightful suburb with a great deal of open space between houses, often not more than two houses on a block, bearing little resemblance to the present typically urban neighborhood which has been swallowed up by the northward spread of apartment houses, stores and business of many varieties. Its spiritual needs, however, were very great at the turn of the century, as the newly organized church found, and its material needs no less urgent. There was need for a church which could be a leaven of Christian life in the community, a bond of union among different kinds of people, a training center for children and young people, and a fellowship in creative worship. Could the Bedford Park Presbyterian Church become such an institution? It was an opportunity which challenged a young minister who was eager to find a chance to give himself utterly through his ministry. It would have had little attraction for the personally ambitious type of cleric with a weather eye out for a comfortable salary, denominational preferment and professional prestige.

Coffin had begun his service in Bedford Park before the little mission had become a regularly organized Presbyterian Church. When he was elected Stated Supply on June 27, 1900, this meant that for one year only he was to fulfill all the functions of a pastor. It was only a few months, however, before the congregation was convinced that it wanted Coffin installed by the Presbytery as its fully accredited pastor. On January 30, 1901, at a special meeting over which Dr. William Adams Brown, of Union Seminary, had been invited to act as Moderator, it was unanimously voted to call Coffin as the church's regular pastor at a salary of fifteen hundred dollars per year. The Service of Installation was held on February 21, 1901, with the Installation Sermon preached by the Reverend Charles Cuthbert Hall.

Even before he became the regularly installed pastor of the church, Coffin had launched the project of securing a church building for his growing congregation. Winghart Hall was only one block from the railroad station. Each Sunday morning a train passed just after the beginning of the sermon and the noise was so great that it was necessary for the preacher to stop and wait until the roar had ceased. In later years Coffin loved to remind the congregation how a group of boys would gather on the steps outside Winghart Hall and roll marbles down the sixteen steps leading up to the door. Each marble was clearly audible as it dropped from step to step, and it took almost superhuman efforts on the part of the preacher to hold the attention of his auditors to the sermon against the natural temptation to count from one to sixteen as each marble made its descent. The chief problems with Winghart Hall, however, were its size and its inappropriateness for worship. From the beginning of his ministry in the district Coffin had called assiduously on the homes of the neighborhood inviting strangers to attend the services. He had even preached on Sunday evenings in the open air near the entrance to the Bronx Zoo when crowds of holiday makers were coming and going, and always invited the passers-by to attend the Bedford Park Church. A larger and more churchly place of worship was needed for the steadily enlarging group of people who were responding to the sincerity and magnetism of the young minister. While Coffin was still serving as Stated Supply, with the aid of the Church Extension Committee of the Presbytery, a site for a new church building was secured on Southern Boulevard (now called Bedford Park Boulevard or 200th Street) and the corner of Bainbridge Avenue. The little congregation raised what money it could and Coffin secured contributions from friends and relatives in the city. The Jerome Park race track was being excavated to make way for a reservoir and it was possible to make an arrangement by which the church secured the stone for its building at no cost except that of transportation. R. H. Robertson gave his services as architect for the building. Coffin found a donor of one hundred and fifty dollars with which to purchase a bell for the small tower. Mr. Morris K. Jesup gave an organ to the church. On August 11, 1900, hardly six weeks after Coffin had become Stated Supply, the cornerstone was laid by Dr. Charles Cuthbert Hall. On December 23, 1900, the congregation met for the last time in Winghart Hall and marched through the street to the new building for the Service of Dedication. It was a simple and dignified structure, somewhat after the fashion of an English parish church. It seemed adequate for the needs of the congregation for a long time to come, although before three years had elapsed, it was to prove too small for the rapidly growing work. As 1900 ended there was satisfaction in the hearts of the people and their minister. Their church had a home of its own.

In December, 1901, *The New York Journal* in its edition for Harlem and the Bronx, carried on its front page a full-length photograph of "Sloane Coffin," as the picture was captioned. The accompanying article, while it made much of Coffin's family background in terms which must have been acutely embarrassing to him, had even more to say about his effectiveness as a pastor who in less than two years had brought "a humble mission" to a new status as a church numbering more than two hundred members worshipping in a new church building free from debt.

When the third annual meeting of the congregation was held on March 18, 1903, the church was growing steadily and was permeated with enthusiasm and confidence. The membership was now two hundred seventy-two and the Sunday School numbered two hundred ninety-three. On Sunday mornings the congregations were larger than the pews of the new little church would hold and it was necessary to put chairs in the aisles. The congregation voted to appoint a committee to confer with the architect concerning the enlargement of the building. The outcome of this was a plan to build a west wing at a cost of five thousand dollars. At a special meeting on May 16 between eight hundred and nine hundred dollars were subscribed by those present. By June 10 it was possible to hold another special meeting at which it was reported that $4700 had been subscribed "with still further kind friends to hear from," and the contract for the work was authorized. There was a general feeling that the church would be better proportioned if the height of the tower were increased. Coffin raised the necessary funds for this improvement from outside sources and the work was done while the west wing was being added. This gave the church exterior the appearance which it has today, except for a Church House which was added in 1929.

There were problems aplenty to tax the patience and wisdom of the young minister, as there are in every church. While the church was still meeting in Winghart Hall, a request was received from the Women's Christian Temperance Union for the use of the Hall for a meeting. Coffin, who served as a member of the Board of Trustees for the first three years of the church's existence, moved that the permission be granted for use when no church meeting was scheduled "provided that the meeting be not held in the interest of any political party." (This question of the relationship of the church and partisan politics was one with which he had to wrestle in various forms all through his active career, and his position was always substantially that which he took in this incident during the first year of his ministry.) When the new church building was being erected the question arose as to whether the pews should be free and unassigned or should be rented. Coffin always believed the rental of pews to be undemocratic and thought that pews in the house of God should be free and unassigned. When the Bedford Park Presbyterian Church was being planned it was decided that pews should be assigned to every regular contributor to the support of the church. Just a year later, however, it was voted that all seats should be declared free after January 1, 1902. There is no record that there was any controversy over the matter or that the decision left any injured feelings in its wake, but the congregation had come to agree with its persuasive pastor who took the time to educate his people on the question instead of making an issue of it. (This also was a problem which Coffin was to meet in a more acute form in his later ministry.)

There were the usual difficulties which most churches face. It was reported to the Board of Trustees that the boys who were using the basement of the church were not conducting themselves properly. The minister was asked to talk with the boys, which he did. There were disturbances created by rowdy elements in front of the church, and more than once the police captain of the precinct was appealed to by the Trustees for help. A sad entry in the Session minutes in 1902 reads: "——, a member of the church, having fallen into grievous sin for the past year, appeared before the Session, and having expressed penitence with a determination with the help of God to lead a good life in the future was again received into the communion of the church." A still sadder record appears in the Session minutes the next year after an office bearer had been charged with immorality and deceit. He appeared before the Session, after which that body "Resolved that his name be deleted from the roll of this church." More frequent than the sad entries in the church records, however, are such items as this in the Session Minutes: "The well-being of the church was discussed and there seemed to be much cause for gratitude and encouragement."

Coffin's liturgical interest, which had been whetted by his work with R. S. Simpson in Edinburgh, found expression in services of worship which were reverent and dignified. Prayers of Confession and Thanksgiving from *The Presbyterian Book of Common Worship* were printed on cards for distribution in the pews and were repeated in unison by the congregation on Sunday mornings. One of his first steps when he became pastor of the church was to organize a volunteer chorus of young people to give leadership to the church's music. He wanted the congregation to sing the best hymns, to hear the fine anthems, and to have nothing in the conduct of the service which would be unworthy of the house of God. There must have been some at the beginning who were more accustomed to the happy-go-lucky ways of the gospel meetings and revival tents, but they learned to appreciate and share his ideals for the worship of God in the beauty of holiness.

During his Bedford Park pastorate Coffin continued to live for part of each week with his family at 13 West 57th Street. He frequently rode the six miles from mid-Manhattan to the Bronx on his bicycle. When that was not feasible, he took the train. This was, of course, before the days of subways. In Bedford Park he boarded with the family of Mr. and Mrs. A. E. Miller on Briggs Avenue. Mr. Miller was an elder in the church and it was in his house that the first Cottage Prayer Meeting had been held in 1899 out of which the church had grown. The house is still standing, a Victorian type of dwelling with a verandah across the front and a cupola on the roof. Here Coffin became at once a much loved member of the household which consisted of Mr. and Mrs. Miller, their adopted daughter and "Grandma Baker." The Millers delighted in his humor and in his rollicking laughter as he would recount the amusing incidents which he encountered during his rounds of parish calls. With an extraordinary gift for good-natured mimicry he would re-enact conversations which revealed queer quirks of human nature or a dialogue with some picturesque character. Long afterwards the daughter could recall no occasion when anyone's feelings had ever been hurt by his humor, although others remember rare instances when someone who had figured in one of his hilarious anecdotes heard it at second hand without unqualified appreciation. What the Miller family enjoyed most was the hour before supper on Sunday evenings. Coffin would come in from his pastoral calls, to which he always devoted Sunday afternoons. He would sit down at the piano and begin to play familiar hymns. One by one the other members of the household would drop in to listen. Coffin would play on until supper was ready. Then after a hurried meal he would be off for the Young People's meeting and his evening service. This twilight hour of hymn playing became a lifelong Sunday habit with him and many others besides the family on Briggs Avenue have remembered the quiet, devotional mood of those hours as revealing a vital aspect of the man who at other times could be so gay, so dynamic, such an avalanche of energy and purposeful activity.

A reporter from *The Mail and Express* went up to the Bronx in 1903 to get material for an article in a series he was publishing on "New York Ministers and Their People." On arriving at the church in the midst of the worst storm of the season, he was surprised to find so many children in the church that he asked an usher if he had stumbled into the Sunday School by mistake. He was told that this was the regular service, and he learned that it was an important part of the minister's aim to build a congregation on the foundation of the children's interest and devotion. A children's sermon which delighted and instructed young and old alike was one of the methods by which this was accomplished. "These children were of all sorts," he wrote his paper, "the children of an evidently well-to-do and better-class sort, and also those of the poor, including a few of color."

A few of the sermons which Coffin preached at Bedford Park were later published in a volume entitled *The Creed of Jesus*.[1] As

[1] Published by Charles Scribner's Sons, New York, 1909.

the title indicates, they were theological sermons, dealing with the basic convictions of the Christian faith. They were serious, thought-provoking sermons which demanded stiff thinking on the part of those who heard them. The illustrations were largely taken from literature and history. There was no attempt to talk down to his congregation or to catch their interest with trivialities. His manifest sincerity, enthusiasm and zeal, however, made them glow when he delivered them, and people whose educational opportunities had been limited were gripped by them as were the more highly trained minds in the congregation. Of course, he did not always carry every member of his congregation with him to the high level on which his preaching moved. One man came home from an evening service which his wife could not attend because of the necessity of looking after their child. "What did Mr. Coffin preach about tonight?" she asked him. With something approaching a groan he answered, "It was Shakespeare again!" But far more often hearers went away with a new sense of power communicated to them by the preacher who seemed to be aflame with zeal for the gospel he proclaimed.

In 1904, Coffin was invited to become associate professor at Union Theological Seminary, teaching classes in preaching and pastoral work one afternoon each week while continuing as pastor at Bedford Park. He accepted the post with enthusiasm after securing the consent of his congregation, for whom the situation was made easy by his declared intention to set aside from his salary from the Seminary a fund to provide an associate pastor for the church. Thus began a relationship with the faculty of the Seminary which continued until his retirement from the Presidency of the institution in 1945. The combination of a pastorate and a teaching post kept him very busy but he enjoyed it. Apparently the students did also, for before the first term was completed they got up a petition asking him to give them an extra hour each week after Christmas. Dr. Marcus Dods wrote from Edinburgh, "You have been born under a good star and when Providence was

tired of turning out failures and resolved for once to do its best
and show what was possible in the line of American men. I knew
you would be fascinated by your work at Union if you gave it
a chance and I am persuaded every hour you spend there will
have its abundant fruit. Don't give it up unless your health
threatens."

Coffin had kept up his Scottish friendships through correspondence and through summer visits to Edinburgh. Particularly with
Marcus Dods the intimacy which had begun as the relationship
between professor and student had ripened into the comradeship
of two men of congenial tastes and a common faith. Dr. Dods,
whose wife had just died, was to come to America to keep
engagements at Montclair, New Jersey, and elsewhere in 1901,
and wrote to Coffin: "Is it too much to ask you to meet me?" They
had long talks together while Dr. Dods visited in the Coffin home
on 57th Street. The next year he wrote begging Coffin to spend
part of the summer with him in Scotland. Coffin had just declined
a call to another church, which his older friend thought had been
a wise decision. "But of course your people will be glad to give
you a long holiday," he wrote. "I have kept myself free from en-
tanglements with greedy, sermon-requesting ministers and would
be overjoyed to spend some of it or all of it with you. . . . I am still
living on the memory of the enjoyment you gave me last year:
and oftener than you know I am in 13 West 57th Street, although,
alas! only in spirit. Do say you will come, and when." On receiv-
ing tidings that Coffin was coming, he wrote at once, "No letter I
have received this century has given me greater pleasure than
that which yesterday reached me and conveyed the information
that you will be here on the 26th July. The calf is not very fat in
comparison with those of New York production, but such as he is
he shall be killed." Echoes of that visit and of the theological discussions in which both men took keen delight are found in a letter
written by Dr. Dods the next year, in December, 1903, when he
was planning another journey to deliver addresses in America.

"If you knew how my 'heart leaps up' when I behold your hand-writing I am sure you would never grudge the time you spend in sending me some account of yourself. I must thank you for your kind offer of hospitality which I shall be very glad to avail myself of. . . . I am very glad to hear that you are in your enlarged church. . . . I am counting on your coming over here when I come back and all your friends here are making ready flags and crackers to welcome you. . . . Certainly I am a little surprised you should be asked to University-preach at Princeton. But this shows how things are moving, and I believe you personally will have a great and I hope quiet part in a great advance of thought and of religion in America." Again the next year, when Dr. Dods had reluctantly declined another invitation to lecture in America, this time at Lake Forest College, he wrote to Coffin: "Certainly after so severe a session, you will need a long rest here. Be sure you come and make a good long stay. It would make us all very happy, and I long for some good talks, which I never get, though I have good friends here." During most of his ministry, Coffin had a large, life-size photograph of Marcus Dods hanging over the fireplace in his study, a symbol of the profound influence which this older friend had exerted upon his formative years. In 1918, when his Beecher Lectures on Preaching, delivered at Yale, were published with the title *In a Day of Social Rebuilding*, Coffin printed on a flyleaf a quotation from a letter which Marcus Dods had written in 1906: "I do not envy those who have to fight the battle of Christianity in the twentieth century. Yes, perhaps I do, but it will be a stiff fight." The volume was dedicated to the memory of his beloved teacher in an ascription which reveals the depth of the relationship which had existed between this modern Paul and Timothy: "To the Memory of an endearing Teacher and enlightening Friend, now with God, Marcus Dods, sometime Principal of New College, Edinburgh, who taught his students to read widely, to face questions with an open mind, to despise cant and be ashamed of laziness, to seek them that are without rather than to please them that are within, to be careful for nothing but loyalty to Christ; and who saw in his friends excellencies neither they nor others saw, and which for his sake they would fain attain."

So his busy, useful life went on in Bedford Park for five years, the church growing steadily and the minister growing also. He spent part of the summer of 1903 as Chaplain at the Profile House in the White Mountains of New Hampshire, where he conducted services and guided parties of guests up the mountain trails. The summer was marred by his becoming ill with pneumonia, which convinced his friends that he had been overworking, although he himself made light of it. Calls came from other churches urging him to leave Bedford Park for other fields—Harlem, Rochester, Berkeley and elsewhere—but he declined them all. "I am anxious to hear what you have done with all your calls," Marcus Dods wrote. "You must not stay too long at Bedford Park, however sore the wrench of parting and of leaving in other hands a congregation you have yourself made." But he was content to plow the furrow to which he had put his hand. Invitations to preach at various colleges—Amherst, Barnard, Princeton, Union and others —and at student conferences, flowed in upon him. He accepted the ones that he could undertake without interfering with his primary responsibility, although they added to the pressure upon him. He read constantly, both in the fields of theology and of general literature. "Do you like poetry?" he wrote to a friend. "I am very much wrought up just now over William Watson. . . . What about George Eliot and Thackeray and Dickens and Scott? I am carrying off *Great Expectations* with me to Princeton. I am half way through." He confessed that he enjoyed poetry so much that he found it "a hard temptation not to be forever quoting it in lectures and addresses."

His Yale classmates and friends were being or had been married and there were times when he felt lonely even though living a public life. After officiating at the marriage of his former roommate, Edward Harkness, he wrote, "All this matrimony business makes me feel like saying with Elijah, 'I, even I only, am left.'"

In November, 1904, Coffin told a special meeting of the congregation that the time had come for the church to assume the support of a missionary pastor. In the light of subsequent world history, there is a poignant interest in the fact that the particular man whom Coffin suggested was at work in Hiroshima, Japan. This specific proposal did not work out but the church voted enthusiastically to support a representative in the world-wide mission, giving evidence of its enlarging outlook and of its readiness to follow the leadership of its dedicated pastor, even when such loyalty involved a sacrificial spirit in which they were just beginning to feel their way.

In January, 1905, came the event which the congregation had known was inevitable, but which everyone had hoped could be postponed as long as possible. Coffin was invited to become the pastor of the Madison Avenue Presbyterian Church on Seventy-third Street in New York City. Calls to pastorates in other cities had found him unresponsive. This, however, was different. The church on Madison Avenue, from which Howard Agnew Johnston had just resigned, had been struggling to keep alive and had seriously considered dissolution, but Coffin foresaw the movement of residential population from further down town up into the neighborhood around the church. He believed that the church had a future. It was in his native city for which he felt a special responsibility and for service in which he was peculiarly fitted by training and experience. He wrote to Dr. George Alexander: "You gave me the charge when I was ordained and have been of inestimable help to me since, so I naturally turn to you for counsel in a serious matter. I am invited to succeed Dr. Johnston. Should I accept? . . . A mistake now would be too costly for that church. Bedford Park is also a question." What Dr. Alexander advised can be inferred from the fact that on April 9 the Session of the Bedford Park Church voted to call a special meeting of the congregation to act upon Coffin's request for a dissolution of the pastoral relationship existing between him and the church. In May the Presbytery of New York received such a request from the congregation, voted to approve the request, and placed in Coffin's hands the call to become pastor of the Madison Avenue Presbyterian Church which he accepted.

The little group which had started in the hall over the butcher shop had become a church of three hundred and seventy members with a Sunday School in which three hundred and sixty-six children were enrolled. "Henry Sloane Coffin Accepts the Call: The Successful Bronx Pastor to Succeed Dr. Howard Agnew Johnston in Madison Avenue" was the heading of *The New York Observer's* account of the Presbytery meeting.

Just before he left the Bedford Park pastorate for his work on Madison Avenue Coffin preached two sermons which made such a profound impression that the congregation requested that they be printed. Quite incidentally in one of them, in his discussion of the New Testament's explanations of the deity of Jesus, he referred to the fact that Mark's gospel implied that the Spirit of God came upon Jesus as a young man when in a crisis in his career he was equipped with wisdom and power. Matthew and Luke, he said, seemed to think that the Spirit of God filled the personality of Jesus at his birth because he had been conceived by the power of the Holy Ghost and was born of the Virgin Mary. The gospel of John, if taken alone, would indicate that "in Jesus the eternal word of God was made flesh and dwelt among men" and that his glory was that of an only-begotten Son of God. No one of these explanations, "nor all three of them together really make Him divine to us. We call Him God for what He is, not because of the way evangelists tell us He became what He is . . . Christ's deity is His love." This statement regarding the divinity of Jesus was to create difficulty for Coffin in the not too distant future.

A copy of the sermons fell into the hands of the Reverend John Fox, a member of the Presbytery of New York, who had a weather eye out for anything that he considered heresy and was eager to leap into the fray against anything that he thought a deviation from strictest orthodoxy. He communicated his displeasure over the sermons to Mr. Timothy Sellew, an elder in the Madison Avenue Presbyterian Church of which Coffin was about to become the minister. Charges of heresy were brought against Coffin by Mr. Sellew and the Presbytery of New York was asked to take action in the matter. By an unfortunate coincidence, the charges were brought at the same meeting of Presbytery at which the congregation of the Madison Avenue Presbyterian Church presented its request that the Presbytery place in Coffin's hands the call to become pastor of the church. Coffin had not previously been notified that the charges were to be preferred, and it was a disturbing experience for him. However, there were wiser heads than Dr. Fox in the Presbytery. The charges were not sustained, the whole matter was quietly dropped, and the Presbytery voted to install Coffin as pastor of the church which had voted to call him.

Years later Coffin and Fox were to meet under very different circumstances. When Dr. Fox lay dying, the one minister whom he wanted at his bedside was Henry Coffin. Coffin was sent for and came instantly. He knelt by the bed of his former accuser and offered a prayer in which all the minor matters on which they had differed dropped out of sight and two men of faith were united before the Eternal God.

CHAPTER SIX

THE FIRST DECADE ON
MADISON AVENUE

A DEVOTED layman who was active in the work of the Madison Avenue Presbyterian Church during Coffin's early pastorate there remarked when he was past seventy: "Those for me were years of romance." So in retrospect they seemed to many, including the young minister. But it required considerable imagination to see anything very romantic in the situation at the time.

The church to which Henry Coffin went as minister in 1905 had a precarious hold on life. It was the result of the merger of two congregations neither of which seemed to be strong enough to survive alone. One of them, the former Madison Avenue Presbyterian Church, had been located for thirty years farther down town, at the corner of Madison Avenue and Fifty-third Street. Soon after it had erected a new building there the Fifth Avenue Presbyterian Church, which had previously occupied a corner at Nineteenth Street, followed the northward trend of the population and built a church at Fifth Avenue and Fifty-fifth Street. This was only three short blocks from the Madison Avenue Church, and with Dr. John Hall, one of the pulpit giants of the era, in its pulpit the Fifth Avenue Church attracted crowds of worshipers. The Madison Avenue Church had less drawing power, and instead of growing, it dwindled. Rather than die, it united with the Phillips Church, a mile farther north on Madison Avenue at Seventy-third Street. This was a small congregation in a neighborhood which at the time was predominantly Jewish. The union did not better matters for either congregation, and it was not long before the roll of the combined churches showed fewer active communicants than either of them had reported before the merger. This was the discouraging outlook which presented itself to Henry Coffin as a challenge from which he could not turn away.

A minister of smaller stature might have attempted to foster the church's growth by promotional devices. That was not Coffin's way. With dedicated zeal he gave himself to the work of preaching and to the pastoral care of his people. The growth of the church followed in a measure which confounded his critics, of whom there were not a few at the outset, and delighted those who had been responsible for his call from the Bronx to Madison Avenue. He had clear-cut goals in mind for the church and when they were translated into reality they combined to produce a growing church. He believed in a democratic church, in which all kinds of people would feel welcome and at home. He envisioned an evangelistic church, going out to all within its reach with an invitation to share in Christian worship and service. He believed in an educational church which would teach young and old the Christian faith and the Christian life. He sought to create a church with a sense of mission to the world, linking its local life with that of the Universal Church. He cherished these goals not because he thought they would draw new members to the church, but because he believed that they were in keeping with the teaching of the New Testament. As a matter of fact, it developed that there were large numbers of people in New York City who wanted the kind of church in which Coffin believed, and they flocked to the standard which he raised on the corner of Madison Avenue and Seventy-third Street.

In June, 1906, Coffin received what was to be the first of many honorary degrees, when the Corporation of New York University made him Doctor of Divinity. When he received the official notification in May he wrote to a friend that he felt like declining the honor because he was far too young to be a D.D. "Honestly, I shall feel very odd to be called 'Dr. Coffin'." As it happened, that is what he was to be called by thousands of people during the next half-century. He was frankly pleased by the honor but not inclined to take himself too seriously because of it. "The one deplorable fact is," he wrote after the event, "that no amount of hoods and initials added to one's name make one's head any fuller of ideas and one's self any abler to do the work he is meant to do."

It took a pioneering spirit to try to establish a democratic church in New York City in the first decade of the twentieth century. As Coffin wrote years later, "Nineteenth Century Protestantism accepted current economic groupings without question. Such divisions were regarded as part of the providential order, and it was silly, indeed wrong, to invite people to seek their religious inspirations above or below their economic status—in which it had pleased God to place them. . . . The American public gave voluble lip service to democracy, but was complacently feudal in its approval of the stratification of folk into economic classes even before Almighty God, the Father of them all." Madison Avenue and Fifth Avenue, one block away, were occupied by the homes of well-to-do people. Park Avenue, one block to the east, was in a state of transition. It had never been a very desirable residential street because the New York Central Railroad had its tracks leading to the Grand Central Station in an uncovered tunnel running down the middle of the Avenue. From this open chasm, smoke and noise poured out making life unpleasant for near-by residents. Now, however, the tunnel was being roofed over and landscaped, and soon the street was to be lined by handsome homes and expensive apartment houses. East of Park Avenue the economic status of the neighborhood took a sudden and radical decline. From Third Avenue to the East River there were some small private houses and substantial apartments, but also many of the shabbiest tenements in the city, in which lived newly arrived Italians, Germans, Czechs, Irish, representatives of

many other European nations as well as American Negroes, along
with people of second-generation immigrant families of varied
national backgrounds. Some blocks contained stables where people who lived on more desirable streets kept their horses and
carriages. The church of which Coffin found himself pastor had
regarded the district between Fifth Avenue and Third Avenue as
its legitimate responsibility. It did, however, feel a missionary
obligation toward the people living farther east, so long as that
did not involve personal identification. Like other well-to-do
churches at the time, it maintained a branch known as "The Good
Will Mission" on East Eightieth Street where a Sunday School
was conducted on Sunday afternoons and preaching services were
held on Sunday mornings and on one week-day evening each
week. It was staffed by a minister and several women visitors who
made calls upon the people in their homes and distributed religious literature. Volunteers from the Madison Avenue Church
helped as teachers in the Sunday School. At Christmas the attendants at the Mission were invited to a festival at the parent
church, but genuine fellowship between the people of the two
institutions was almost non-existent. This seemed an undesirable
and less than Christian arrangement to an impetuous young
minister on fire with enthusiasm for a democratic church. He regarded it as intolerable that when a child applied for admission
to the Sunday School at the Madison Avenue Church he was
promptly asked to give his address. If he came from east of Third
Avenue, he was given a card directing him to the Good Will Mission on East Eightieth Street. Officers of the church felt that if
children from the tenements were admitted, families living on the
more fashionable streets would not send their boys and girls to
the church where, it was feared, they would be exposed to germs
and vermin. Coffin felt that germs of snobbishness were even
more to be feared. But he initiated no revolution. As he later
described the changes which were brought about: "We took the
Madison Avenue congregation as we found it; and asked for no

radical changes. Our call was far too precarious for that, and we had first to become established in their confidence. Our task in this, as in many other matters, was education; and education requires time to produce results. The kingdom of heaven is 'like unto leaven,' and to employ it as T.N.T. is apt to bring on explosions which destroy rather than transform. It is a strain on the patience of the eager to move slowly, but a congregation is an unwieldy group which develops an individuality of its own with a distinctive flavor; and it 'moveth altogether, if it move at all.' Secessions of those who disagree strongly with a policy are evidences of defects in educational skill and disregard for feelings on the part of those who are leading. The pace of change is always a difficult matter to determine accurately. To advance too slowly is to irk, and perhaps lose, the ardent; to advance too swiftly angers the conservatives. Both types, and many shades of temperament in between, appear indigenous in any company of God's people."

Coffin began by getting to know the families already in the congregation. With the help of a Senior student from Union Seminary, Frank L. Janeway, he called on every person whose name appeared on any church list. Gradually, however, he introduced children from the East Side into the Sunday School. He was alert to discover providential possibilities in what sometimes seemed like awkward situations. The minister at the Good Will Mission asked for the dismissal of one of his women visitors whom he accused of insubordination. Coffin admired Florence Weir greatly as a woman of ability and spiritual depth, although her fundamentalist theology was not his. He asked her if she would be willing to work with him at Seventy-third Street in spite of his more liberal theology. She was ready to do so, and was transferred by the church Session to Madison Avenue. Not long afterwards, another similar situation developed at the Mission on Eightieth Street and Anna E. Andrus also joined the staff of the parent church. With these two devoted visitors, Coffin set out to canvass the blocks of apartments to the east of the church. It involved the endless climbing of tenement stairs, often with ten fruitless visits to everyone which had any visible result. But a surprising number of children were discovered who had no church connection. They were cordially invited to attend the Sunday School on Madison Avenue, and, convinced of their welcome by the obvious sincerity and friendliness of the dynamic young minister and his aides, they came in ever-increasing numbers. So the victory for a democratic church, or at least the first phase of the struggle, was won without a battle, and the time came when those who had been most firmly opposed to the removal of social and economic barriers were those who were proudest of being part of an inclusive church.

Criticism of the open door policy did not die out all at once, but Coffin met objections with patience and frequently with humor that disarmed the critics. One Monday morning he met a gentleman who was an elder and strong supporter of a church on Fifth Avenue. He told Coffin bluntly that he was ruining the Madison Avenue Church. "Why, yesterday my wife and I went to see how things were going. After a few minutes she caught sight of all those children, and said: 'Do you notice the smell'?" Coffin retorted that the smell was "the odor of sanctity" and mischievously added that the gentleman and his wife might be unfamiliar with that particular odor in the sedate sanctuary which they regularly attended. In order to meet objections from aristocratic parents who feared for the health of their children, Coffin studied the weekly bulletins in which the Board of Health reported all cases of infectious illness in the area. One week it was reported that there were a dozen cases of scarlet fever in the blocks between Fifth Avenue and Third Avenue but not a single case farther east. Coffin called this fact to the attention of the congregation on the following Sunday morning, and, not without a measure of impish glee, asked parents of children in the affected neighborhoods to see that they did not unduly expose those from more easterly homes. A look of mystification spread over the faces in the congregation, followed by a broad smile which indicated that the point had gone home. One of the distinguished physicians of the city, Dr. Theodore C. Janeway, united with the congregation, and when he was told that fear of infection was prevalent among some of his neighbors whose children attended the Sunday School at Madison Avenue, remarked: "The young Janeways can be counted on to export as many germs as they import." This was reassuring to many fearful souls.

"Our aim from the start," Coffin said, "was to make the church serve as many elements in the neighboring population as could be induced to respond." He was fortunate in having as superintendent of the Sunday School a business man, William W. Hall, who shared his vision, although Mr. Hall was somewhat skeptical as to the possibility of combining the children of Fifth Avenue and First Avenue in one Church School. However, he was willing to work for it. He had time to give to the work, was an indefatigable visitor, knew the city streets thoroughly, met people of all conditions with an outgoing friendliness which won their confidence, and proved to have a genius for recruiting both young and old for the church. He brought children into the Sunday School and their parents followed them into the church. He helped to organize classes for men and women as well as for the boys and girls. For many years he was the moving spirit in an afternoon Bible class for men who drove milk delivery wagons. Because of their hours of labor they could not attend morning or evening church services, but they could and did gather each week for instruction in the Bible followed by a social period. Coffin called Hall's cooperation during the early days of his pastorate "our richest asset."

Coffin's sermons had intellectual vigor and spiritual fervor. They reflected the liberal outlook in which college and university graduates had been trained to think. Moreover, he was abundantly endowed with the personal gifts and abilities to make him a persuasive religious leader among the cultured people who were moving in steadily increasing numbers into the neighborhoods along the streets in the Seventies and Eighties west of Third Avenue. The sanctuary in which he conducted services of worship had nothing to commend it from the standpoint of architectural or aesthetic distinction. He had some changes made gradually which toned down its more glaringly ugly features, making it restful and worshipful, but it was never a beautiful church. Surroundings were forgotten, however, when he led the congregation in worship. His prayers had the cadences and the elevation of the King James Version of the Bible, in which he steeped himself. He led men into the Presence of God. Striking in appearance in the pulpit and out of it, fascinating in conversation wherever people met him, gay and bantering on all occasions in which humor was appropriate, no more inclined to despise the rich than he was to patronize the poor, he was uniquely equipped to be the minister of people to whom good taste, good manners, good education as well as Christian grace were important. And they came in constantly growing numbers.

It was more difficult to draw into the church people from the humbler homes who came out of different national backgrounds. They were accustomed to being called "foreigners" and as a protective precaution were reluctant to go into places where they feared they might not be welcome or where they might not understand what was going on. The largest national group in the vicinity was made up of Czechs who had come from what was then called Bohemia, part of Austria-Hungary. The Czechs at home were unwilling subjects of the Empire, as their actions later on during World War I amply demonstrated. Their rebellion against their political rulers carried over into hostility to the Roman Catholic Church with which their rulers were identified. Many of the Czechs who had come to the United States to escape from Austro-Hungarian rule were hostile to all forms of organized religion. There were several strong Czech societies called Sokols in the neighborhood of the Madison Avenue Presbyterian Church. One of them demanded of its members a promise to have nothing to do with any church. Even in the families of this group Coffin was a welcome guest and it was not unusual, when a death occurred, for him to be asked to hold "a little mass," which he would do quietly at an hour when the Sokol leaders were busy at their work elsewhere. Immigrants were pouring into the United States at the rate of a million each year, and thousands of them remained in New York City, many in the area which the Madison Avenue Presbyterian Church, under Coffin's leadership, was coming to regard as its parish. Language and customary ways of living set them apart from the older population of the district. Even their dress identified them as newcomers, the women often walking the streets with shawls over their heads in marked contrast to the more conventionally attired. On Madison Avenue it was still the custom for men to go to church wearing frock coats and high silk hats while ladies regarded Sunday morning appearances as times when elaborate apparel was essential. Coffin mulled over the problem of making his East Side friends feel comfortable and at home in a congregation where their differentness was so conspicuous and, it must be acknowledged, was so exposed to condescension on the part of some who did not understand or appreciate their pastor's eagerness to build a democratic church.

He decided that half-way houses had to be discovered. A Bible class for women was organized to meet in a large second-story room over a stable between Lexington and Third Avenues. This was made possible by a loyal member of the church, a coachman, who secured his employer's consent to the use of the property. Coffin said that "there was something eminently New Testament in being housed in a stable." The class flourished under Miss Weir's competent leadership. Mr. Hall began organizing meetings for men, which met at first in the homes of the members. This, too, had precedent in the "house churches" of the New Testament. The classes outgrew their meeting-places, and it became imperative that larger quarters somewhere be found. The Sunday School and the groups which had been meeting in the basement and sup-

plementary rooms of the church were also growing too large for
the space available for them. A group of men met in 1910 to discuss what could be done. Coffin's former room-mate at Yale,
Edward S. Harkness, who had become a member and a trustee of
the church, came to the rescue. Acting anonymously, as he frequently did in his philanthropies, he purchased and gave to the
church a large private garage which was providentially located
on Madison Avenue on property adjoining that of the church.
There was a large main floor which could be used for a gymnasium, another good-sized room on the second floor suitable for
meetings, some living quarters where church visitors could be
given a home, and a roof which could be adapted for open-air
services on summer evenings. A class of young men had been
meeting on Sunday mornings in the back gallery of the church.
Now they were provided with a more adequate room for their
discussions and for Friday evening social gatherings around "Old
Ironsides," as a huge coffee-pot was affectionately called. A large
Bible class of young women met in the workers' apartment for
informal friendly discussions of all manner of subjects of personal
concern to them. Promising young men and young women were
recruited for teacher training classes to provide competent leadership for the ever growing Church School. In 1907 the Sunday
School numbered 565. By 1908 the Sunday School had enrolled
714 members, and by 1910 its membership numbered more than
a thousand.

Obviously, this expanding program and growing constituency
necessitated a larger staff, even though Coffin was a prodigious
worker and was enlisting a fine group of volunteer lay men and
women in the church's work. He turned quite naturally to Union
Theological Seminary, where he was still teaching one afternoon
each week, and enlisted the services of students who could give a
few hours during each week as well as leadership on Sundays.
The first student to be so associated with Coffin was Charles W.
Gilkey, a Baptist, who was later to have a distinguished career in

the Hyde Park Church of Chicago and as the Dean of the Chapel at the University of Chicago. He was joined in 1906 by Robert S. Steen, a Princeton graduate who before entering the Seminary had taught for three years at what was then called the Syrian Protestant College at Beirut. Steen's untimely death seven months after he had become the minister of the Hillside Presbyterian Church in Orange, New Jersey, was a heavy blow to Coffin. Not only did he feel keenly the loss of a younger friend in whose companionship he took great delight, but he mourned the loss to the church of a gifted leader on the threshold of a promising life of service. When a volume of Steen's sermons was published in 1908, Coffin wrote a biographical sketch as a Foreword in which he revealed something of his own philosophy as well as his estimate of Robert Steen, saying: "He had a clearly defined ideal for the church but he had that rare quality of leadership which enabled him to guide his people without their being aware that they were led."[1] He added a tribute which has been often quoted: "Earth was richer for many of us while it numbered him in its population, and heaven seems more to be desired now that he is among its citizens."[2] These men, together with the two women visitors, made an effective team, but it was apparent that with the expanding activities and the increasing number of families in the congregation there was need for another minister who could give full time to the administrative responsibilities of the church.

~ The right man was found in William Raymond Jelliffe, who joined the staff in 1908. Jelliffe had been a friend and classmate of Coffin's at Union Seminary. Like Coffin, he was a native New Yorker and knew the city's life thoroughly. His experience had prepared him admirably for an administrative ministry in which he was to systematize the work of a growing staff of visitors and volunteers, introduce the keeping of exact records and formulate

[1] *The Strength of Quietness* by Robert Service Steen, Dodd, Mead, and Co., 1908, p. xii.
[2] *Ibid.*, p. xvii.

plans for a steadily enlarging complex of activities. Before studying for the ministry he was for a time engaged in business, which
he always felt had been a valuable preparation for a vocation
which sometimes tended toward the impractical. On graduating
from the Seminary he had become a member of the staff of the
Church of the Sea and Land on the Lower East Side, where he
had grappled with the problems of families and young people
living under the most unfavorable circumstances. The minister of
that church, Dr. John Hopkins Denison, accepted a call to the
Central Congregational Church in the Back Bay district of Boston, and persuaded Jelliffe to join him there. Coffin felt that
Jelliffe was the ideal man to be his colleague in the ministry of
the Madison Avenue Presbyterian Church. Jelliffe came to New
York, looked the situation over and accepted the post which was
offered him. The exact relationship between the two ministers
was never defined, and it was a tribute to both men that such
delimitation of functions and responsibilities was never necessary. The church bulletin carried the names of the two men as its
ministers and that was sufficient. Coffin later wrote of Jelliffe: "The
church little suspected the leader he was to prove in the years
ahead. . . . He had a genius for system, introduced exact records,
had his colleague and other visitors report to him frequently and
conserved the information garnered in their calls. . . . He possessed
a fertile mind which set itself to devise plans for every group in
the church's heterogeneous constituency. Men and women with
time or funds to invest sought him out, and with informed in-
genuity he opened doors for them, and communicated his own
enthusiasm. . . . He multiplied himself many times in those whom
he sent into the church's tasks. . . . If the church displayed inven-
tiveness, thoughtful individual care and businesslike planning
through the next two decades, behind and in it all was his versa-
tile and consecrated mind and heart." In subsequent years, when
he was asked how to go about developing a program of church
activities, Coffin would reply, "The first thing to do is to get a man

like Jelliffe." Coffin and Jelliffe supplemented each other in a remarkable way and it proved to be an ideal combination of talents.

Even with so efficient a colleague, however, Coffin felt the need
of a larger staff. It was characteristic of him that in the expansion
of the church's work he should have sought the aid not primarily of
enlarged equipment or of a busy church office with more type-
writers sending out more and more letters and notices. He felt
the need for more people establishing and developing more personal relationships with people who needed the church and whom
the church needed. In 1910 he increased the number of Seminary
student assistants to five and the next year he had seven. As he
preached in men's and women's colleges, he was frequently consulted by students who were interested in opportunities for
Christian service. This made it possible for him to select young
men and women who impressed him as good material for his
church staff. From among men who were planning to attend
Union Seminary he chose future student assistants. In the
women's colleges he found fine additions to the staff. Gladys
Streibert came from Wellesley and Gertrude Hunter from Barnard. By 1913 there was a team of seven women, each of whom, in
addition to teaching and club leadership, had a list of families on
whom monthly calls were made as well as a constantly changing
list of families who it was hoped could be interested in the church.
Each worker had regular conferences with Mr. Jelliffe and a brief
prayer service at the beginning of each day united ministers and
staff in intercession for the tasks to which they were committed.

From the very beginning of his pastorate Coffin was troubled
and felt himself hampered by the Madison Avenue Church's practice of renting pews. This was common among middle-class
churches of the period, except in some where pews were owned
outright, being bequeathed like any other real estate at the death
of the owner. The practice was cherished by many as making for
family religion, it being felt that identification with a particular
pew strengthened a family's loyalty to the church. Coffin's father

and mother, who had rented a pew in the Madison Avenue Church when their son became its minister, felt this strongly. The rented pew system, however, owed its vitality chiefly to the fact that it commended itself to a commercial people as good business. It seemed to provide an assured, predictable income for a church. By calculating the number of sittings and pricing them on the proper scale, the church's budget could be covered in much the same way that any business enterprise would be planned. To Coffin, eager as he was for a democratic church, the system was repugnant and, he thought, un-Christian. Soon after he assumed the pastorate on Madison Avenue a man who had recently moved to the city from Nova Scotia began to attend the church with his wife. They had been loyal and active members of the church in their native town and hoped to be the same in New York. After they had attended a few Sunday morning services they were invited to become pew-holders. An overly zealous member of the pew committee, anxious to make the best possible bargain for the church, showed them a pew which was for rent on the middle aisle. The man was stunned. He was a factory-worker and the rental was the equivalent of his total earnings for three months! Only the tactful intervention of a less commercially minded officer of the church persuaded the prospective member that he really would be welcome anywhere in the Madison Avenue Church. He and his wife did stay—in a less expensive pew—and eventually became devoted and useful participants in the church's work. This incident, however, accentuated Coffin's dislike of the whole rented pew system. He particularly abhorred the necessity of facing a congregation on Sunday mornings visibly graded as to wealth or poverty by location in the church. As in theaters, the most expensive seats were on the center aisle in the middle of the church, with cheaper pews on the side aisles and still lower prices prevailing in the galleries. In the spring and autumn when the holders of the pews in the center of the church were frequently out of the city for week-ends, the obligation to hold the best seats

for them until the service started seemed particularly objection-
able. Coffin quoted from the second chapter of the Epistle of
James: "If there come into your assembly a man with a gold ring,
in goodly apparel, and there come in also a poor man in vile
raiment; And ye have respect to him that weareth the gay
clothing, and say unto him, Sit thou here in a good place; and say
to the poor, Stand thou there, or sit here under my footstool: Are
ye not then partial in yourselves, and are become judges of evil
thoughts?" St. George's Protestant Episcopal Church, on Stuyvesant Square at Sixteenth Street, under the prophetic leadership
of Dr. William S. Rainsford, had abolished pew rents. One of
Coffin's predecessors, Dr. Charles L. Thompson, had attempted to
bring about a similar change in the Madison Avenue Presbyterian
Church while it was still on Fifty-third Street. He was fond of
quoting, "Rich and poor meet together: the Lord is the Maker of
them all." But with many empty pews, the church clung to the
rentals of those that were occupied. Even in the early years of
Coffin's pastorate the church was not ready to make the change.
He precipitated no crisis over the question, but waited. The general acceptance of the system of renting pews, he felt, "was an
indication of the saturation of even Christian minds with the
American commercial spirit, where prosperity was hailed as a sure
token of God's favor and of man's virtuous industry." It was a
dozen years before the church was ready to give public notice that
"All pews are free and unassigned."

Coffin was anxious to have the boards of the church represent
the various elements of whom the congregation was made up. At
a time when formal dress was still the Sunday morning habit of
the well-to-do on Madison Avenue, two men who did not fall into
that category were suggested in a meeting of the Session as
possible nominations for membership in that body. One elder
strongly objected, saying that the men in question would probably
not appear at the Sunday services in cutaway coats. "Of course
they all wore them in the Upper Room," said Coffin and the argument was ended before it began.

Coffin was also troubled in his early days on Madison Avenue by the chasm between the Sunday School and the worshiping church. Boys and girls attended classes of instruction and joined in the prayers and hymns in Church School assemblies, but were for the most part unfamiliar with the church's service of worship. In Scotland, Coffin had been trained to include a brief Children's Sermon in the Sunday morning service. He had followed this practice at Bedford Park where it had been found helpful to young and old alike. It proved equally appealing to children farther down town. So long as the five-minute talks dealt with important themes, as they always did, even the most sophisticated adults found the simple presentations helpful, and there were always some adults in the congregation incapable of carrying away the message of the longer sermon who felt that the sermon directed to the children was manna from heaven for them. And the children delighted in them and came to church in droves, leaving in orderly fashion during the singing of a hymn when their part in the service was concluded. It should be pointed out that Coffin had a rare gift for establishing instant rapport with young people of all ages. He never talked down to children and yet he was never over their heads when addressing them. Frequently he had some visible object with him in the pulpit to serve as an illustration of his theme. He was once quarantined for several days on a Japanese ship in a harbor, when the only book on board in English was a volume containing the international signal code.[3] He amused himself by studying the signal flags displayed by ships entering the harbor and by drawing copies of them. On his return home he had cardboard flags made and used their messages as starting-points for children's sermons: "I need a pilot," "Have you any combustibles on board?", "How much water do you draw?", and warnings regarding various types of hazardous weather. He recognized the danger that the objects might simply call attention to themselves and never communicate spiritual truth, but contended that the risk must be taken, as Jesus did when he spoke in

[3] *The Public Worship of God,* Westminster, pp. 170-171.

parables. He deliberately used his gift of humor to capture the attention and commitment of the children in his congregations. This was criticized by some of the more sedate older people but he defended the employment of humor:

"Preaching to children has to be intimate with a personal relationship quickly established. One can tell instantly by their faces whether they are or are not listening and with what degree of attention. Such preaching cannot in thought or language be the least bit dull, and humor supplies a sparkle which grips young minds. A face with a smile is a sure indication of genuine response. . . . The Creator made man capable of laughter, and some of the most threatening evils can be effectively punctured with satire and some of the most serious lessons learned by seeing the incongruity of our conduct with professed standards. Thackeray's daughter described humor as 'thinking in fun while we feel in earnest.' Shakespeare provided bits of comedy as relief in the midst of awesome tragedies, and lighter moments in public worship enable minds to concentrate with fresher zest on God and the issues with which he faces us in the moments which follow. It was one minister's experience that for every person who ever thanked him for a sermon prepared for adults he was thanked by ten for some of these simpler and very much lighter five-minute talks to boys and girls. The mental age of most grown-ups is over-estimated, and this generation, accustomed to absorb so much through the eye at moving pictures, profits by the picturesque presentation demanded if the attention of the young is to be caught and held."

Although the sermons to children were appreciated by most of the adult members of the congregation, there were some irreconcilables. Two elderly ladies kept up a continuous stream of correspondence maintaining that the talks were irreverent and utterly out of place in the house of God. The services of their church, they said, were being ruined for them. Coffin talked with them, tried to explain to them the evangelistic purpose behind the sermons to children, but failed to win their approval. Finding them adamant in their opposition, he courteously suggested that they might be happier in some other church. He suggested another church where he felt sure their sense of decorum would not be disturbed. He was mistaken, for, on the first Sunday on which they attended the church he recommended, the minister twice provoked laughter on the part of his hearers. He was therefore pronounced flippant by the critical ladies. Coffin patiently suggested another church where he was confident that no humor could creep in. This time he was correct in his appraisal, the demure women were satisfied and remained, to their contentment and his. His subsequent comment was characteristic of him: "The problems of combining two ladies with such outlook and several hundred small children with little or no religious background seemed insoluble, and as these good women could 'read their titles clear' to their future mansions, it did not seem the church's urgent duty to please their taste and neglect the children." Coffin's persistence in his policy was justified by the crowds of children who listened eagerly to his messages and learned to feel at home in the church's worship.

As the membership and the facilities of the church grew, new organizations and activities were added to the program. Coffin never believed in using social and recreational activities as bait to lure people into the church. He did believe that the church should minister in a variety of ways to help its constituents develop the fullest possible lives. When he became pastor in 1905 he found the women of the congregation organized in Home and Foreign Missionary Societies, in a Mary and Martha League, and in a project known as the Helping Hand. The women did some visiting on needy families connected with the Good Will Chapel. They packed boxes with cast-off garments and with new ones which they made, the boxes being then shipped to the families of pastors serving on meager salaries under the Presbyterian Board of Home Missions. The Mary and Martha League was a combination of prayer meeting and social effort. The Helping Hand gathered together women from poorer families who were provided with materials and instruction for the making of garments for their families. These were the conventional activities of churches at the time. Coffin was eager to try new ventures in meeting the needs of the particular neighborhood he served. In addition to the classes and clubs for young men and women, the work for children and adults was expanded. When the Church School at the Good Will Mission was, with the exception of classes for the youngest children, transferred to Madison Avenue, a horse-drawn bus was secured to make the rounds Sunday mornings and bring to the Sunday School children who lived too far away to walk. An island off the Connecticut shore, rechristened "Treasure Island," was purchased in 1911 for use as a vacation spot for mothers and children. Groups of girls also enjoyed its simple life and found refreshment in its sea breezes and bathing. In 1912 a camp for boys was started at Tottenville on Staten Island, later transferred to Lake Hopatcong in New Jersey and eventually to Sharon, Connecticut. During the summer months Monday mornings were busy times at the Church House as excited parties of children and adults set out for their happiest weeks of the year at one or the other of these camps. A woman who spoke Czech was added to the staff in 1912 and a Bible class in that language was begun for those to whom English was still uncomfortably strange. A Men's Association was launched, with a weekly social gathering and a monthly meeting at which some topic of social or religious importance was discussed by a speaker whom Coffin's prestige drew to the church. It was discovered that there were many men employed as butlers and housemen in the more luxurious homes of the district and a special Bible Class, meeting on a weekday afternoon, was set up for them. A Hungarian Men's Bible Class was inaugurated. Then it was discovered that there were a considerable number of men in the neighborhood who worked at night, for whom meetings at the usual hours were out of the question. A Night Workers' Class, meeting in one of the homes, was begun for them. Coffin would sometimes attend these gatherings, carrying a little portable organ with him. After a Bible lesson he would sit down at the organ and lead the group in hymn singing. From the standpoint of musical quality the singing left a good deal to be desired but it carried into nearby apartments an atmosphere of hearty masculine fellowship which drew new members into the organization. In 1915 a third Sunday service of worship held in the afternoon was begun for those whose hours of work or family obligations made it impossible for them to attend services on Sunday mornings or evenings. The hours of labor required in some occupations at the time is indicated by the fact that in 1916 an Evening Bible Class was organized for men who worked seven days a week.

In June, 1910, a World Missionary Conference was held in Edinburgh and Coffin was invited to address one of the evening meetings. This Conference brought together twelve hundred missionary leaders as delegates and several hundred others, missionaries and lay leaders, from all over the world to plan cooperatively for the world mission of the Protestant Churches. It was the first of the great ecumenical gatherings which have been distinctive landmarks on the path toward Christian unity in the Twentieth Century. One of its crowning achievements was the creation of a Continuation Committee to carry forward its purposes. Probably none but the most optimistic foresaw at the time that a movement was being launched which would eventually result in a World Council of Churches embracing most of the Protestant and Eastern Orthodox Churches of the world, although the Conference rose and sang "Praise God from Whom all blessings flow" when the Chairman, John R. Mott, announced that the vote in favor of the Continuation Committee had been unanimous.

Coffin made his address at an evening meeting on June 15. The hall was crowded with three thousand people. Professor W. P. Paterson spoke on "The Finality of the Christian Religion" and

Coffin followed with an address on "The Finality of the Christian Ethic." Mr. J. H. Oldham, one of the assistant secretaries in the department which organized the Conference, had written Coffin that the purpose of his address was "to assert afresh the right of Christianity to be a missionary religion. It was felt that there is a widepread hesitancy and uncertainty on this subject due partly to the rise of the science of comparative religions. Even among those who would not maintain the position that other religions than Christianity are sufficient for those who have been brought up in them, there is apt to be an underlying doubt whether the scientific study of other faiths has not weakened the position of Christianity." Coffin's address made a deep impression upon the more intellectual delegates to the Conference who were eager for fresh thought upon a fundamental subject expressed in something other than the traditional terminology. To some of the more conservative delegates his views sounded radical. On the following Sunday morning, Coffin preached to a crowded church in Free St. George's Church, West, where the venerable Alexander Whyte and Coffin's intimate friend John Kelman were colleagues in the pastorate. That evening he preached, again to an overflowing congregation, in the United Free High Church, where in his student days he had been assistant to Robert Simpson. One of the Edinburgh newspapers reported that "a young minister from New York, Dr. H. S. Coffin, who took no part in the debates, has been hailed as a coming leader of the churches by those who heard his revolutionary address at one of the evening meetings and his no less revolutionary sermon at the United Free Church on Sunday." Alexander Whyte called the address brilliant, and the two sermons no less so.

An unexpected necessity for an important decision confronted Coffin there in an urgent invitation to become co-minister with John Kelman at Free St. George's, West. Alexander Whyte, unwell and advanced in years, was about to retire and the congregation had voted unanimously to call Coffin to be Kelman's co-minister. But Coffin was convinced that his mission was in his own country and felt that he must decline. Coffin went to the Edinburgh Conference a marked man among the younger American ministers. He returned to New York a recognized leader in the budding ecumenical movement, with the assurance that his Scottish friends believed that the promise which they had seen in him as a student had in one short decade been fulfilled.

The year 1910 also saw the publication of the hymnbook, *Hymns of the Kingdom of God,* edited by Coffin in collaboration with his friend, Ambrose White Vernon, minister of the Harvard Congregational Church of Brookline, Massachusetts. Coffin's interest in a more dignified and more religiously healthy worship led him to study the church's heritage in hymnody. He found the theology of many hymns in common use unacceptable, was appalled by the sentimentality of many of the hymns which were popular in Presbyterian churches and was grieved by the number of majestic hymns which were unknown in American churches. Vernon shared his interest and his convictions. They expressed the prevailing liberalism of the day in their Editor's Note at the front of the book: "Each generation of Christians emphasizes a particular aspect of the everlasting Gospel. Our own lays the stress upon the Kingdom of God." They declared that it had been their aim "to include only hymns which are poetically beautiful, which express a normal and healthy spiritual experience, contain no divisive theology, and are specifically Christian in religion." Coffin was especially fond of some of the ancient Greek hymns which had been translated into English by the Reverend John Brownlie in Scotland. He included several of these which have since found their way into the best American hymnals. The German chorales also had a strong appeal for Coffin and Vernon, both of whom had studied in the land of Luther. Their predilection is evidenced by the large number which they included, thus putting their influence behind the growing popularity of German hymnody in American churches. *Hymns of the Kingdom of God* never became a popular hymnal, probably because the churches were not ready to limit their choice of hymns for use in public worship by the exacting standards which Coffin and Vernon set up. It has, however, had a profound influence upon other hymnals and introduced to American churches a number of fine hymns which had not previously been widely known.

Coffin's second book appeared in 1911 with the title, *Social Aspects of the Cross*.[4] His dominant concerns were revealed in the four sermons which he included in the little volume, all of them interpretations of some aspect of the crucifixion of Jesus. The four chapters were entitled "Sin," "Duty," "Man" and "God." Running through the whole volume is the emphasis upon the individual Christian's responsibility for helping create a society in which Christian life and character can develop and thrive, which was an obligation so heavy upon his own heart.

In 1913 Coffin was sent by the Presbytery of New York as a delegate to the annual meeting of the General Assembly of the Presbyterian Church in the U.S.A. The Assembly met in Atlanta, Georgia, as the denomination, while predominantly northern since the Civil War, had some churches scattered through the South. Coming from New York with its cosmopolitan population, Coffin wrote, "This city surprises me by its thorough 'Americanism.' I have not heard a word in a foreign tongue since I arrived. I am also impressed with its prosperity and the charming characteristics of most of its inhabitants. They are a splendid lot of God-fearing, courteous people." He was also deeply impressed by the rugged character of the men who made up the Assembly. "The Assembly," he wrote, as the session opened, "is a strong body of earnest, sober, stedfast men, without much polish and without many superficial refinements, but typical of the great mass of genuine American citizenship. They are ill-fitted to discuss modern theology, but well adapted to push forward practical enterprises." Before the Assembly adjourned he was to become

[4] George H. Doran Co.

profoundly depressed over its theological backwardness. He was
made Chairman of one of the Standing Committees, and also
leader of a group organized to defend the Graded Sunday School
Lessons with which the denomination's educational department
was attempting to meet the demands for something better than
the Uniform Lessons which had traditionally been used. As a
member of the Board of Home Missions he found himself in the
thick of a controversy over its policies, extreme conservatives
objecting to what they regarded as its liberal tendencies, Dr. Mark
Matthews of Seattle leading the attack. "I had to take the floor
for the Board," Coffin wrote, "and for the first time in my life I
found myself working parliamentary dodges and circumventing
the enemy. Some of our ardent supporters are down on me for
calling off a fight, but I made Dr. Matthews interpret his Commission's action exactly in the sense in which our Board wished
it; and then I staved off a row in order to save the Assembly's time
and to have no sore feelings." Coffin was most disturbed, however,
by an attack made upon Union Seminary by a faction which had
never been satisfied by the Seminary's resumption of its complete independence of ecclesiastical control after the Briggs trial
in 1891. It was a conservative Assembly meeting in the theologi-
cally conservative South and a majority of the delegates supported
the Seminary's critics and voted to appoint a committee to go
further into the property matters involved. The Seminary's president, Francis Brown, defended Union's position, and was, Coffin
thought, "superb—clear, dignified, gentlemanly, Christian," but to
no avail. In the end nothing came of it, but Coffin spent a sleepless
night after the debate, which had been shut off before he had
been able to get the floor. "We are terribly depressed," he wrote
home. "However it is darkest before the dawn and no doubt help
will come to us. We have been led through tight places before and
I do not doubt that we shall come out again in peace."

In his own church, in the Presbyterian communion and in the
Church at large as well as in University circles, Coffin was com-

ing to be recognized as one of the foremost religious leaders of the day. The membership of the Madison Avenue Church which had been 506 in 1906 had risen to 1541 in 1916 and the Church School which had numbered 565 in 1906 had by the end of the decade enrolled 1598 children and young people. In addition to the three or four Seminary students and the seven women visitors, a third minister, Hugh C. Burr, had been added to the staff, as well as a layman to direct men's activities, and a physical director to be in charge of the gymnasium and the summer camp for boys and men. To them all Coffin communicated his own vision and enthusiasm, his spirit of dedication and comradeship. It was a happy family who knew that they were engaged in an important pioneering undertaking and did their work well.

CHAPTER SEVEN

EXPANDING HORIZONS

O N September 6, 1906, Henry Sloane Coffin and Dorothy
Prentice Eells were married in San Anselmo Chapel at Ross
Valley, California. He was twenty-nine years of age. The bride
was nineteen. The marriage was the culmination of a friendship
which had begun when Dorothy Eells was a girl of fifteen, had
developed on her visits to the Coffin family in New York, was continued through a correspondence of growing seriousness and was
brought to a whirlwind climax at the altar when he visited California in the summer of 1906. It was the beginning of a partnership
of singular happiness.

James Coffin, Henry's uncle, lived in San Francisco. His daughter, Marion, had married John Shepherd Eells, Dorothy's brother,
the son of Charles Parmelee Eells, a prominent attorney in that
West Coast city. In 1902, Mr. and Mrs. Edmund Coffin invited
Marion's younger sister, Natalie Coffin, to spend the winter with
them in New York. Thinking that she might find their home somewhat lonely, occupied as it was by two older people whose sons
were away, one at Yale and the other in his parish in the Bronx,
they suggested that she bring her friend Dorothy Eells with her.
So at the age of fifteen Dorothy became for a winter a member of
the Coffin household on 57th Street.

The elder Coffins were enchanted with her. Henry, on his

weekly visits from the Bronx, found it pleasant to have a charming young girl as a member of the family, but seems to have regarded her as a child whom it was good fun to tease. When Spring came and her visit was about to end, he told her to go home and grow up. But before long they began to write letters to each other, at first in a bantering vein, then gradually finding themselves in a different mood in which they shared their serious as well as superficial interests. He wrote about his work, his love of poetry and books of all sorts, his theological views which had been labelled "heretical," his troubled conscience because his family background was one of luxury in a city where so many families lacked necessities. She wrote about her family, her social life in San Francisco and at Ross Valley, her comments on books which he had suggested, and her interest in the life he was leading as a Presbyterian minister in the Bronx, so different from her own in an Episcopalian family vibrating between their city and their country homes. Gradually there crept into his letters the realization that he was corresponding not with a little girl but with a thoughtful woman whom he was eager to see again. That opportunity came in February, 1905, when on her way to Europe she again stopped in New York for a visit with the Coffins on 57th Street. Henry declined a dinner invitation elsewhere for the evening of February ninth in order to be at his parents' home when she arrived. She visited the Coffins again in October on her return from Europe. On both visits there was a great deal of joking and teasing when Henry came down from the Bronx, but no interruption of his regular heavy schedule of work. Then she returned to California, leaving him suddenly aware of the depth of his feeling for her. He wrote to her hinting that he would like to come out to the West Coast the following summer, and from that time their weekly letters, which were becoming more and more a sharing of their most deeply cherished interests were pointed toward that projected journey.

In April, 1906, San Francisco was almost destroyed by the

earthquake and the devastating fire which followed. The Eells family were in San Francisco at the time but were able to cross the Bay on the ferry and take refuge in their home in Ross Valley. In New York the Coffins spent sleepless nights until word came that their California relatives and friends were safe and well. For Henry it was an experience of terror such as had never before come into his fortunate life, as he waited for the news that the person in whom his thoughts and hopes had come to center had been spared. When the word came the immediate relief was very great, although followed at once by concern for those who had met great losses and by sympathy for his friends who were surrounded by so much devastation.

Months before the earthquake it had been mutually decided that he would start for California at the beginning of July. As the date approached he felt with increasing intensity an acute loneliness of spirit although his days were spent in public. He went through a period of self-criticism and soul-searching, wondering if anyone could fully understand him since he had such difficulty in understanding himself. He lived from one letter from California to another. In other words he displayed the usual symptoms of a man in love. Marcus Dods wanted him to come to Edinburgh for the summer, but on learning that it was to be California rather than Scotland that year, replied: "Possibly Frisco contains your fate." Late in June he was laid low with a case of ptomaine poisoning while on a visit to Bayshore, Long Island, and was plunged into depression by the fear that his journey West might have to be postponed. However, he was able to start on the appointed date. Not long after his arrival he wired his parents that Dorothy would return with him in September as his wife. No tidings could have been more welcome to them or to his friends. When Marcus Dods received the news he wrote to the prospective bride: "Were all the world searched, I believe you could not find a man so likely to give a woman pure and unalloyed happiness. . . . If you two do not realise the ideal of happy married life, then I think all human foresight and forecasting may cease." His mother wrote him a letter overflowing with happiness, at the same time cautioning him to remember that his young bride would want a wedding like other girls while she knew he would try to have extreme simplicity. On all such arrangements, she pointed out, he must yield to the wishes of the Eells family.

A continent lay between the home in which the bride had grown up and the home to which the jubilant groom was to take her. It was therefore the obvious part of wisdom to set an early date for the wedding in order that the marriage could take place before Coffin had to plunge into his winter's work in New York. So they were married in the first week of September in the Episcopal Chapel in Ross Valley, near the country home of the bride's family where the reception was held after the ceremony. Coffin's parents came on for the wedding, as did his brother, William Sloane Coffin, who acted as best man. The bride's two older sisters were among her attendants. It was a joyous day for both families.

Coffin's parents hoped that the newly married couple would make their home with them at 13 West 57th Street for the early days of their married life and went so far as to have the third floor of their home fitted up as an apartment for them. Coffin found himself in an embarrassing situation, as he did not wish to seem ungrateful and yet felt strongly that he would be greatly handicapped as pastor of the Madison Avenue Church unless he had a home of his own nearer the church. He explained his predicament to the elder Coffins who regretfully accepted the situation as he saw it. A house at 36 East 62nd Street was rented as a temporary home until a house was built at 129 East 71st Street, where the younger Coffins lived until 1926, when they moved to the President's House at Union Theological Seminary at the corner of Claremont Avenue and 122nd Street.

It was something of an adventure for Dorothy Coffin to move from the West Coast to the East as the wife of a New York minis-

ter ten years her senior. She had been brought up in the Episcopal Church of which her mother was a member. She herself had
been confirmed in that Church at the usual age. She had never
had any direct contact with a Presbyterian Church, although her
grandfather Eells had been a Presbyterian minister, the distinguished President of Lane Theological Seminary in Cincinnati.
She had never had any experience in the kind of church activity
in which the wife of a Presbyterian minister usually engages, but
she was determined to learn and to play her full part in the church
life in which her husband was so thoroughly at home. Soon she
was teaching a class of girls in the Church School, was actively at
work in the Women's Societies although as a matter of principle
she would never accept any office in them, and was making personal contacts with the congregation which enabled her to bring
her husband information as to what the lay people were thinking
and feeling. She was not long out of school at the time of her marriage, unfamiliar with the world of higher education in which he
was and was to be so influential. Endowed with a quick mind and
great intelligence, she soon acquired through reading and conversation the broad intellectual background which made her a stimulating addition to the academic circles into which her new life took
her. Her beauty and charm won the hearts of people who had little
taste for the ordinary stereotype of a professionalized "minister's
wife." As the years went on she was increasingly recognized as an
able leader in her own right and rendered great service as a
member of the National Board of the Young Women's Christian
Association and in the Women's Division of the Federal Council
of the Churches of Christ in America. Her greatest service, however, was to provide for her husband the kind of home in which
he could find happiness and relaxation. Her interests in music, art
and the drama provided a wholesome foil for his absorption in
theological and ecclesiastical concerns and broadened his outlook. To an extraordinary degree they supplemented one another
and shared a rich and interesting life.

"One twenty-nine East Seventy-first Street" was to become something more than an address to a great many people from all over the world. It became for them a symbol of hospitality at its delightful best. Coffin never had a study at the church and while he made appointments there to see some people who wanted to consult with him, he saw most of them at his home. They came from all walks of life in New York and beyond. Friends from Scotland and England and Germany came. Missionaries home on furlough came to talk with him about their work. Students from colleges where he preached came with their personal problems and with their questions regarding future vocations. Ministers from across the nation asked for interviews when they were in New York, seeking an opportunity to talk with him about their plans and perplexities. The luncheon table was seldom set for two. A steady stream of guests brought the concerns of the world to it and found there two eager minds and sympathetic hearts with whom to share those concerns. The guest room on the third floor was a temporary home for many a visiting minister from overseas and for a wide variety of people. John Kelman's daughter, Mrs. John Hayes, came down with measles while visiting the Coffins just before the birth of her first child and the baby was born under the Coffins' roof. Students who had been ill at the Seminary around the corner or in the nearby Presbyterian Hospital were brought to "129" and convalesced in its friendly atmosphere. Thanksgiving dinners brought together groups of students away from home who soon felt at home around a long family table. Once a year the faculty of the Seminary were invited in for a buffet supper followed by an informal talk by some distinguished scholar of Coffin's acquaintance. The Coffins enjoyed their home and shared it generously and widely.

No group found greater pleasure there than did the Seminary students who served as assistants in the Madison Avenue Church. In the early days they lived on the third floor of the house during the summer months when the Seminary was closed. When the

Coffins went off for their vacation, the student assistants occupied the house by themselves. But it was the Sunday evening suppers which these men in later years cherished as one of the happiest memories of an association rich in memories. At six o'clock they would arrive at the house, often to find Coffin at the piano playing hymns. The peak of a busy Sunday was past, although they would have to slip away early for meetings of the Young People's society, and Coffin still had the sermon at the evening service to preach. He would be in a relaxed mood, full of stories and jocular comments on the events of the day and of the preceding week. Sometimes the atmosphere would become hilarious as he would indulge in good-natured mimicry of well-known figures in the local or the larger church. Beneath all the fun, however, lay a serious concern for each student and his work. It was a rare Sunday evening when any student left the house without some friendly inquiry about his work at the church and at the Seminary or without some helpful suggestion to aid him in meeting his problems. Most of them came to look back on the informal discussions about the Coffins' Sunday evening supper table as their most illuminating course in pastoral theology, although no formal syllabus was even dreamed of and learning took place at the furthest possible remove from the usual procedures of the classroom. Coffin selected his student assistants with great care and brought out the best in them. Some of them became ministers of very large influence. Among them were: Frank L. Janeway, Robert S. Steen, Charles W. Gilkey, John E. Steen, Chester Emerson, Melville B. Gurley, Anton T. Boisen, William M. Fincke, George C. Hood, Harold R. Chidsey, Kenneth D. Miller, Frank J. Scribner, Kenneth B. Welles, Philip S. Bird, James M. Howard, Hugh C. Burr, T. Guthrie Speers, James Gordon Gilkey, Arthur C. McGiffert, Jr., Earl T. Douglass, Marcus A. Spencer, Morgan P. Noyes, Arthur A. Rouner, Henry P. Van Dusen, A. Meredith MacColl, G. Barrett Rich, Theodore C. Speers, Erdman Harris, Hugh Moran, Bradford H. Burnham, Ray Gibbons, John M. Currie, Loy Long, William H.

Hudnut, Jr., and others. During the twenty-one years of Coffin's
pastorate at the Madison Avenue Church, forty-three Seminary
students enjoyed this privilege. In 1936, ten years after Coffin had
relinquished the pastorate for the Seminary presidency, twenty
of them gathered at a New York club for a dinner in honor of
their former chief, to express the gratitude and affection in which
he was held by them all. In his reminiscent remarks that evening
Coffin reminded the group that for a decade and a half of his
pastorate there had been no children in his home. The student
assistants had been "his boys," sons in the faith, filling a large
place in his life. After 1923 there were two children in the home,
Ruth Prentice Coffin and David Douglas Coffin, who brought
great happiness into the family life which was already full of
many-sided interests.

In the Coffin home each day began with family prayers. Immediately after breakfast the household including the servants and
whatever guests might be there at the time gathered in the draw-
ing-room. Coffin read a brief passage from the Bible after which
the group knelt while he offered prayer. His spontaneous devo-
tions in this intimate circle had the same deeply moving sincerity
and beauty of expression which characterized his conduct of public worship for which he carefully prepared. No guest who had
found lodging for the night in this Christian home ever went out
to face the day without a new sense of the reality and nearness of
God. After the family prayers Coffin would hurry around to the
church for another brief service with the Church Staff in the
Chapel. Then a few words with one worker or another and he
was off to the Church Office to dictate replies to letters which
awaited him there. Nine-thirty or ten o'clock found him back
home in his study at work on his sermons for the following Sunday. He had a remarkable capacity for doing creative work on
schedule. Wednesday noon would usually see his Sunday morning
sermon completed, pounded out on his own typewriter. Friday
noon would find the evening sermon finished, in outline at least,

and the prayers for both services prepared (although he usually offered them from memory). His assistants who marvelled at his seemingly inexhaustible flow of ideas were occasionally relieved to find that he was only human after all and that once in a long while "the sermon would not come" and he would be obliged to complete it under pressure toward the end of the week. Such delays, however, were rare. After lunch, except for the days when he taught at the Seminary, the hours were devoted to pastoral calling. He enjoyed getting into the homes of his people, believed in the major importance of this aspect of his pastorate, and jealously guarded his afternoons from the multitude of encroachments which nibble away any minister's daylight hours if he gives them a chance. His evenings were frequently sought for by various church groups, but he saved some of them each week for calling and for dining out in the homes of the congregation. After there were children in the home he tried to save at least part of each Saturday for them, and trips to the Zoo, to the parks or to other places of interest gave him relaxation and the companionship of the youngsters to whom he was devoted. Saturday evenings were reserved for his home. He made no engagements, accepted no invitations and spent the evening quietly by his own fireside.

A new source of pleasure and refreshment came into Coffin's life in 1919 when he spent his first summer at St. Hubert's, near Keene Valley, in the Adirondack Mountains in the northern section of New York State. While he was in France in the summer of 1918 Mrs. Coffin, who spent most of that summer serving as a hostess at a U.S. Army cantonment on Long Island, made a brief visit with friends at St. Hubert's. Twenty miles from the railroad, it lay, a cluster of summer cottages scattered through the forest around the Ausable Club, in a valley surrounded by Giant Mountain, Noonmark and other wooded peaks. A few miles away, accessible only by buckboard or on foot over a road through the woods, was Lower Ausable Lake and a mile farther on, to be reached only on foot over a mile-long carry, Upper Ausable Lake with Gothics Mountain looking down upon it and Mt. Marcy, the highest of the Adirondack Mountains, not far distant. She was enchanted with the region and the friends who spent summers there made it all the more attractive. The next two summers the Coffins rented Icy Brook Camp, a house made of logs, where they had their meals on a verandah overlooking a running stream. Coffin found the mountain air a tonic, greatly enjoyed the mountain climbing and camping at the Upper Lake, found congenial companionship in the colony, and went back to the city in September reinvigorated. In 1921 the Coffins built their own cottage which they named Phantom Height because of its location on a rise of ground crossed by a path through a line of white birches which had come to be known as Ghost Walk. Here they spent seventeen happy summers. As usual they shared their home with a steady stream of guests: relatives, church staff, students, and visiting ministers and theologians from abroad. Their presence in the community was greatly appreciated by their summer neighbors who delighted in the rollicking humor and sparkling conversation which they came to expect in every gathering of which the Coffins were a part. The Sunday when Coffin preached annually in the Keene Valley Church was an occasion when a crowded church could always be counted on. When a community Sunday service was inaugurated at the Ausable Club, Coffin was its moving spirit and guiding genius. It was the custom for a number of families to gather in one or another of the cottages on Sunday evenings for hymn singing and Coffin was generally at the piano. One of the Coffins' neighbors was Dr. Felix Adler, the kindly head of the Ethical Culture Society, with whom Coffin had long talks about the world and its problems, the two men approaching them from different theological viewpoints but sharing a common passion for human welfare. Another old acquaintance with whom Coffin renewed his friendship at St. Hubert's was Henry L. Stimson who had been Secretary of War in the Cabinet of President Taft and was subsequently to become Secretary of State in the Cabinet of President Hoover and again Secretary of War under President Franklin D. Roosevelt. One memorable day Coffin and a few other friends climbed Mt. McIntyre with Stimson and ate their sandwiches on the top while Stimson told stories of his adventures as a young man in what had been little traveled regions in Montana and Wyoming.

The wild flowers which grew in profusion on the mountains were a never ending source of fascination to Coffin. It was a rare mountain climbing expedition from which he did not return with some specimens in his pack basket. He studied carefully the conditions under which they grew in their native habitats, gathered plenty of soil with them when he removed them, and planted them among the trees around Phantom Height in situations as nearly as possible like those from which he had taken them. He had great success in transplanting them and soon had his home surrounded by a wild flower garden quite unique in its variety. Guests would be taken out to see some new flower which had just opened up, Coffin calling it affectionately by its Latin name and recalling in detail the circumstances under which he had made it his own. When in 1937 Phantom Height was sold and the Coffins bought a home in Lakeville, Connecticut, with a view to future retirement there, the choicest of the plants which were suitable for moving went with them.

CHAPTER EIGHT

THE END OF AN ERA

AS a preacher, Coffin had conspicuous gifts and graces which gained him a hearing from many people not ordinarily within the range of messages from a pulpit. In his early days his voice had been somewhat high and thin, but in Edinburgh he had put himself under the instruction of a teacher who had helped him master the art of tone production. This, combined with the intensity and wide range of feeling with which he spoke, gave flexibility and a moving quality to his utterances on all sorts of occasions. Nearly three decades after his graduation from Yale, a classmate wrote to the *Yale Alumni Weekly*, describing an informal talk which Coffin had given at a class dinner, saying, "Even if his subject matter had not been so well chosen and skilfully handled his voice is so well cultivated, the tones so pleasantly modulated, and his command of words so graceful and easy that it would be a pleasure to listen to him recite a timetable or describe a paving stone." Behind the voice, of course, was the man, handsome and striking in appearance, who arrested attention instantly anywhere. But what made him a preacher of power was the transparent reality of his own spiritual life, the vigorous honesty of his approach to the intellectual problems of religion, and the social passion with which he brought his religious convictions to bear upon the perplexities of the changing society in which his hearers were involved.

Before he had been ten years in the Madison Avenue pastorate, three volumes of his sermons had been published in response to many requests from people who had heard them and wished to ponder them further. In 1914 *University Sermons,* published by the Yale University Press, brought to a wider public fifteen sermons which had been preached in the chapels of Yale, Harvard, Princeton, Columbia, Brown, New York and Chicago Universities, and of Williams, Dartmouth, Wellesley, Vassar, Mt. Holyoke and Bryn Mawr Colleges, as well as at student conferences at Northfield, Massachusetts, and at Silver Bay, New York. Here were straight-forward discussions of such basic questions as "The Finality of Jesus," "The Claims of the Church upon Christians," "The Christian Thought of God," "The Reality of God," "Religion —A Load or a Lift?" and a penetrating examination of the influence of Darwinism entitled "The Fallacy of Origins."

In 1915, Coffin gave two more volumes of sermons to the public. One of them was a series on *The Ten Commandments*[1] which had been preached in the Madison Avenue Presbyterian Church. The full title included the phrase "With a Christian Application to Present Conditions." He dedicated the volume to Edward S. Harkness, with a quotation from Augustine's *Confessions,* Book IV, Paragraph IV: "Non est vera amicitia, nisi cum eam Tu agglutinas inter inhoerentes Tibi."[2] He made it clear that he believed that "Our Lord has not left us a fixed law, but a living Spirit." In the light of the ancient wisdom of the Commandments and of the teaching of the New Testament, he discussed such issues as polytheism and monotheism, art and idolatry, honesty and reverence, working hours, relations between parents and children, war and peace, marriage and the home, the treatment of wrongdoers, reverence for life and personality, property and the

[1] Doran, 1915.
[2] "True [friendship] it cannot be, unless in such as Thou cementest together, cleaving unto Thee." E. B. Pusey's translation. J. M. Dent and Sons, London, (E. P. Dutton, New York), 1907, p. 54.

individual and society, gossip and slander, covetousness and greed. His genius for the crisp condensation of truth is revealed on every page, as when he begins his opening chapter on the First Commandment with the sentence: "Were this commandment to be phrased today, it might read: 'Thou shalt have at least one God'"; or when in discussing the Fifth Commandment he observes: "One would like to insert *Commandment No. 5A,* 'Fathers and mothers, prove yourselves honorable.'"

The tenth anniversary of his installation on Madison Avenue also saw the publication of a volume with the title *Some Christian Convicitions.*[3] It consisted of a series of lectures on the fundamental beliefs of Christianity which he had given to various college and university groups and to other thoughtful persons elsewhere who were seeking enlightenment in religious matters. Disclaiming any pretense of making any contribution to scholarship, he stated their aim as "the less difficult, but perhaps scarcely less necessary middleman's task of bringing the results of the study of scholars to men and women who (to borrow a phrase of Augustine's) 'believe in thinking' and wish to 'think in believing.'" All the material in the lectures was preached in sermon form to the congregation on Madison Avenue on Sunday mornings.

The liberalism of the period has frequently been criticized as being excessively optimistic. It is said to have put its emphasis on man rather than on God, on human goodness rather than on man's sin, on automatic progress rather than on redemption, on the benevolence rather than the judgment of God. Coffin's lectures on theology in 1915 were characteristically liberal in spirit in that they plead for open-mindedness to truth wherever it might lead, they accepted the results of modern scholarship in Biblical studies, they urged the re-statement of Christian doctrines in the light of scientific discoveries, and they summoned Christians to sacrificial effort to re-mould society, protesting "against any fea-

[3] Yale University Press, 1915.

tures in prevailing conditions that do not disclose Christlike
love."[4] There was, however, no overlooking of the tragic aspects
of human existence, no blindness to the terrible reality of sin.
"Golgotha convinces us of the ruinous forces that live in and
dominate our world; it faces us with the suicidal elements in
men's spirits that drive them to murder the Christlike in themselves; it tears the veil from each hostile thought and feeling that
enacts this tragedy and exposes the God-murdering character of
our sin. Sin is deicidal. When that Life of light is extinguished,
we find a world about us and within us so dark that its darkness
can be felt."[5] "Christians label any un-Christlikeness sin, and
they vastly darken the world with a new sense of its evil, and
are themselves most painfully aware of their own sinfulness."
Concurrent with his indictment of the evil in existing individual
and corporate life, however, was an emphasis upon higher possibilities because of God's forgiveness, renewing power and eternal
purpose. "Jesus confers His confidence in the alterability of human relations. Christians believe in the superiority of moral over
material forces, in the wisdom and might of love. . . . His followers in every age have seemed fools to many, if not to most of
their judicious contemporaries; but cheered by His confidence,
they venture on apparently hopeless undertakings, and find that
He has overcome the world."[6] In later years the emphasis in
Coffin's theological preaching and teaching may have shifted
somewhat as new problems came to the fore in the public mind,
but in this volume in 1915 he stated the essential position which
was the substance of his preaching throughout his ministry.

The finest and clearest statement of the heart of his message is
found in the Closing Address which he gave to the students at
Union Seminary on May 18, 1915. "The Practical Aims of a Liberal
Evangelicalism" was the title. No address was ever a clearer

[4] *Op. cit.,* p. 170.
[5] *Op. cit.,* p. 143.
[6] *Op. cit.,* p. 105.

revelation of a man's deepest convictions and most passionate faith than this. "Liberal Evangelicalism!" he began. "Note which word in our title stands merely in the qualifying position of the adjective and which occupies the position of eminence as the noun. We are first and foremost evangelicals—evangelicals to the core of our spiritual beings. We own ourselves redeemed by and we worship God in Jesus Christ; we loyally hold fast to the Scriptures as the authoritative Self-revelation of God, and confidently believe that, when we read them under the guidance of the Spirit of Christ, they are to us the self-accrediting standard of God's life with us and of our life with one another in Him; we reverently turn to Calvary as the supreme disclosure both of the world's tragic sinfulness and of God's redemptive love, who suffers with and for His children; we are convinced that He who wrought by His Spirit in believers of old, renewing, enlightening, sanctifying them, works in our day, bringing light and life and power to all who yield themselves to the Lordship of Jesus." He was on guard against a shallow liberalism which in its enthusiasm for freedom became a negative attitude, casting aside what Coffin regarded as essentials of the faith. "Any attempt to belittle Jesus, to reduce Him to a mere Teacher, a sage superior to other sages but one among many, not the unique Saviour of the world; to substitute any other standard for the Bible as the authoritative expression of God's life with men; to regard the cross as anything less than the power of God and the wisdom of God for a world's redemption; to trust to human effort alone for salvation, personal or social; runs counter to our deepest instincts and convictions, and seems to us, as such attempts have seemed to our fathers in the faith, to depreciate the Christian religion and to rob it of its vital force. We are evangelicals." It was, however, in no sense a compromised liberalism for which he stood. "And we are liberals —not liberals in the sense that we cultivate freedom for its own sake, but for the Gospel's sake. . . . We are loyal to truth, and our Gospel in order to be *good* news must be *true* news. Our allegiance to Christ includes an allegiance to veracity, a constant endeavor to seek for and state 'truth as it is in Jesus.' Consequently we keep our minds hospitable to every movement of human thought."

On June 23, 1915, Yale University conferred upon Coffin the honorary degree of Doctor of Divinity. He had already received the degree from two other institutions of learning, and he was to receive many more degrees during his career, but the accolade from his own Alma Mater touched him deeply. With character-istic self-dedication, he regarded it as a summons to further service to the cause of religion at Yale. At the Alumni Luncheon following the conferring of the degrees, Coffin in his remarks pled for the retention of the traditional requirement of attend-ance at daily and Sunday chapel services, arguing that in an institution founded for the advancement of Christian learning this was not an infringement of personal liberty.

Before Coffin had been very long at the Madison Avenue Church the congregation had become interested in establishing and supporting a mission station in China. It came about quite naturally. The city fathers in Nanhsuchow in Anhwei Province were eager to have for their community the humanitarian and educational services which they had seen rendered by the mis-sionaries in Hwai Yuen, a few miles away. They offered to pro-vide the land required for such a mission. Coffin's friends, Edward C. Lobenstine, James B. Cochran and others suggested that the Madison Avenue Church should sponsor such a project. Coffin responded enthusiastically and he communicated his enthusiasm to his people.

Coffin set about at once recruiting personnel and raising funds for the enterprise. Thomas F. Carter, a graduate of Princeton University and of Union Theological Seminary, who in his latter years was head of the department of Chinese at Columbia Uni-versity, was enlisted to head the mission, ably assisted by George

C. Hood, another Union Seminary graduate. Two temples which were not in use were put at the disposal of the mission for school purposes, the ancient images being carefully covered over with waxed paper. One became a boys' school and the other one for girls. A simple church was built, and before many years a dispensary and a small hospital under the direction of Dr. James W. Wiltsie. When land outside the city wall was made available for an agricultural experiment station, J. Lossing Buck, a graduate of the Cornell Agricultural School, came to bring the resources of modern science to bear upon the ever present problem of feeding the teeming population. Chinese preachers, teachers, doctors and farmers were recruited to aid in the work and to assist the missionaries as they itinerated over a wide surrounding area, carrying to other towns and villages their knowledge, compassion and Christian faith.

In 1916 Coffin and his wife visited the station. After trips to Hawaii and Japan, they landed at Shanghai and went directly to Kuling, a mountain resort where missionaries and members of the foreign colony gathered for their summer holidays. There he lectured for a week on "Social Aspects of the Gospel" with a thousand men and women in the audience at each lecture. At the first lecture he was introduced by an elderly missionary of rather conservative views who had been somewhat dubious about Coffin's coming. When the lecture was finished he rose and solemnly announced, "Our apprehensions are allayed!" At the urgent request of missionaries in the north of China, the lectures were then repeated at Peitaiho, a seaside resort in that region. Then the Coffins journeyed inland to Changsha where they saw the expanding work at Yale-in-China and he dedicated a newly completed chapel. At Nanhsuchow he visited the schools which had been opened by the mission and also spoke to three hundred boys and young men at the Government School. A meeting of leading citizens of the city was arranged at which he spoke on "Christian Ethics and Western Civilisation." At a dinner given in his honor he met the President of the Chamber of Commerce, the head of the Board of Education, the Collector of Taxes, the Postmaster and other civic leaders. They praised the mission for what it was doing for the people of the city and urged further expansion of its services. Coffin told them frankly that further help depended upon their helping themselves. This produced instantaneous results in the offer of the land for agricultural experiments and in the formation of a committee to secure land for a hospital. A crowded Sunday followed, in which he preached at the morning service, gave a Communion Address in the afternoon, met with a Bible Class of young men and took a walk about the city. Then the night train took him on to Chufu, convinced that his church was making a good investment at Nanhsuchow. Later events vindicated his judgment. The work grew steadily in scope and usefulness, through civil war as well as days of peace, until the mainland of China came under Communist rule and the missionaries had to leave.

In the summer of 1914 the peaceful world in which Coffin and his contemporaries had been educated and had begun their careers came to an end. Thenceforth the grim possibilities or realities of war constituted the background of life for his generation. "The outbreak of the Great War in the summer of 1914 seemed to many to set us abruptly in the midst of another age," he wrote in the Preface to the volume of sermons on *The Ten Commandments* which he preached in the winter of 1914–1915. "We had come to think of ourselves as living in an earth which, with all its selfishness, was slowly but surely responding to the touch of the Spirit of Christ. Americans looked upon the huge armaments of Europe as absurd anachronisms; the growth of intelligence and the spread of Christian ideals had made a conflict between the great powers unthinkable. We were startled and appalled to find ourselves suddenly thrust back into a day of pagan horrors."[7] The blow came with even greater shattering

[7] P. 7.

force to Coffin's hopes because of the many friends he had made
during his student days in both Britain and Germany, and because
of the numbers of people in his New York congregation who were
natives of both countries.

He had never been and never became a thorough-going pacifist,
but his whole nature revolted at the slaughter going on in Europe.
For many months, until Germany's unrestrained submarine war-
fare against American shipping convinced him that the United
States had no choice except resistance or subjugation, he was
opposed to his country's participation in the conflict. In 1916 when
President Woodrow Wilson urged the building up of American
military and naval power and "preparedness" was the slogan of
the hour, Coffin believed that this was a mistaken policy. On May
13, a huge Preparedness Parade marched up Fifth Avenue to
arouse enthusiasm for the President's program. A member of the
Madison Avenue Presbyterian Church, General Charles H. Sherrill, a former United States Minister to the Argentine Republic,
was the Grand Marshal of the parade. Coffin felt that the demonstration was a step in the direction of militarizing America and
announced in advance in his church paper that on Sunday, May
14, he would preach a sermon on "A Christian Nation's Preparedness." That sermon was subsequently printed as a pamphlet and
widely circulated. Taking for his text the plea in I Peter 4:1, "Arm
ye yourselves also with the same mind," he argued that "there is a
preparedness of the nation's soul . . . that the Christian Church
must press upon the consciences of American citizens. . . . It must
hold up the ideal of a nation armed with mind of Christ."[8]
With his friend General Sherrill sitting in one of the front pews,
he referred to the parade of the day before and said, "As a protest
against the donothingism of many of our fellow-citizens, as an
awakening to the realization that we possess treasures of which
we are stewards for posterity and for the race and which we
dare not suffer to be endangered, as a reassertion of loyalty to this

[8] *The Preparedness of a Christian Nation,* (Pamphlet), p. 3.

country it had its value. But so far as it was a demonstration for military preparedness it was a march into yesterday."[9]

The sermon caused great excitement in his congregation, and was the subject of heated discussion in a much wider circle for a long time. Not many in Coffin's congregation shared his point of view. One of his most loyal supporters said at his dinner table that Sunday, "Much as I love Henry Coffin I would gladly see him go to jail for preaching this morning's sermon." Until April, 1917, in sermon after sermon he opposed what he interpreted as the growing militarism of the country with such vigor that not a few of his hearers ticketed him as a pacifist. Some of them felt let down when he ultimately supported President Wilson's request to Congress for a Declaration of War. On the Sunday morning following that historic event, Coffin from his pulpit declared that the country had no alternative but to resist German aggression, and urged that the war be prosecuted with the utmost vigor and brought to an end at the earliest possible moment so that the world could get on with the constructive tasks of peace.

As the young men of his congregation went off into various forms of military service and the people of his congregation were caught up in a wide variety of war services, he was eager to do his part in the common endeavor. During the Spring and Summer of 1917 he made frequent trips to the posts where the newly re-cruited American army was in training, speaking and preaching under the auspices of the Young Men's Christian Association. Accustomed as he was to the services of the church where the setting, music, and atmosphere were all aids to worship, he found it difficult at first to adjust himself to speaking under all sorts of circumstances, frequently more conducive to anything else than to worship. Soon, however, he was thoroughly at home on any kind of platform, or on none, bringing the Christian message with persuasiveness and power. One June evening he had been asked to speak to a gathering of new recruits at the Brooklyn Navy

[9] *Op. cit.*, p. 2.

Yard. When he arrived he found a large tent filled to capacity with young men in uniform. Two well-known vaudeville performers, the Dolly Sisters, were putting on a song-and-dance program to the huge delight of their audience. The ill-advised Y.M.C.A. secretary who had arranged the affair had thought that he could lure a crowd into the meeting by advertising the Dolly Sisters without mentioning the fact that the main feature of the evening would be a religious address. When therefore, after a particularly popular number, he announced that this concluded the musical part of the program and that now the meeting would be addressed by the well-known Presbyterian minister, Dr. Henry Sloane Coffin, a shout of outrage followed by groans went up from the boys, who quite properly felt that they had been brought together under false pretenses. No speaker ever faced a more hostile audience or a more difficult situation. Although he subsequently expressed his opinion of the affair in quite definite terms, Coffin betrayed no confusion or embarrassment at the time but proceeded at once with the address on the meaning of religious faith which he had planned to give. Within seconds he had the attention of the crowd and very soon they were listening as though this was what they had always wanted to hear. When he finished a burst of applause swept the tent and little groups gathered around him to talk until he had to hurry back to Madison Avenue and another busy day in his parish.

The realities of the war were brought home to Coffin with new force during the Summer of 1918 which he spent in France on a special assignment as a speaker to the troops, again under the auspices of the Young Men's Christian Association. His brother, William Sloane Coffin, was in Paris, having left his business in New York to become one of the directors of Foyers des Soldats, the Y.M.C.A.'s service to the French army. The brothers met there in June. The younger brother gave the older a briefing on the situation in France and Henry Coffin went off for a strenuous two months of speaking, often several times a day, in all sorts of places and under all manner of circumstances. He spoke in Y.M.C.A. halls, in public squares with all the turmoil of traffic and restless humanity as a background, in ancient palaces which had been taken over by the army, in hospitals and rest areas, in *cafés chantants* and cinemas, on hill-sides and in open fields within sound of the guns or with the drone of airplanes overhead, to men just out of the trenches and to men just about to go into battle. On one occasion he was sent up to one unit near the front and was obliged to leave immediately as he found them just preparing to go into the line. At another place he terminated his address hurriedly in the middle because orders arrived summoning his audience into action. Sometimes near the front he found himself in hospitals or relief stations where the wounded were being brought. At such times he devoted himself to rendering practical help in any way he could, moving about among the sufferers, writing letters for them, distributing coffee, sandwiches and cigarettes and bringing his friendliness and faith into the cheerless atmosphere. Not infrequently he would hear his name called and would find a young man from his own congregation or one who had heard him preach at some college chapel or someone from New York City who knew him by reputation. Sometimes it would be a German soldier to whom he spoke in his own language.

By the end of August he had spoken at 93 meetings, with a total attendance of 33,000 and an average attendance of 351. Everywhere he had met with a responsive attitude on the part of the men whom he addressed and with cooperation on the part of their officers. In general he thought the chaplains and Y.M.C.A. workers to be men of fine calibre. Occasionally he was amused by ecclesiastical pretensions. In one instance a young chaplain who was just out of seminary and greatly impressed with his own importance said to him, "Dr. Coffin, when you speak to me I would be grateful if you would address me as 'Father'." "Certainly," Coffin replied, "I will call you 'Grandfather' if you want me to." He felt under great pressure to make the most of his opportunity to bring the Christian message to his audiences without diluting it or toning it down. "What a chance I am having to speak to men—thousands of them every week—and what a chance to preach the Gospel!", he wrote to Mrs. Coffin. "I introduce my address with local allusions or with a story or two from men I have met, and then go straight to a message of the Living God as a present comrade, and what His companionship means." At the end of a crowded week, which he described in a letter to his church paper at home, he said, "We have had between seven and eight thousand men in all at services throughout the week, and while I have tried to put things simply, I have given every whit as thoughtful addresses as I would use in a University Chapel at home."

Although cut off from books and a study, his own intellectual activity never flagged, and he found stimulus in a new way in the Bible. "I have been reading Jeremiah lately, and making notes," he wrote in mid-July. "He fits in with the war background and his own moods have modern counterparts." "I have been reading Daniel through yesterday," he wrote in August, "and found a number of good texts. It is a book worth studying." "I have no books but the Bible, but that really proves quite a new book against this war background—especially Psalms and Prophets."

When his period of service in France drew to its close in late August, efforts were made to have him extend it, or to agree to return to Europe the following winter. He felt, however, that his primary obligation, even in war time, was to the church of which he was pastor, especially since one of his associate ministers, Paul D. Moody, was serving as a Headquarters Chaplain in France, and his other associate, William R. Jelliffe, was eager to enlist. So, after a brief trip to England and Scotland, where he had fleeting visits with H. R. Mackintosh and John Kelman and put in a full Sunday preaching in one of the Scottish churches, he returned to New York in September. The Armistice which was signed on

November 11, 1918, relieved him of any further obligation for
service with the troops overseas.

No one who saw the war at first hand came out of the experience unchanged. Many ministers reacted by taking a pacifist
pledge never again to lend their support to war in any form.
Coffin was not of their number. What the war did create in him,
or strengthen in him, was a life long passion to work for the spiritual bases of peace and for the international framework which
would make wars less likely. He was not naïve enough to imagine
that an orderly world could be easily achieved. He had said in
his Lyman Beecher Lectures at Yale in the Spring of 1918: "You
are not likely to hear progress talked of as though there were some
principle resident in men and things that fated them to improve
and to work out right—a view of life that excludes judgment and
redemption. We know that we live in a vastly more tragic world
that we had supposed, where things that are wrong, if unchecked,
get worse and work out to hideous catastrophes. The world moves
in no steadily advancing evolution; sin brings on inevitable doom;
unless redemptive forces produce radical changes, nothing remains but a certain fearful looking for of judgment."[10] As the
country tried to forget the war and settle down to what was
called "normalcy," Coffin in sermon after sermon pleaded for the
changes which would justify the sacrifices of blood and treasure
which had been made during the conflict. He summoned his
people to generosity in aiding the victims of the struggle. He held
up the ideal of America as a servant nation, in contrast with the
growing mood of national selfishness. He preached the gospel
of a Universal Church, transcending nationalistic lines and drawing together people of all nations. He was a staunch advocate of
the League of Nations as the next step in the establishment of a
reign of law in international affairs. While the war was still raging,
ex-President William Howard Taft and President A. Lawrence
Lowell, of Harvard University, had advocated a League to En-

[10] *In a Day of Social Rebuilding*, Yale University Press, 1918, pp. 2-3.

force Peace. Coffin endorsed the proposal and invited Mr. Taft to speak on the subject at a mid-week meeting in the Madison Avenue Presbyterian Church. After the war, in the face of growing isolationism in America, Coffin's sermons consistently stressed the obligation of a Christian nation to assume responsibilities for the world's peace and urged membership in the League of Nations as a clear duty.

Colonel E. M. House, who had been President Woodrow Wilson's advisor and personal representative during the war and at the Versailles Peace Conference, lived around the corner from the Madison Avenue Church during the immediate post-war years and attended Sunday services there. On November 11, 1923, the fifth anniversary of the Armistice, he wrote to Coffin:

"I want to thank you for the pleasure your sermon of this morning gave me. . . . I left your church with the wish in my heart that your words might be broadcasted throughout the world. . . . It is the clearest, the most logical and most convincing argument I have yet heard in favor of peace and of our assuming our obligations to help maintain it."

How heavily the burden of war weighed upon Coffin's spirit was perhaps unconsciously revealed in a passage in one of his lectures on *The Meaning of the Cross* which he delivered to various groups of theological students and ministers during the decade following the war and published in 1931. He said: "Those who lived and ministered during the years of the Great War may have shared the experience of the writer, who month after month found haunting his mind the text: 'God gave unto us the ministry of reconciliation.' Amid the passions and hatreds of that appalling day when by every device imaginable men were butchering one another on a wholesale scale, what could a minister of the Gospel do to discharge this God-committed duty? The text burned itself into his heart and was a daily discomfort and misery to him."[11]

Through the discouraging years of European disintegration

[11] *The Meaning of the Cross*, Scribners, 1931, p. 147.

and American isolationism, Coffin continued to believe in international cooperation as essential to peace. He liked to repeat a remark made to him by William Howard Taft at a time when the League of Nations had become pathetically weak and seemed almost futile. Coffin was preaching in Washington and Mr. Taft, at the time Chief Justice of the United States, asked him to go for a walk with him. In the course of their conversation, Coffin ventured to ask the Chief Justice: "What do you think of the League now?" Mr. Taft stopped, turned and faced Coffin, and said: "You ought to know that in our world the best things get crucified; *but they rise again.*"[12] Coffin shared this indomitable hope.

[12] *God Confronts Man in History,* Scribners, 1947, p. 149.

CHAPTER NINE

THE SECOND DECADE ON
MADISON AVENUE

THE first decade of Coffin's pastorate in the Madison Avenue Church was one which saw steady and somewhat spectacular growth in the congregations which attended the services, and especially in the number of children, young people and adults who attended the Bible School. The church building had become inadequate for the crowds which flocked to it. Especially the remodelled garage which had served as a Church House was too small for all the classes and clubs which were crowded into it on Sunday mornings and evenings, to say nothing of the other six days of the week. John Steen had once written a jingle describing the Madison Avenue institution as

> *"The light church,*
> *The bright church,*
> *The seven day and night church."*

By 1916 it had become apparent that a larger and better equipped Church House was a necessity. On February 11, 1916, the church paper, *The Weekly,* carried the picture of an architect's drawing of a proposed new Church House, a seven-story structure with an open roof where summer evening services could be held. It was announced that the cost of the building had been pledged "on condition that the congregation add fifty thousand dollars to the endowment and increase the envelope contributions to church support for next year by twenty-five hundred dollars." (The anonymous donor of the building was again Edward S. Harkness.) The congregation promptly pledged its share of the necessary funds and on May 11, 1917, the new Church House was dedicated. It contained two gymnasiums which could be used also for Sunday School assemblies and classrooms, a swimming pool, rooms for social gatherings and meetings of various sizes, a small office for the two secretaries and one for the Men's Work Director. It was simply furnished and was obviously meant to be used. It towered over the lower structures which then lined Madison Avenue, and could be seen for many blocks bearing witness to the church's desire to minister in a wide variety of ways to the lives of its people.

Coffin had not changed his view with regard to the function of the Church. On September 26, 1912, in an address at Union Seminary he had said: "There is need for a clear definition of the Church's distinctive mission. It is not its task to supply wholesome recreations, or to furnish sanitary dwellings, or to sell cheaper groceries, or to provide education for a community, or to take up the scale of wages in shops and factories. There may be, there unhappily are, circumstances under which it becomes necessary for the Church to do such things because no other agency is meeting an imperative need. . . . But the Church's proper task, like her Lord's, is to hold up the ideals, furnish the motives and convictions, and provide the devoted men and women who through the State, or private companies, or benevolent societies shall render this social service. And the Church's function is to inspire, not to direct."[1] There was a growing feeling in some circles that the Church ought to serve the community around it in any way possible. There was also an idea in some churches, seldom explicitly declared but subtly influential, that recreational facilities could be used as bait to attract into the church young

[1] "The Religious Opportunity of the Present Social Awakening," delivered in the Chapel of the Union Theological Seminary, p. 12.

people for whom opportunities for religious instruction and worship would otherwise make faint appeal. Coffin was unmoved by either of these popular theories. He insisted that the primary purpose for which the new Church House should be used was religious education and that the facilities of the building were intended to supplement formal teaching by providing opportunities for the young people of the church groups to live well-rounded lives in every aspect of which the Christian spirit would be developed and expressed. In a striking sermon at the dedication[2] of the Church House on May 11, 1917, he took as his text Revelations 11:1, "And there was given me a reed like unto a rod: and the angel stood, saying, Rise, and measure the temple of God, and the altar, and them that worship therein." It was a plea for a church with a varied program in which nothing should be allowed to overshadow the altar or the spiritual life of the worshipping people.

In April, 1918, two months before he went to France, Coffin had delivered the Lyman Beecher Lectures on Preaching at the Yale Divinity School. This was the first of the lectureships which he was to hold at various institutions of learning throughout his career. Coffin gave his lectures the title, "In a Day of Social Rebuilding." Speaking as he was in the midst of the war, he was already looking forward to the changed world which would follow the conflict and the obligation resting upon the Church to bring the resources of religion to bear upon international relations, industrial problems, educational work and personal life. Specifically, he discussed "The Ministry of Reconciliation," "The Ministry of Evangelism," "The Ministry of Teaching," and "The Ministry of Organization," with penetrating surveys of the contemporary world and keen analysis of the demands of the times upon ministers of the gospel. Two of the finest lectures, "The Ministry of Worship" and "The Ministry of Friendship," were profound discussions of subjects transcending the circumstances

[2] *The Weekly,* May, 1917.

of any particular era and constitute valuable contributions to the standard literature on the liturgical and pastoral ministry.

With the war in Europe in the forefront of his mind and on his heart, it was natural that he should have considered the effect that the war would have upon men's thinking and upon their attitudes toward human affairs. He began his final lecture by saying:[3] "In the memoirs of Nehemiah there is a striking description of his first inspection of the ruined Jerusalem, when he had returned to take up the task of its rebuilding. . . . We began this course of lectures with a similar survey of our world in pieces, and the darkness of night is still about us as we scan the ruins. As to Nehemiah the destroyed city seemed clearly a judgment of God, so to the eyes of faith this catastrophe can have no other interpretation. . . . Never before have international relations been so searchingly scrutinized, and the disease spots in imperialistic commerce, tariff discriminations and threatening armaments exposed. Never before has it been so generally recognised that a new heart and a right spirit must govern nations, or all devices to preserve international order are futile. And the probe has been put into other relations, notably those of industry, with far-reaching disclosures. . . . Men of social insight are aware that public control, however valuable, will not better matters much unless new motives come into play, and men become socially-minded. Never was the supreme need of the social spirit so patent. It is the day of the Church of Christ as the Fellowship of His Spirit, with the task of spiritualizing every sphere of human society."

With the growing congregation and expanded program at the Madison Avenue Church, a larger staff of ministers was needed to share with Coffin and Jelliffe the administrative responsibilities and the pastoral care of the parish, while leaving the major part of the responsibility for preaching upon Coffin's shoulders. In 1917, Paul D. Moody, younger son of Dwight L. Moody, was called from the pastorate of the Congregational Church in St.

[3] *In a Day of Social Rebuilding*, Yale University Press, 1919, pp. 188-190.

Johnsbury, Vermont. Before he had assumed the post, however, the regiment in the Vermont National Guard of which he was Chaplain was ordered to France and he felt it his duty to accompany them. In France he had a distinguished career, most of it in association with Bishop Charles H. Brent as Headquarters Chaplain. He had not been very long in service at the Madison Avenue Church after the war before he was called back to Vermont to become President of Middlebury College. His place was taken in 1922 by George Stewart, who had been General Secretary of the Yale University Christian Association. Later on John Hopkins Denison, an older man with whom Jelliffe in his early ministry had been associated at the Central Congregational Church of Boston, joined the group. Each of them was a man of great ability, although they were very different from one another. They worked well together, not without occasional strain, but as Christian men dedicated to a common purpose.

The first major sorrow in Coffin's life struck suddenly on February 17, 1919, in the death of his mother. In order to be nearer their son the elder Coffins had sold their home on 57th Street and had built a handsome new house at 110 East 71st Street, on the same block with the Henry Coffins. The house was completed during the summer of 1918 while Henry Coffin was in France. They had occupied it for only a few months when Mrs. Edmund Coffin died of a heart attack. The family were all together as they customarily were for Sunday dinner. They had just walked from the dining-room to the drawing room when she was stricken and died almost instantly. Coffin remembered afterwards how his father had stood by the body of his wife and solemnly announced to the others in the room, "This is death." This was the first break in a family which had always been very close to each other. They accepted it with the stoicism of well-bred people not accustomed to make outward display of grief, except for the wearing of the conventional mourning arm-band. In a far more profound way they accepted the blow with a triumphant Christian faith, demonstrating the validity of the gospel Henry Coffin had preached by meeting their responsibilities steadily and generously with no time out for self-pity or luxuriating in the sense of loss. For a few weeks the Henry Coffins moved in with Edmund Coffin and William Sloane Coffin, the younger son who at the time was still unmarried. Then they went back to 129 East 71st Street, keeping in daily touch with the bereaved father but resuming their normal habits of life.

Raymond Jelliffe once said that one of the secrets of Coffin's helpfulness as a pastor was that he had "an intuitive capacity for entering into the experiences of other people which he had never been through himself." To his classes at the Seminary Coffin used to point to the verse in the first chapter of Second Corinthians in which St. Paul gave thanks to "the Father of mercies and God of all comfort, who comforteth us in all our tribulation, that we may be able to comfort *them which are in any trouble,* by the comfort wherewith we ourselves are comforted of God." A man does not need to have been through every sorrow in order to comfort people passing through it, he would say. If he has been comforted *in any tribulation* he knows what the comfort of God is and is able to mediate it to those passing through troubles which he himself has never experienced. But after February 17, 1919, he knew for himself the keen edge of bereavement.

This capacity for entering sympathetically into the experiences of other people and for expressing the affirmations of the Christian faith applicable to those experiences was undoubtedly one of the ingredients in his extraordinary helpfulness as a pastor. When one of the Presbyterian board secretaries was in the hospital about to undergo a critical operation, a group of his ministerial friends were one day sitting with him in his room when Coffin came down the corridor bringing with him an atmosphere of confidence and cheer. He entered the room, chatted for a moment and asked if he could offer prayer. The patient gratefully begged him to do so. Coffin voiced a brief prayer and immediately took his leave.

"There was nothing more to say," said one of the men who was present. "He had said exactly what every man there would have liked to say if he could have expressed what was on his heart." Brief notes which he wrote to people in sorrow were preserved and treasured. To a young man whose fiancée had died he wrote on a Sunday evening at the end of a crowded day: "I have just learned of the very great sorrow that has come to you. It could not be a sorer loss. You have my heart with you in tender sympathy. There is nothing to say but that God remains, and He is Home for those who go and for us who stay, and in Him we still meet and are one. Your life as it moves along in His purposes will never be remote from hers yonder." To a woman whose husband had died he wrote: "You must think of him as with God and that is never far away. One learns, I think, to feel that God is Home and that in Him we are always close to those who serve Him yonder. But it still remains yonder and we are here, and the adjustment of one's life to a great loneliness cannot be easy. With a very earnest prayer that you may have daily renewals of strength and courage, I am, Faithfully Yours."

One of the elders of the Madison Avenue Church, a native of the north of Ireland, attended a meeting one evening at the church at a time when he was going through great troubles. Coffin had returned from Union Seminary where he had recently become President, to speak at this meeting. As the man came out of the church after the meeting he saw Coffin sitting with his wife in an automobile at the curb, apparently just ready to start home. A shy and reticent man, the elder started to walk down the street thinking himself unnoticed in the night, but before he reached the corner he felt an arm around his shoulder and there stood Coffin beside him ready to take his hand. "*He did not say anything,*" the man recalled many years afterwards. "What was there to say?"

During the war Coffin had felt that its tragic losses and destruction could only be justified by the elimination of social injustices and the creation of a more fraternal society when the conflict ended. Woodrow Wilson had said that the aim of the war was "to make the world safe for democracy." Coffin felt the challenge to put Christian foundations under the democracy which had been saved. The period immediately following the Armistice of November 11, 1918, was one of acute unrest throughout the United States. The Peace Conference at Versailles dragged on, while the opponents of the League of Nations in the Senate were blocking President Wilson's efforts to persuade the United States to join it. There was unemployment and unrest in the ranks of labor. There was a widespread fear of bolshevism which sometimes resulted in suspicion of anyone advocating brotherhood. In this situation Coffin announced early in 1920 that he would preach a series of sermons on Sunday mornings bearing on the theme, "A More Christian Industrial Order." They were published under that title the next year. Disclaiming any purpose of drawing a blueprint of a Christian society, Coffin addressed himself to the task of defining the next steps which he believed should be taken in that direction. He contended that service of the community rather than the making of profits ought to be the pervading motive of industry and commerce for all involved in their enterprises.[4] He felt it essential that people should have "a feeling of proprietorship and obligation in their work, a voice in its control and a knowledge of its policies, with an appeal in it to their hearts to do their utmost for the service of the community."[5] He was not critical of the Stock Market as an institution but criticized "types of brokerage which do not assist production but help gambling in stock or cotton or real estate."[6] (A broker in the congregation good naturedly took exception to this view and sent Coffin a volume on economics by Professor Frank W. Taussig of Harvard. Coffin was delighted to find a statement in the book corroborating the opinion he had expressed.) He argued that the community should "de-

[4] *A More Christian Industrial Order,* Macmillan, 1920, p. 10.
[5] *Op. cit.,* p. 12.
[6] *Op. cit.,* pp. 6-7.

termine a minimum standard of living and see that no family lacks a chance to earn that,"[7] and condemned the exploitation of labor through low wages, excessive hours and unhealthy conditions of work. He held that "some form of public control of essential industries" was necessary. He accepted the distinction between "property for use" and "property for power."[8] He stressed the importance of having every member of society a property owner, but maintained that every man is really a steward and God the real owner, since He "loans possessions to the community of His children, and to individuals through the community."[9] He identified himself with no particular social movement but left the working out of his principles to the consciences and practical policies of his hearers and readers. In all these matters, Coffin was simply expressing in the light of conditions at the end of the war convictions which were basic with him all through his ministry, convictions which had a theological foundation for him in what in 1911 he had called the *Social Aspects of the Cross.*[10] "I once assumed that Dr. Coffin depended on Rauschenbusch's treatment of the idea in *A Theology for the Social Gospel*," John C. Bennett has written, "but his first published discussion of the subject with which I am familiar came out six years before Rauschenbusch's book. . . . If Henry Sloane Coffin were not so well known for other interests and achievements he would be recognized as one of the most forthright and consistent champions of the social interpretation of Christianity."

Dr. Jonathan Day, the Minister of Labor Temple on Second Avenue at Fourteenth Street, heard one of the sermons and remarked as he left the church, "I think that was the most courageous sermon I ever heard in New York." Many members of the Madison Avenue congregation did not agree with Coffin's views

[7] *Op. cit.*, p. 23.
[8] *Op. cit.*, p. 37.
[9] *Op. cit.*, p. 32.
[10] G. H. Doran, 1911.

on social questions. For the most part they believed in him and respected both his honesty and his humanity. They did not go all the way with him but they listened and in their own way were moved nearer to the ideals of the Kingdom of God.

During the period of almost hysterical popular fear of radicalism which followed the end of the war, Coffin remained staunchly true to the principles of freedom for thought and speech to which he had given allegiance in less stormy times. When the New York Legislature voted not to seat certain elected members because they were affiliated with the Socialist Party, Coffin joined with other leading citizens of the state in protest, and voiced his objections from the pulpit, disclaiming identity of views with the ejected men but defending their right to be seated in spite of the unpopularity of their political position. When a crowd attacked the office of the *New York Call* and the Lusk Committee by subpoena authorized a raid on the Rand School in which books, papers and other documents were carried off leading to requests for the withdrawal of the School's charter Coffin joined with a group of clergymen in issuing a statement urging that "calm counsels prevail" in dealing with radicals. They united in condemning a situation in which "violence employed in the name of patriotism has been allowed to go unpunished by the authorities and has even been praised by leaders in the government." The *New York Evening Globe* commended the statement editorially, saying: "The five prominent clergymen of New York City who have united in a protest against the methods used in combating the influence, teachings, and general activities of radicals in this country can hardly be accused of oversympathy with the Rand School or with the I.W.W. It is seldom that any public statement is made with more backing of sane and respected authority than this. The Rev. Arthur C. McGiffert, president of Union Theological Seminary; the Rev. Howard C. Robbins, dean of the Cathedral of St. John; the Rev. Charles R. Brown, dean of the Yale School of Religion; the Rev. Henry Sloane Coffin, of the Madison Avenue Pres-

byterian Church; and the Rev. William Austin Smith, editor of
the *Churchman*, make up a list of men whose opinions on any
social subject must be taken seriously and carefully weighed. And
they have spoken out against two varieties of opposition to radicals in this city—the sort of violence that may be typified by the
attack upon the *Call* offices May 1, and the strictly legal proceedings of the Lusk Committee. We are all against mob action to
punish any member of the community, and it has been clear in the
public mind that such action, whether for or against the radical
elements, was subversive to our liberties. There is no similar
unanimity of opinion about the raid on the Rand School. Such
action is legally justifiable. . . . But it is probably just as bad policy
as the other. As the statement from the National Civil Liberties
Bureau says, it will not pay us to drive criticism underground. We
can safely leave the teachings of any school of political thinking
which does not advocate the use of force to the jury of public
opinion." Coffin's expression of belief in a free market for ideas
and his defense of the right of other men to advocate views with
which he did not agree was in line with what was to become a
lifelong practice based on deep conviction.

Coffin's discriminating judgment and his shrewd blend of enthusiasm and wisdom were repeatedly tested in the exposed position which he occupied as pastor of one of the most influential
churches in New York. In 1917, in spite of great pressure put upon
him to support the Billy Sunday Evangelistic Campaign which for
weeks drew great throngs to a Tabernacle erected in uptown New
York, Coffin refused to have anything to do with it. Evangelistic
to the core though he was, he did not believe that the Christian
gospel could be advanced by a circus atmosphere and preaching
which lacked solid content. The meager results of the meetings
and the subsequent general revulsion of feeling against their irrev-
erence and sensationalism vindicated his stand. For quite other
reasons he refused to cooperate in the Inter-Church World Movement which denominational leaders launched immediately after

the war ended. The movement was a drawing together of campaigns for advance in missionary and benevolence giving on which most of the Protestant Churches had embarked as evidence of their desire to build a new world after the holocaust of war. It was hoped that it would bring them into closer fellowship in a variety of activities and so promote the ultimate unity of Christendom. Coffin was thoroughly committed to the cause of Christian Unity but he was suspicious of the grandiose plans, the high-powered promotional methods and the administrative cost of the Inter-Church World Movement. When it was proposed to put many millions of dollars into a great building to house the Movement in New York City, in what he regarded as a misguided attempt to make an impression on the secular world, he would have none of it. When the Movement collapsed, he deplored the fact that its obligations had to be paid off out of funds which had been contributed for the missionary work of the churches. Having seen his own churches grow in membership and strength as the result of faithful pastoral service and preaching in the great tradition, he had little faith in the short cuts to the Kingdom of God through highly organized movements, of which he saw the rise and fall of many during the years of his ministry. Some of his friends felt that he was too reluctant to participate in such ventures. In later years he was active in the Federal Council of Churches and then in the National and World Councils of Churches, but never with the same abandon with which he threw himself into work more closely connected with the parish.

Chapel services sponsored by college and university authorities were a familiar experience for Coffin and he delighted in the opportunity they afforded him to present the Christian faith to students. In 1920 he was challenged by an invitation to speak at Yale at a series of evening meetings sponsored by students themselves. It was proposed to hold the meetings in Woolsey Hall, the largest auditorium in the University, and it seemed like a daring venture to hope that there would be enough interest in the meetings to justify the ambitious plans of the youthful sponsors. Religious life was at a low ebb throughout the country after the World War. Coffin was not one to turn his back on an opportunity to present the claims of Christianity when a body of students asked him to do so and he accepted the invitation even though he had qualms about the wisdom of some of the plans being made. The event proved that the students were not too optimistic in making large plans for the meetings. The response of the University was overwhelming. Woolsey Hall was packed for the opening gathering on February 22 and continued to be full for four nights as Coffin spoke simply and directly on "The Message of Christianity for the College Man of Today." A Committee of Two Hundred had been organized under the Chairmanship of Henry P. Davison, Jr., later to become President of J. P. Morgan and Co. It is interesting today to read over the prospectus of the meetings and to note some of the names of those who as students were members of this committee: Britton Hadden and Henry R. Luce, who were to be founders of *Time* Magazine; Amos N. Wilder, poet and professor at the Harvard Divinity School; Frederick W. Hilles, head of the Department of English at Yale; Malcolm Aldrich, President of the Commonwealth Fund; Juan T. Trippe, President of Pan-American Airways, and many others. They advocated "Facing Religion as a Part of One's Education" and called "Dr. Coffin the Right Man for the Task," "a man fitted in personality, in intellectual capacity and in the temper of his life to lead such a series of meetings." Four professors presided, one each evening, at the meetings: William Lyon Phelps, George H. Nettleton, Robert N. Corwin, and Edward B. Reed. The University Glee Club Quartette sang at each session. For four evenings prior to the series, group meetings were held in the dormitories to explain their purpose and to prepare the way for them. Recent graduates of the University returned to lead these group meetings, among them Allan W. Ames, H. M. Baldridge, Norman Donaldson, Arthur Howe, Sidney Lovett, and Charles P. Taft II. George Stewart, Jr., as General Secretary of the University Christian Association, was a moving spirit behind all the planning and the execution of the plans. Coffin made himself available for personal interviews as well as for the major addresses, and was deeply impressed by the sincerity and eagerness of the young men who brought their intellectual and spiritual problems to him. He returned to New York saying that he did not see how any men could have carried out such a project more effectively than the student leaders had done and that he was deeply gratified by the response which he and his message had received.

When Arthur T. Hadley announced that he would retire from the presidency of Yale University in 1921, Coffin unexpectedly found himself in a position which was at once embarrassing and puzzling. The thought that he might be chosen as President Hadley's successor had never entered his mind. For the Twenty-fifth Reunion Record of the Class of 1897 he wrote, "I haven't planned or hoped for anything but to be a useful Christian minister wherever I seemed to be wanted." But his name began to appear prominently among those being publicly discussed as eminently qualified for the post. Presidents of Yale University are elected by the Corporation, a body made up of ten "Successors to the Original Trustees," six Fellows elected by the alumni for six-year terms, together with the Governor and the Lieutenant Governor of the State of Connecticut and the President of the University who are *ex officio* members. The election of a president takes place in executive session, and votes are never made public. However, James R. Angell, who was elected to succeed President Hadley, wrote in 1945: "It is, I believe, no secret that at the time of Mr. Hadley's retirement several members of the Corporation were strongly disposed to restore the earlier practice of selecting a clergyman for President and urged that Dr. Coffin be chosen for the part. Other views prevailed, but no one can doubt that Coffin would have made a wise and effective leader of the University."

Whatever may have taken place in the Corporation Room, there was widespread discussion among alumni and faculty members who favored Coffin as the next president and made their conviction known to the Corporation. The discussion crept into the public press and the *Boston Transcript* took the unusual step of advocating editorially the election of Coffin, saying: "We hope that the Yale Corporation, when it assembles to elect the fourteenth president of Yale, will conscript for that office Dr. Henry Sloane Coffin of New York, as the man best fitted to be the chief executive of one of the greatest of the national universities of the United States, at a time when the nation has greater need of its services than ever before. . . . Dr. Coffin has repeatedly demonstrated that he possesses a rare power of personal leadership. As a scholar he takes a prominent rank among present-day American preachers. Dr. Coffin, moreover, is not merely a leader of men. As pastor of one of the largest and most important churches in New York City he has shown marked executive and administrative ability, qualities which are indispensable to a university president. The selection of Dr. Coffin would be in accord with the ministerial traditions which featured the first two centuries of Yale's history. What is of more fundamental import, his selection would bring to the Yale presidency a minister who is in full sympathy with the liberalizing spirit of twentieth-century religion."

Coffin received a steady stream of letters from Yale graduates expressing their hope that he would be their next president, all of which put him in a difficult position. With characteristic modesty he did not think he would be chosen, and he did not know what reply he would give if he were. He shrank from the thought of leaving the Madison Avenue Church, and he questioned whether he would find the New Haven position congenial. He was not a candidate for the post, but did not want to make any statements which might be interpreted as declining a position which had not been offered him. He suffered acutely over the feeling that he was being discussed and dissected and wished that the whole matter were settled. Dean Charles R. Brown of the Yale Divinity School came to him, assuring him of very strong support from the Yale faculty and expressing confidence that he would be elected. He begged Coffin to give some indication that he would accept the position if chosen. Coffin still refused to commit himself to such unofficial overtures, but the combined pressures tended to break down his skepticism with regard to the possibility of his election and also his doubts about the wisdom of accepting if elected. It was a genuine disappointment, although a short-lived one, when the Corporation elected, not any of the men who had been widely discussed but a distinguished psychologist, Dr. James Rowland Angell, President of the Carnegie Corporation, who was to become one of Coffin's staunch friends. The two men were destined to work together in Yale affairs for many years to come. In the meantime Coffin went on unperturbed in the great work of his pastorate until leadership in theological education claimed his conspicuous abilities. As he reached the high tide of his powers in the theological field for which all his training and experience so admirably equipped him, he and his friends were grateful that in 1921 he had not been called to labor in another sphere.

Yale, however, was not willing to be without Coffin's services and on January 9, 1922, Coffin came home from a meeting of ministers to find that New Haven had been trying all afternoon to get him on the telephone. When he made the connection it was to be told that the Yale Corporation had that morning elected him as one of the "Successors to the Original Trustees." This meant a life membership on that body, limited by a gentlemen's agreement among the Fellows to retire voluntarily at the age of sixty-eight. Coffin hesitated to accept. He was told that membership would involve his being in New Haven once a month from Friday afternoon to Saturday noon in addition to special committee work and ceremonial occasions. It seemed like a formidable demand upon his time. There was also a slight feeling of embarrassment about becoming a member of a board which had been so thoroughly analyzing and "dissecting" him throughout the previous year. He talked the matter over with his father who advised him to accept. He tried to consult Edward S. Harkness and William E.S. Griswold, both of whom were officers in his church. The Yale authorities were anxious for an immediate reply, and after a barrage of telephone calls urging his acceptance, he sent word the next day that he would serve. So began an official relationship with the University which continued for twenty-three years, culminating in his service as Senior Fellow of the Corporation and by common consent its most useful member. President Angell wrote after both had retired: "No executive who has had at once to lead and to defer to a Board of Trustees will fail to understand the tremendous satisfaction and sense of confidence which it gives to know that one, at least, of your group can always be counted upon to bring keen intelligence, sympathetic understanding, caution, tolerance and inflexible courage to any question which arises. If you add to that the assurance of a liberal and open mind, you have an asset of incomparable value in the deliberations of a governing body. Dr. Coffin brought all these qualities to the business of the Corporation and made the life of the President immeasurably happier and more effective, saving him again and again from wasteful expenditure of time and energy in forestalling premature or injudicious actions, or in clarifying and expediting wise and essential measures. There were many men of marked wisdom and intelligence in the Corporation but none more gifted in the adroit presentation of diverse facets of controversial issues, none more skillful in persuasive formulation of lines of procedure."

Coffin's reputation as an effective speaker to college students involved him in many more invitations to preach and lecture across the country than he could possibly accept. For the most part he held himself rigidly to his primary obligations in his pastorate. In March, 1921, however, he gave a series of addresses to the student body of Purdue University at Lafayette, Indiana. He went with considerable interest in seeing the prairie country of the Middle West and in becoming acquainted with its people.

Cosmopolitan though he was, thoroughly at home in Europe and Asia, on the West Coast and the Eastern Seaboard, he had never had much first-hand contact with great sections of the United States between the Appalachian Mountains and the Rockies, although in later years he was to know them well. He was very favorably impressed. "I found the students a very serious and earnest lot of men, nearly all of whom are helping themselves through by their summer work and are looking forward to careers in which they will use their education, so that study is gone into with a zeal not found in Princeton or New Haven," he wrote home. On his arrival he found a difference of opinion as to the kind of meetings he was to conduct. The Y.M.C.A. leaders wanted an evangelistic campaign with decisions registered by the signing of cards. The President of the University wanted "a clear and intelligent presentation of the Christian religion with no emotional appeal." Coffin gave the type of address he had given at Yale and elsewhere, with the result that the students packed the auditorium at every meeting, stayed on to ask questions after the formal gatherings had adjourned, invited him to their fraternity houses for discussions, and seized every opportunity to find out how the Christian religion could be stated by so clear, so intelligent and so devout an adherent as he. When the final meeting had been held, he wrote to his wife, "We closed with another crowded hall last night—men and girls all over the steps, in every passage and a fair number of late comers standing throughout. I don't think we have had many less than two thousand at every meeting. That is more than two-thirds of the resident students." He was deeply impressed by the down-to-earth character of his hearers and questioners. "These fellows are eminently practical, hard-headed Hoosiers with no training in philosophy and not speculative or mystical. They seem to want to 'hustle' the Kingdom of God along. It is a different psychology than any to which I am used, but very interesting."

The next year, in April, 1922, Coffin gave the Merrick Lectures at Ohio Wesleyan University in Delaware, Ohio. This was an endowed lectureship the deed of gift for which prescribed that the lectures should deal with "practical and experimental religion." Somewhat like the Beecher lectureship at Yale, this was a foundation which had gathered distinction through the years by reason of the distinguished leaders of thought who had held it. Taking as his cue a question asked him by a group of young people in a town on the banks of the Hudson River, "What is there in religion, anyhow?" to whom he had replied with a counter question, "What is there in the Hudson River anyhow?" Coffin pointed out that in both river and religion may be found refreshment, cleansing, power, fertility, serenity and adventure, change and permanence. With additional chapters, the lectures were published under the title "What Is There in Religion?" A resolution of gratitude passed by the faculty of Ohio Wesleyan University included the comment: "These lectures on experimental religion have also been practical. The chief criticism of Professor William James' charming book on *The Varieties of Religious Experience* was that his illustrations were so largely of an abnormal and exceptional character. Dr. Coffin, on the other hand, has instanced the experience of sane, strong and well poised leaders in all departments of human endeavor, and his book might be called, What the ordinary, normal man may expect in the way of a religious experience."

Harvard University conferred the honorary degree of Doctor of Divinity upon Coffin at its June Commencement in 1922, citing him as "a preacher of the gospel, who, in his words, has all the fervor of the prophet illumined by the light of common day." That evening the *Boston Transcript* reported his remarks to the alumni with the head-line, "Yale Man Discusses Enforced Feeding and Optional Praying." Coffin had pointed out that when a freshman arrived at New Haven he was told that his presence at daily and Sunday chapel was required. At Harvard the freshman was told that he might attend chapel if he pleased, but that he must take his meals in the freshman dormitories. "In other words," he said, "you have enforced feeding and optional praying, while we have required prayers and voluntary eating." This, of course, was typical Coffin banter. In serious vein he reminded his hearers that "Harvard and Yale were founded for the avowed purpose of furthering religion, as the seals of both universities remind us." "How," he asked, "may a university founded as were these two Puritan colleges with a distinctive religious aim, fulfill this portion of their obligation under present conditions?" He had three suggestions to make. First, they could keep steadily before their students the fact that religion is one of the fundamental perennial interests of mankind. Second, they could through chapel and classroom furnish adequate instruction in historic religion and offer a Christian interpretation of life in terms of contemporary thought as a subject of which no educated man could afford to remain ignorant. Third, they could recognize their special responsibility to produce leaders in pulpit and education, in commerce and statesmanship able to inspire the Commonwealth with Christian convictions and ideals.

The Harvard doctorate was the first honorary degree which Coffin received from an institution outside New York City in which he had never been a student. It was, however, the first of many, and during the following sixteen years he was the recipient of honor upon honor until by 1938 a doctor's hood of one sort or another had been placed on his shoulders by no less than eighteen colleges and universities. It is an impressive list of institutions of higher learning which honored him year after year, as follows:

Doctor of Divinity:

  1906, New York University; 1915, Yale University; 1922, Harvard University; 1925, Princeton University and Columbia University; 1926, Glasgow University; 1928, Union College; 1935, Episcopal Theological Seminary; 1944, Bowdoin College.

Doctor of Laws:

  1927, Amherst College; 1932, Wabash College; 1934, St. Andrews University; 1938, Hamilton College.

Doctor of Letters:

1931, College of the Ozarks; 1937, Western Reserve University.

Doctor of Sacred Theology:

1937, Jewish Theological Seminary.

Doctor of Theology:

1930, University of Marburg; 1938, University of Paris.

In February, 1926, Coffin journeyed to Scotland to deliver the Warrack Lectures on Preaching in New College, Edinburgh, and in the Colleges of the United Free Church of Scotland in Glasgow and Aberdeen. He was the first American to be invited to hold this lectureship, regarded in Scotland as perhaps the outstanding honor which the churches could confer upon a minister. His Edinburgh friends welcomed him with open arms. "It is like coming home to be here and the affection and friendship are quite overpowering," he wrote home. "For conversation, Edinburgh is still unsurpassed." He had lunch with Principal Martin and other friends at the University Club, where they "had much talk. This is the land for that."

His lectures had as their general theme the somewhat awkward title, "What to Preach."[11] In his opening paragraph he explained its choice: "A youth, who nearly thirty years ago sat where you now sit, found himself again and again haunted by the misgiving that he would never have enough to preach to keep him ministering to a congregation week in and week out. He had not spoken in public for more than ten or fifteen minutes on any theme. He had found himself barely able to fill five minutes with ideas on even the greatest subject. How would it be possible for him, twice on a Sunday, forty odd weeks every year, to preach interestingly and enrichingly for half an hour? During his course in divinity he received much useful counsel on *how* to preach; but he would return to his room to be tormented by the old perplexity *what* to preach." With a glint of his characteristic humor he continued in reminiscent vein: "This embryonic divine felt that no utterance

[11] Doran Co., 1926, pp. 11-12.

of his had been or was ever likely to be oracular. Occasionally he had things to say which he wished to say very much, and he could usually say them in a very few minutes, but they were not in the habit of coming to him periodically at seven-day intervals, nor in such measured abundance as to furnish him with a twenty-five or thirty-minute sermon Sunday morning and evening, not to mention fragments that remained over to be served up at the weekly prayer-meeting." In the light of his own experience he proceeded to discuss various types of preaching—expository, doctrinal, ethical, pastoral and evangelistic—with a wealth of suggestions concerning themes, texts, illustrations and methods to be used in each type of sermon. In each college the response was enthusiastic and the lecture halls were crowded with eager, grateful listeners who increased in numbers with each succeeding lecture. Principal Martin wrote to a friend in New York: "His utterances on the inexhaustible theme—*Christian Preaching*—have had all his own freshness, vitality and force; and better still, if possible, and even more impressive and memorable, has been the heightened conception he has left in his hearers' minds of what it is to be a Christian minister. I am profoundly thankful that our men have been, if even for only these few hours, in contact with so concentrated and consecrated a nature."

A pleasant surprise awaited Coffin when he returned to New York on the *Majestic* in early March. He came back prepared to plunge at once into the annual campaign to raise funds for the financial support of the Madison Avenue Church and its benevolences. On the steamer he had written two sermons, one for Sunday morning and one for the evening, presenting to his congregation the reasons why the sum of $179,392 was needed. When he reached his home at 129 East Seventy-first Street, however, he found on his desk a note saying that in his absence the entire budget had been raised. A committee of laymen representing the Deacons, Trustees and Elders of the church had sent out a letter to the congregation two weeks before. "For twenty years," they said, "Dr. Coffin has borne the burden of this church, and has been forced to appeal to us each year for the necessary support. This year offers our opportunity to provide without suggestion from him for the continuance of the work throughout the twenty-first year of his ministry with us." The budget was $5,000 larger than the preceding year, but it all flowed in without pressure from a loyal congregation. "You will have to put up with an extemporaneous sermon," Coffin said in the pulpit on Sunday morning. "The two sermons I had prepared to set before you the claims of our budget I have simply put in my waste-basket."

CHAPTER TEN

STANDING FAST FOR LIBERTY

C OFFIN'S experience as a preacher in colleges and universities and his many interviews with students in the institutions which he visited made him keenly aware of the intellectual difficulties which the Christian faith encountered in the minds of countless thoughtful people in a scientific age. In his sermons and conversations he sought to meet these difficulties. He was profoundly disturbed when in the second decade of the Twentieth Century a renascent fundamentalist movement attempted, as it seemed to him, to magnify those difficulties by insisting that peripheral beliefs actually held by a minority of Christian believers were essentials of the faith. As the fundamentalist controversy developed and dragged on, Coffin came to be regarded by common consent as the leader of the liberal forces in the Presbyterian Church and in the Church at large.

His memories of the controversy over the teaching of Professor Charles Augustus Briggs, which he had observed when hardly more than a boy, made him wary of Biblical literalists when they embarked upon a crusade. When he was a student in Scotland, he was told that the question of the verbal inspiration of the Bible had ceased to be an issue there after the controversy over the teaching of William Robertson Smith in 1881. But he had not forgotten the charges of heresy which had been brought against him in 1905. In 1911, when William Adams Brown was attacked in the Presbyterian General Assembly because of theological statements made in an article in the *Harvard Theological Review,* Coffin gave an interview to the *New York Evening Post* in which he defended Professor Brown as a "true conservative." Saying that, "Many educated people have broken away from the Presbyterian Church because, while they sympathize with the religion and purpose of Jesus, they are unable to accept the traditional forms in which the church's Christianity has been expressed," he insisted that William Adams Brown attempted to show such people "how in new theological forms all that was vital in the church's older doctrinal statements is conserved, and to win them back to their allegiance to the church by putting its teachings in forms which they can accept heartily and intelligently." He was not unprepared when fundamentalism as a movement began to gain in influence in the Protestant Churches in 1910 or thereabouts.

In that year the Presbyterian General Assembly adopted a resolution stating that Biblical inerrancy, the virgin birth of Christ, his substitutionary atonement, his physical resurrection and his miracles ("making changes in the order of nature") are essential doctrines in the Presbyterian Church. It directed presbyteries to refuse to license candidates for the ministry who did not affirm belief in these "five points." It was pointed out in many presbyteries that the action of one General Assembly could not amend the Confession of Faith unless confirmed by two-thirds of the presbyteries and agreed to by the General Assembly next ensuing. The Church had never defined "essential doctrines" in this way. Nevertheless the Assembly of 1916 repeated the action of 1910 in passing this resolution with the direction to the presbyteries regarding ordinations. Coffin and likeminded ministers protested in sermons and published writings against this attempt of particular Assemblies to define the doctrinal standards of the Church in ways that went beyond the Church's historic position.

After the First World War, in May, 1919, a World Conference on Christian Fundamentals was held in Philadelphia. At this conference it was charged that the Churches had failed because they had departed from the "fundamentals" and had embraced "modernism." The conference named as the "fundamentals" the "five points," including in its interpretation of them an affirmation of belief in the imminent return of Christ in physical form to the earth. It adopted a broad program avowing its purpose to eliminate from leadership in the churches and other religious organizations those who did not adhere to this fundamentalist point of view. On May 21, 1922, however, a voice was raised in the pulpit of the First Presbyterian Church of New York City which was destined to be heard throughout the land. Harry Emerson Fosdick preached his famous sermon entitled "Shall the Fundamentalists Win?" He called attention to the "great mass of new knowledge" which within a generation had come into man's possession, new knowledge regarding the physical universe, human history, and the ancient religions of the world. He appealed to the Baptist and Presbyterian Churches in particular, and to all churches by implication, to keep their membership and posts of leadership open to "reverent Christians who have been unable to keep this new knowledge in one compartment of their minds and the Christian faith in another."[1] The title of the sermon was more provocative than its substance. Actually, it was a calm, lucid statement of the fundamentalist position and of the reasons why it was unacceptable to multitudes of liberal men and women trained in modern science and in history. The spirit of the sermon was embodied in the prayer with which it closed, "Hear us this morning as with eager prayer we lift up our hearts and seek from Thee the grace of magnanimity, the ability to differ and yet love, the beauty of tolerance and of a large heart. Grant Thy church this grace, possessing which alone we may be disciples of the Master who said, 'By this shall all men know that ye are my

[1] "Shall the Fundamentalists Win?" Privately printed, p. 4.

disciples, if ye have love one to another.' "[2] Nevertheless, the sermon was the match which lit the flames of a controversy which embroiled the Protestant Churches of America for several years and was most acute in the Presbyterian Church in the U.S.A. where the liberals turned instinctively to Coffin for leadership.

As the war was coming to an end three Presbyterian churches in downtown Manhattan had united, taking the name and worshipping in the building of the First Presbyterian Church at the corner of Fifth Avenue and Twelfth Street. The General Assembly had been urging the Presbyterian churches to promote Christian unity, and the newly constituted church wanted to call as its minister Dr. Harry Emerson Fosdick, a professor at Union Theological Seminary, already known as an outstanding preacher and as the writer of widely read religious books. Dr. Fosdick, however, was a Baptist and did not wish to become a Presbyterian. An arrangement was made, with the approval of the Presbytery of New York, whereby Dr. Fosdick was appointed Special Preacher without any change in his denominational affiliation. The arrangement was highly satisfactory to all who were immediately concerned. Sunday after Sunday the church was crowded with eager congregations who found the preacher's interpretation of Christianity stimulating and helpful. But the fundamentalists in the Presbyterian denomination were not pleased to have one of its historic churches a conspicuous center for liberal theology. After Dr. Fosdick in his sermon, which was widely quoted in the press, had seemed to throw down the gauntlet to the fundamentalists, Dr. Clarence E. Macartney, minister of the Arch Street Presbyterian Church of Philadelphia, became the spokesman of those who wanted the General Assembly to take action. Dr. Macartney was the author of an overture passed by the General Assembly meeting in Indianapolis in 1923 directing the New York Presbytery to correct the preaching in the First Church. The Assembly of that year reiterated the 1910 and 1916 assertions of the five

[2] *Ibid.*, p. 15.

points as essential doctrines of the Presbyterian Church. The New York Presbytery was ordered to report to the next Assembly what it had done to carry out the Assembly's directive.

Coffin immediately took his stand publicly beside Dr. Fosdick in so far as theological beliefs were concerned. He issued a statement to the press in which he said: "In the face of the action taken by the majority of the General Assembly, it is impossible for those of us who stand in the pulpits of the Presbyterian Church to remain silent, and I feel that I owe it to my own congregation and to the Presbytery to state plainly that if any action is taken which removes Dr. Fosdick from the pulpit of the First Church on account of his interpretation of the Christian Gospel, I cannot honestly be allowed to remain in the pulpit of the Madison Avenue Church, for I share fully his point of view. . . . Dearly as I love the Church of my fathers, I love truth and human beings more. I cannot teach what the Assembly has set forth as essential. While I will not voluntarily withdraw from the Presbyterian ministry and leave the Church to those who appear to me to misconstrue its standards and repudiate its Protestant heritage, I wish to make my own position plain."

When the Assembly met in Grand Rapids in May, 1924, Coffin was a delegate representing the New York Presbytery and its spokesman in the controversy. All through the year the issues of fundamentalism versus liberalism had been discussed in pulpits, ecclesiastical gatherings and in all manner of periodicals, religious and secular. There was a widespread fear that the Presbyterian denomination was about to split apart, as it had divided into the New School and Old School Assemblies in 1837. Coffin had been in frequent conference with denominational leaders and with fellow liberals, seeking to hold the Church together on terms which preserved the traditional liberties of Presbyterianism. He had been one of the prime movers in the preparation of a document which was published shortly before the meeting of the 1924 Assembly, entitled, "An affirmation designed to safeguard the unity and liberty of the Presbyterian Church in the United States of America." Generally known as *The Auburn Affirmation* because it was issued from Auburn Seminary, some of whose faculty members were active in its preparation, it was signed by thirteen hundred ministers of the denomination from all sections of the country. Affirming their loyalty to evangelical Christianity and their adherence to the Church's Confession of Faith as given at their ordinations, they cited the history and law of the Church to show that liberty in the interpretation of the Confession and of the Scriptures had always been the constitutional right of Presbyterian ministers. They rejected Biblical inerrancy as not being a teaching of the Bible, the Confession of Faith, the ancient creeds or the Reformation. They denied on constitutional grounds the authority of the General Assembly alone to declare particular doctrines essentials of the faith. The whole document gives clear evidence of Coffin's influence. In particular he was the author of its title, stressing two of his major concerns, unity and liberty, as well as of a paragraph which was the heart of the Affirmation: "This opinion of the General Assembly attempts to commit our Church to certain theories concerning the inspiration of the Bible, and the Incarnation, the Atonement, the Resurrection, and the Continuing Life and Supernatural Power of our Lord Jesus Christ. We all hold most earnestly to these great facts and doctrines; we all believe from our hearts that the writers of the Bible were inspired of God; that Jesus Christ was God manifest in the flesh; that God was in Christ, reconciling the world unto Himself, and through Him we have our redemption; that having died for our sins He rose from the dead and is our ever-living Savior; that in His earthly ministry He wrought many mighty works, and by His vicarious death and unfailing presence He is able to save to the uttermost. Some of us regard the particular theories contained in the deliverance of the General Assembly of 1923 as satisfactory explanations of these facts and doctrines. But we are united in believing that these are not the only theories allowed by the

Scriptures and our standards as explanations of these facts and doctrines of our religion, and that all who hold to these facts and doctrines, whatever theories they may employ to explain them, are worthy of all confidence and fellowship. We do not desire liberty to go beyond the teachings of evangelical Christianity. But we maintain that it is our constitutional right and our Christian duty within these limits to exercise liberty of thought and teaching, that we may more effectively preach the gospel of Jesus Christ, the Saviour of the world."[3]

The Auburn Affirmation exerted a profound influence upon the Church at large and in the end probably had a good deal to do with settling the controversy in the Presbyterian denomination on the basis of mutual tolerance and an inclusive Church. Still, when the General Assembly met in 1924 it was obvious that the fundamentalists were in control. William Jennings Bryan nominated Dr. Clarence Macartney for the post of Moderator, saying, "It was his vigilance that detected the insidious attack upon our doctrine. It was his courage that rallied the forces to fight for our standards. It was his leadership which placed the church back on the rock of the Holy Spirit . . . I appeal to you to vote for one whose name is a guarantee that he will not yield to modern thought and substitute it for the inspired word of God." Dr. Macartney was elected and immediately appointed Bryan Vice Moderator. Coffin was plunged into gloom, a rare mood for one so buoyant and high spirited as he. On Sunday, May 25, he preached in the Park Street Congregational Church to a crowded congregation which included a large number of Commissioners to the Assembly. He used a sermon which he had preached in March in the Madison Avenue Church. Taking as a text Acts 27:31: "Except these abide in the ship, ye cannot be saved," he urged that if the Church were to render its full service to a needy world it must keep both conservatives and liberals on board and not succumb to divisive

---

[3] From "Leader of Liberal Protestantism" by Robert Hastings Nichols in *This Ministry*, Scribners, 1945, p. 49.

tendencies. He was heard with breathless attention, and became so stirred as he preached that he added extemporaneously to the sermon as he had originally written it, and found when he sat down that he had preached ten minutes longer than his usual thirty-five minutes. (The sermon was later published in *The Christian Work*[4] and made a deep impression on a much larger public than that which was present in the Grand Rapids church.) But he observed rather sadly that those who most needed its message were not there. The next day he pleaded the cause of New York Presbytery before the Judicial Commission but thought them unresponsive. He became convinced that a split in the Church was coming, or, if not a division, that he and his closest associates would be put out of the Presbyterian ministry. In the end, however, the outcome was far happier than he had expected, and he left Grand Rapids with high hopes that the controversy had been brought to a satisfactory conclusion. The Assembly rejected the proposal that office-bearers be required to give assent to the five points. It voted "no action" with regard to the Auburn Affirmation. In dealing with the complaints which had been levelled against Dr. Fosdick's preaching in the First Presbyterian Church of New York, the Judicial Commission side-stepped the theological aspects of the case and simply called attention to the Church law which obviously did not intend that ministers of other denominations should supply Presbyterian pulpits indefinitely and invited Dr. Fosdick to become a Presbyterian in the manner provided for in the Form of Government. This seemed reasonable to Coffin and it did not occur to him that Dr. Fosdick would have objections to taking the step suggested for him. He left Grand Rapids weary but happy, and went up to rest in the Adirondacks, convinced that the goals for which he had contended had been achieved.

Dr. Fosdick was in Scotland when the Assembly's action was taken. He had preached in Scottish Presbyterian churches and

[4] Issue of March 15, 1924, pp. 334 ff.

before Presbyterian official bodies in Scotland and had been enthusiastically received. Coffin cabled him expressing the hope that he would not answer the Assembly's invitation until there had been an opportunity for the two of them to discuss the matter. As Fosdick's steamer came into New York harbor on his homeward voyage a long letter from Coffin was put into his hands urging him to accept Presbyterian status. This Dr. Fosdick declined to do. Coffin, with Presbyterianism in his blood and firmly convinced that the historic Presbyterian traditions and Form of Government assured the liberties of Presbyterian ministers, could not understand Fosdick's objections and wrote again to him, pleading for his acceptance. Fosdick again declined to change his ecclesiastical affiliation. He wrote to Coffin on December 11, 1924, from the Preachers' Room at Harvard University:

"My dear Coffin,

"The enclosed letter, written day before yesterday, was still lying unmailed on my desk here when your second letter came about the Presbyterian affairs. I appreciate your most fraternal interest and urgency in the matter. But if ever a resolution were built into a man's mind, fabric of its very fabric, the resolution never under any circumstances to be an ordained Presbyterian minister is built into mine. I simply do not talk your language about theological subscription. I read what you say, not so much disagreeing with it as not understanding it. I simply could not make the sort of even formal assent required of all candidates for your denomination's ministry. I would choke—for, rightly or wrongly, I should feel as if I were lying like a rogue. I never could look at myself in a mirror again—no great loss, you well may say, but nevertheless a great inconvenience. The thing is for my conscience an absolute moral impossibility. My wife would disown me if I did it; I would disown myself; and as for preaching a sermon thereafter on love of the truth—'out of me!' I write thus, not to grieve you, whose own persuasion in the matter I thoroughly respect, but to let you see how prohibitive my own deep-seated feeling is to any such move as you suggest.

"Moreover, while I should doubtless remain a Presbyterian had I been born one, I will not in middle life, with my eyes open, walk into the hands of an extra-congregational authority with power over my liberty. I never have raised a rumpus, but I should do so at once, as a test of my honesty, if I found myself in the novel position, hitherto unthinkable, of facing a *possible* heresy trial. No practical chance of immediate service could ever justify what would seem to me a surrender of my moral integrity and my intellectual freedom.

"I rejoice immensely in the forward movements which you mention. In brains, in devotion, in money, the Presbyterians are one of the greatest hopes of the Church. I should think you would be proud to be one of them. I should, *were* I one of them. But I am not—and the polity and discipline of the church interpose an insuperable barrier to my ever becoming one.

"Bless your dear heart—I love you!

Harry Emerson Fosdick."

Coffin was profoundly disappointed and was never quite able to understand why Fosdick was unwilling to subscribe to the Confession of Faith in the terms required of Presbyterian ministers. Perhaps he was so deeply rooted in Presbyterianism that he never quite understood why everyone did not want to become a Presbyterian! At any rate, in spite of the fact that the General Assembly had avoided the theological issue in the Fosdick case, he was not long under any illusion as to the situation in the Presbyterian Church. He knew that the fundamentalist movement was still very strong and that the misunderstanding of the historic Presbyterian liberties was very widespread. On November 16, 1924, he preached a notable sermon in the Madison Avenue Church on "Freedom in the Presbyterian Pulpit" and followed it the next Sunday with its sequel on "The Pulpit's Use of Its Freedom."[5] "Recent events," he said, "have turned the thought of all Protestant Christians, and particularly of Presbyterians, to the

[5] *The Weekly,* November 28, 1924, and December 5, 1924.

questions of freedom in the pulpit. The determined effort, on the one hand, of a large and dominant group in our Church to exclude from the ministry any who do not share their interpretation of the Gospel, and on the other hand the refusal of a most brilliant and useful preacher to accept the vows required of Presbyterian ministers on the ground that to subscribe an ancient creed and interpret it in modern terms is 'perilous to honesty and hampering to the free leadership of the Spirit' makes it fitting that all our people should know what our constitution requires in this matter of their ministers and other office-bearers."

This sermon on "Freedom in the Presbyterian Pulpit" was printed as a pamphlet[6] and distributed from coast to coast by a "Correspondence Committee," a group of some thirty Presbyterian ministers who were, as they stated, "united in a common desire to maintain the unity, liberty and peace of the Presbyterian Church in the United States of America." Pointing out that at the time of the Reformation the question uppermost in Christian minds was, Where is the supreme authority in religion? and reminding his hearers that attempts had been made to claim such authority for the Church speaking through the Pope, and, at a later date, for Tudor and Stuart kings who claimed divine right to rule the Church, Coffin insisted that the Protestant tradition maintains that "the supreme authority in religion is God speaking directly by His Spirit to the consciences of men in and through the Bible." He reviewed the history of the Westminster Confession of Faith, revealing a profound knowledge of the discussions which preceded its adoption, and making it clear that great care had been taken to safeguard individual liberty in the Adopting Act by which the Confession had been accepted as a standard by the American Church. "Several times in our history," he went on, "once in the middle of the Eighteenth Century and twice in the first half of the Nineteenth, those who believed in a strict interpretation have tried to force their view on the Church and have

[6] The Jacobs Press, Auburn, New York 1925.

caused a disruption. And each time when the dissevered portions of the Presbyterian Church came together again, it was on a basis which allowed both the stricter and the freer views in the reunited Church. . . . Several Assemblies lately have issued deliverances naming certain interpretations of doctrinal points 'essential and necessary.' A deliverance of an Assembly is merely the expression of its opinion and is not part of the law of the Church. Some of us are persuaded that these five points are not essentials in the system of doctrine set forth in the Bible, and we have said so. At the last Assembly an attempt was made to require theological professors and the members and officers of our Boards to subscribe the Confession with these interpretations. But the Judicial Commission decided that this was unconstitutional, and the Assembly sustained its verdict. Our standards conserved our liberties." The pamphlet containing this sermon was useful to a large number of Presbyterian ministers who were not so learned in their Church's history as Coffin was. They found in the precedents which he cited the guarantee of their right to be liberals in the Presbyterian Church.

But Coffin did not believe that liberty in itself was always a blessing. "Freedom may be either a bane or a blessing according to the use which is made of it"—so he began the sermon on "The Pulpit's Use of Its Freedom." Admitting that there were groups of religious men who labeled themselves "liberal," "many of whom do not accord Jesus Christ supreme and unique authority, and preach a Gospel which omits the saving power of His cross and the renewing work of His Spirit, and which is devoid of evangelistic passion and missionary ambition," he maintained that in the Presbyterian and similar communions freedom was desired for no such intent. "We claim and wish to employ our liberties, exactly as did our spiritual ancestors in every generation in the Church, to render the Gospel appealing and convincing to the thoughtful folk of our time." "Yes, we claim our historic Christian and Protestant right to freedom; and along with that claim we are prepared to give any pledge which may be suggested that we purpose with God's help to use that freedom solely in the service of Christ."

When the next General Assembly met in May, 1925, in Columbus, Ohio, it was presented with a judicial case which involved no question of church polity as Dr. Fosdick's indefinite occupancy of a Presbyterian pulpit had done. The New York Presbytery had licensed and ordained two young men, one of whom, Henry Pitney Van Dusen, was later to become Coffin's successor as President of Union Theological Seminary. Neither of them had been able either to affirm or deny belief in the Virgin Birth of Jesus. A fundamentalist minority in the Presbytery sought to have the Presbytery's action set aside by the Synod of New York, the organization of the Presbyterian churches of the state, and failing in that court carried their complaint to the Judicial Commission of the General Assembly. Coffin was again elected a delegate to the Assembly and in association with a lay delegate, Mr. John Foster Dulles, at the time a lawyer in the City of New York, was charged with the responsibility of representing the Presbytery before the Commission and the Assembly. Coffin was cheered by the manifest desire for peace and harmony which he found among the ministers and lay elders when they assembled at Columbus. After appearing before the Judicial Commission, however, and answering theological questions from its lay members for a solid hour, he was depressed and felt that the outlook for a break in his beloved Church was darker than it had been the year before in Grand Rapids.

On Sunday Coffin preached in the pulpit of the First Congregational Church, a pulpit made famous in the preceding generation by Dr. Washington Gladden. One-third of the delegates to the Assembly crowded in to hear him, Dr. Clarence Macartney sitting in the front row. He preached a sermon which he had delivered in New York before going to Columbus on "What Liberal Presbyterians Are Standing For." Emphasizing again the inclusive nature of the Presbyterian Church and reviewing its history of tension

between liberals and conservatives which had always been resolved on the basis of mutual tolerance and guaranteed freedom,
he pleaded for unity and liberty. "In the light of the intention
of the framers of our standards," he said, "we would interpret
them to make place inside our Presbyterian ministry for every
God-owned interpreter of Christ. Indeed we question whether
we have any right to call ourselves a Christian Church, if we exclude from its ministry any whom Christ manifestly does not exclude from the gift of His Holy Spirit." A dozen men came to him
before Sunday asking him to tone down his sermon or not to
preach at all the sermon on the topic he had announced. Older
and wiser leaders in the Church, not identified with the liberal
movement, whom he consulted, said to him, "Go ahead and say
every word of it." It was not his nature to tone down the expression of his convictions, and he took the better counsel.

Still, the threatened division in the Church bore heavily upon
his spirit. In its desire for peace, the Assembly had defeated the
fundamentalists' candidate for the Moderatorship of the Assembly, although he was highly respected for his ability and character, and elected Dr. Charles R. Erdman, a professor at Princeton
Theological Seminary, a conservative in theology, but a man
known for his irenic spirit, non-partisan churchmanship, and gracious Christian life. Coffin had a two-hour conference with Erdman, discussing possible modes of procedure if the Judicial
Commission should rule against the Presbytery of New York. He
warned the Moderator bluntly that any attack on New York Presbytery would mean a split in the Church, although it might be
staved off for a year or two. He was prepared, if a decision against
New York Presbytery were handed down, to lead the New York
delegation and their friends out of the Assembly after the distribution of printed statements explaining their position. This Erdman
did not want. In a Presbyterian General Assembly the decision of
a Judicial Commission cannot be debated. The Assembly simply
votes to confirm or to reject the decision. Erdman agreed, how-

ever, that if a negative decision were announced by the Commission, he would recognize Coffin and permit him to read a protest from the platform. This is what happened on Tuesday afternoon. The Judicial Commission announced its decision, which the Assembly ratified, stating that the New York Presbytery had "erred" in ordaining the men in question and remanded the case to the Presbytery "for appropriate action." It stated that the doctrine of the Virgin Birth was "the established law of the Church" and asserted the power of the General Assembly to revoke a license given a presbytery. There have probably been few more dramatic moments in ecclesiastical assemblies than that which followed the General Assembly's vote sustaining the decision. Before a hushed and anxious Assembly, Coffin went to the platform of the huge Arena where the meetings were held. He was pale and showed the effects of the strained and sleepless nights during which he had been in conference seeking to avert this action. In a firm voice he read a prepared statement on behalf of the Commissioners of the Presbytery of New York protesting the decision as contrary to the constitution of the Church and declaring the purpose of New York Presbytery to maintain its constitutional rights in licensure. He was followed immediately by a representative of the Synod of New York who read a similar statement on behalf of that body. The Moderator of the Assembly then took the floor and moved the appointment of a commission to inquire into the causes of unrest in the Church. That evening Erdman attended a hastily called informal meeting of liberal delegates, many of whom were alarmed and saw no future for men of their views except expulsion or resignation from the Presbyterian Church which they loved. He pleaded for patience until his Commission of Fifteen could make its study and report to a later Assembly. Coffin joined in this plea and it was his influence which was largely responsible for preventing a walk-out of the liberals from the Assembly. Dr. John H. Finley, editor-in-chief of the *New York Times,* was one of the commissioners from New York who attended that meeting. At its close he rose and said, "Dr. Erdman, when the decision of the Judicial Commission was announced today, I left the Assembly. I felt so deeply that I could not stay. Now in the light of what I have heard tonight I am ready to come back and fight on under your leadership."

The next Sunday, back in New York, Coffin preached on the text: Ephesians 4:3, "Giving diligence to keep the unity of the Spirit in the bond of peace." He had nothing but praise for the fine spirit which had prevailed in the Assembly in spite of the deeply felt differences and for Dr. Erdman's "admirable tact, tenderness, good judgment and manifest fairness," so generally recognized that "no member of the Assembly could help loving him and thanking God for a so conspicuously worthy representative of the great Head of the Church." But, he said, the decision on the Complaint against the licensure of Mr. Van Dusen, while a mild decision in that it did not attempt to touch his standing as a Presbyterian minister nor censure the Presbytery, was un-Protestant in its demand that a man accept what the Church teaches whether he understands it or not. If it were allowed to become a binding interpretation of the law of the Church, there would be no safeguard for the freedom of any minister, elder or deacon. And, he maintained, it went beyond the constitution of the Church in assuming that "deliverances" of General Assemblies were ipso facto "the established law of the Church." "Instead of the Headship of Christ it points to the headship of that party in the General Assembly which happens to have the majority of votes. The tyranny of an infallible Pope is offensive to all Protestant Christians; but in practice Popes very rarely use their alleged infallibility. Only once in a great while and under most careful conditions does the Supreme Pontiff utter a doctrinal interpretation which the faithful are under obligation to accept. But Presbyterian General Assemblies meet every year. . . . They pass resolutions ranging from the condemnation of Sunday newspapers to the assertion or non-assertion of the salvation of infants dying in childhood. These 'deliverances' have always been considered expressions of opinion to be regarded for what they are worth. Now we are solemnly told that when the Assembly votes upon the importance of clear and positive views concerning a matter upon which in the nature of the case it is extraordinarily difficult to have any views at all, all candidates for the holy ministry must forthwith proceed to have such clear and positive views. If I must choose between the authority of a Pope, speaking rarely and under many safeguarding provisos, and the authority of a majority of the General Assembly, give me a Pope every time." He pointed out that by the same logic Mr. Bryan could prevent the ordination of any man who did not believe that the world was created in six days and could bar the Presbyterian ministry to any man who believed in evolution. "The pathetic element in this situation is the gross misunderstanding of the liberal position on the part of sincere and earnest fundamentalists . . . Mr. Bryan, for example, has been saying publicly that these modernist ministers believe that when Jesus died on the cross that was the end of Him and that we hold out no hope of future life to our people." Then the impish Coffin came to the surface even in so serious a discussion. "I do not think that Mr. Bryan intentionally tells an untruth. Probably he has been so busy boosting Florida real estate to bathers and near-bathers at a remuneration which seems to mere preachers of the gospel beyond the dreams of avarice that he has not had the opportunity to inform himself of the facts." The sermon concluded with a summons to his people to carry forward the work of the Church with greater vigor, in the faith that as the different elements in the Church kept working side by side they would feel how indispensable they were to each other and how tragic separation would be. Then a final word to the fearful: "Some timid folk have been asking me whether our property may not be in danger. I began my ministry in this city in a small hall above a fish market with an old oyster counter for a pulpit. I would sooner continue it in some similar surroundings with an unstultified mind and a conscience void of offense towards God than preach in the finest imaginable cathedral in a Romanized and Bryanized Church. Let us not talk about property. We are contending for a great principle—for the principle that nothing shall be made essential which Jesus Christ does not make essential, in order that with as much as in us is we may freely proclaim Him with His emphases and His present power to save the world." *Time* magazine reported the sermon in considerable detail and commented: "Dr. Coffin went to the General Assembly, as he had often gone before, one of the many commissioners from the Presbytery of New York. He returned the acknowledged leader of the Liberal elements in his church, and the potential leader of Liberals in all Evangelical Churches."

The next year when the General Assembly met in Baltimore Coffin was again a Commissioner and found himself in an entirely new atmosphere. The churches had sent Commissioners who were determined to have peace in the Church and to avoid a rupture. A minority in the New York Presbytery brought a complaint that their Presbytery had failed to comply with the directions given it by the preceding Assembly but the Judicial Commission dismissed the complaint as unfounded. An attempt was made to prevent Coffin's re-election as a member of the Board of National Missions, and some solicitous ministers tried unsuccessfully to persuade him to withdraw, but he was continued on the Board by an overwhelming vote of the Assembly. The Commission of Fifteen, which the Assembly of 1925 had created, made its report which Coffin considered "magnificent." "It is a splendid beginning on which better things can be built," he said in an interview with a reporter for the *New York Times.* "It absolutely supports the protest which the New York Commissioners made at Columbus last year. It forms the basis on which all differences in the Church can be ironed out." Dr. Clarence Macartney had attempted to persuade the Assembly to reject the Commission's report and to dissolve the Commission, basing his objection on the paragraph in the report which asserted that "a principle enunciated in a court of last resort is always subject to challenge when it is sought to apply that principle in later cases." He saw clearly that this vindicated the liberals' contention that the deliverance or decision of one Assembly does not automatically become "the established law of the Church." The Assembly, however, voted overwhelmingly to adopt the report. As the Assembly closed Macartney congratulated Coffin on going home with everything he wanted. In 1927 the Commission made its final report which the liberals felt assured them of the liberties for which they had contended. It was adopted almost unanimously by the Assembly of that year. The so-called "fundamentalist controversy" in the Presbyterian Church in the U.S.A. was practically at an end.

How effectively the spirit of unity had been established was demonstrated sixteen years later when the General Assembly of 1943 elected Coffin as Moderator. The vote was 291 for Coffin, 159 for the other nominee. Coffin was elected not as the leader of a party in the Church, but as a leader whom the whole Church delighted to honor. He welcomed the election as a sign that the years of controversy were over and the unity of the Church established. He also welcomed it as a sign that the breach between Union Theological Seminary and the Presbyterian Church had been healed when a President of the Seminary could be chosen Moderator of the Church.

Coffin had deplored the necessity for controversy, although he had felt himself called to stand fast for Christian liberty in the Church. At the end of the Christmas season of 1923 during which the newspapers had been filled with vehement statements which had been made in the pulpits of the city for and against the doctrine of the Virgin Birth of Jesus, Coffin wrote to a friend, "Despite the Christmas rowing in the papers over the Virgin Birth this has been a good Christmas, I think, with much religious interest. I confess that I hate the rows for I happen to have had a number of tragic cases of religious need and the rows seem so trivial and irrelevant in face of the Christ and what He can do when trusted."

CHAPTER ELEVEN

SEMINARY PRESIDENT

IN April, 1926, Coffin was elected President of the faculty of Union Theological Seminary. Ten years before, after the death of President Francis Brown, he had been asked to assume the post and had declined. At that time, having just completed a decade at the Madison Avenue Church, he did not feel that he ought to leave his work there. Dr. Arthur C. McGiffert, a great scholar and brilliant teacher in the field of church history, who had been serving as Acting President during President Brown's long illness, had been persuaded to retain the presidency on a permanent basis. Now he was not well and was ordered by his physician to retire, a step, incidentally, which made it possible for him to publish in two volumes the heart of his lectures on *The History of Christian Thought* which had delighted and enriched generations of students. Coffin took counsel with his church officers and with friends. To leave the pastorate which he loved was a wrench, even though his interest and loyalty were so deeply invested in the Seminary. Dr. McGiffert wrote assuring him of the unanimous desire of the full professors at the Seminary and of his own deep desire that he should become the Seminary's leader. The Board of Directors pressed him to accept. He felt acutely the urgency of the need for well-educated, religiously developed, sincerely dedicated ministers for the churches in a critical time. The call had come to him. "One wishes decisions like this did not have to be faced, but there is no dodging, and one must work while it is called Today," he wrote one friend whose advice he had solicited. He accepted the call and prepared to move from 129 East 71st Street to the President's House in the Seminary Quadrangle at the corner of Claremont Avenue and 120th Street.

It was not an easy time in which to become the head of a theological school. P. Whitwell Wilson, who interviewed Coffin for the *New York Times* and published his record of their conversation in the Magazine Section of the paper that autumn, did so with the comment: "Few indeed have been the men to hold an office of such strategic importance at a crisis of faith so perplexing." Coffin himself, at least in that interview, attributed the religious decline during the Twenties to two circumstances: the extraordinary increase in wealth which made men feel that they had no need for God, and the backwash of the World War, which like all wars was followed by a period in which ideals were at a discount. At student conferences since the war he had observed that fewer men attended than in the pre-war years and that, although there were outstanding leaders of great ability among them, the general average was not so high. It was obvious that what Walter Lippmann was in 1929 to characterize as the "acids of modernity" had eaten into the foundations of a generation's faith. One element in the student world, as in society in general, was attempting to forget its disappointments and to conceal its despair under the guise of reckless frivolity. Idealists who had hoped to see their country assume new international responsibilities in the League of Nations were discouraged, sometimes cynical, because the United States had repudiated the organization which it had urged other nations to accept. The country by and large was disillusioned because the war had not been followed by the millenium and was content to withdraw into isolationism and to seek no higher good than what the first post-war

American president had called a "return to normalcy." Coffin
felt that the national temper presented a challenge to the Christian Church and emphasized the need for adequately trained
ministers, but he must have reflected often on that sentence from
one of Marcus Dods's letters which in 1918 he had printed inside
the cover of his Lyman Beecher Lectures: "I do not envy those
who have to fight the battle of Christianity in the twentieth century. Yes, perhaps I do, but it will be a stiff fight."

There were also difficulties within the Seminary to be faced
by the new President. Dr. McGiffert had written him that he
hoped that Coffin's coming would mean a greater emphasis on
training men for the pastoral ministry, and had also pointed out
that the curriculum needed revision, always a difficult task in
every educational institution in view of the sincere conviction of
its own paramount importance on the part of each department.
The Board of Directors had expressed to him its concern for a
strengthening of the spiritual life of the student body, as well as
for a closer relationship between the Seminary's training and the
life of the Church. For Coffin these were congenial objectives.
He could not achieve them, however, without giving and experi-
encing some pain. He was disturbed by the number of men
enrolled in the Seminary and enjoying all its facilities who were
not and had no intention of being servants of the Church. By
tightening the requirements for dormitory residence he drastically
reduced their number, thereby causing an outcry of angry as-
tonishment and giving rise to the charge vehemently made but
soon forgotten, that he was unsympathetic with graduate study
and serious scholarship. He set out at once to make the daily
Chapel services more helpful and more attractive. Although attendance at Chapel was voluntary he did not hesitate to lay
the obligation of participation directly upon the consciences of
faculty and students alike as he met them informally in his office
or in the corridors. Occasionally someone thought that he was
making the Seminary too pietistic, but for the most part he got

the cooperation of the whole Seminary community and soon the services which had been sparsely attended became what they were intended to be, the Seminary as a family at worship. This result was facilitated by his radical innovation of enlisting women students for the choir, which improved the musical part of the service greatly, and by making greater use of those members of the faculty who were most gifted in the leadership in worship. A more perplexing problem had to do with the location of the responsibility for pastoral training. His election as President occurred just when he was engaged in a friendly controversy with the Religious Education Department over this matter. Harrison S. Elliott, who had just become the head of that department, felt that training in psychology was the essential qualification for those who were to teach the conduct of public worship, pastoral care of individuals and parish administration. Coffin insisted that while the religious education department could be of great assistance, the primary responsibility for courses in these subjects should be in the hands of men who themselves had been pastors and who knew, as he put it, "the Church as it is, not some possible revised church of tomorrow." (The capital letter C is where he put it!) Dr. McGiffert marked time on the question, but when Coffin succeeded to the presidency, the line of demarcation between the Religious Education Department and the Department of Practical Theology remained where it had been before the issue was raised. (Although they did not agree on some matters, Coffin had no more loyal friend on the faculty than Harrison Elliott.) A difficulty in the same general field arose when Coffin did not give his backing to the Union School of Religion. This was a Sunday School conducted on Sunday mornings in the Seminary buildings, administered and taught for the most part by faculty and students in the Department of Religious Education. It provided a thoroughly modern and liberal religious program for children in the neighborhood, and gave Seminary students an opportunity to gain experience in teaching under the supervision of their teachers. Coffin had two criticisms of the School. He believed that children should receive religious education as part of their life in a church, not in an unrelated Seminary, however expert the instruction the latter might provide. He also felt that the School used the Bible as a source for illustrations of ethical and religious principles rather than as the unique Book through which God speaks to men. Coffin refused to send his own children to the School, desiring for them the continuance of a church relationship. The difference between him and the School, while amicable, was fundamental. When the Riverside Church was opened across the street from the Seminary, there was obviously no need for two Sunday Schools on one block, and the Union School of Religion was absorbed into the educational program of that church. The leaders of the School were happier under the new sponsorship, and Coffin also was happier because of the new arrangement.

Coffin was inaugurated as President of the Seminary on November 4, 1926. Friends on the faculty—James Everett Frame, Hugh Black and William Adams Brown—with four from the Board of Directors—William M. Kingsley, William P. Merrill, Robert Russell Wicks, and Walter Russell Bowie—took part in the service. Inaugurations of presidents and professors at Union had traditionally been of Spartan simplicity. Coffin, at home in the academic and ecclesiastical dignities of Scotland, made more of the occasion, not as an opportunity for self-display but in order to strengthen the Seminary's relationships with the educational world. *Time* magazine, which carried Coffin's picture on the cover of the next issue, featured the inauguration with a vivid description of the event:

"The chapel of Union Theological Seminary, long famed training school for divines, was most reverently crowded. Upstairs, in a room on the second floor, was an overflow of people, radio-attentive. As the organ struck into 'The Church's One Foundation,' a flashing, gleaming pageant advanced in academic rhythm, most steps firm, assured, a few a trifle embarrassed by glory, to the chancel. There were hoods of scarlet, hoods of green, hoods of orange, purple, blue, set off by touchs of spotless white, the whole toned down to harmony by the austere background of a white granite pile. Among the robe wearers were forty university, college and seminary presidents, including two women, Mary E. Woolley (Mt. Holyoke), and Ellen F. Pendleton (Wellesley). In a gown a cardinal hue, symbol of University of Glasgow honors, was the Reverend Henry Sloane Coffin, D.D. (N.Y.U., Yale, Harvard, Columbia, Princeton, Glasgow), who was there to be inaugurated as President. Whence came he to this post of eminence and ecclesiastical danger?

"From Yale, in 1897, a brilliant youth of twenty was graduated. Of prosperous and socially impeccable Manhattan parentage, he did not forsake his youthful religious enthusiasm, but committed himself at once to the ministry. He was urbane, witty, talkative, diplomatic—even then having something of the Giorgione monk in his deep eyes and strange eye-brows. A gypsy, for less than a quarter, might easily have predicted for him an easy path to a Manhattan bishopric. But the gypsy could not have guessed how passionately Presbyterian he is—this modern liberal; and the radical honesty of the man would sooner lead him to be anything but Society's parson. . . .

"If the distinguished visiting educators of last week were hoping to hear things of good repute about the ministry, they were partially mistaken: 'The intellectual level of the ministry of an American church is pathetically low. Recent controversies could hardly have arisen had our pulpits been filled with men abreast of current thought and seriously teaching their people. The number of college professors and leaders in the professions who show no interest in the Church is an alarming sign of the inability of our clergy to grip the minds and stir the imaginations of many of our educated people. A rift between teachers of religion and foremost thinkers along other lines constitutes a grave national peril.'"

In his Inaugural Address, Coffin declared that the Seminary had a threefold function: to be a training school for Christian ministers, to be a school for graduate study, and to carry on extension education in theology for a wider public. "Of its three functions, all of them valuable," he said, "the first is the most important." The four ideals which he defined at the outset and by which during the nineteen years of his administration he was consistently guided were scholarship, churchmanship, worshipfulness and a passion for the world-wide Kingdom of Christ. "What a day for a theological seminary, free from the domination of any single sect and committed to serve all the churches, neighbor to a great university with all the stimulus of its pulsing intellectual activity and held firmly to vital Christianity by leadership vested in a board and faculty of churchmen; with a noble tradition of fearless pursuit of truth and of fervent devotion to Jesus Christ, the Son of God and Redeemer of the world, with an unrivalled equipment haunting those who use it with misgiving lest the resultant product be not worth the investment; with the teeming and throbbing life of the greatest city on the American continent surrounding it, challenging faculty and students so to interpret their gospel that it charms, persuades and transforms all sorts and conditions of men and provides a Christian solvent for the social perplexities of this cosmopolitan industrial community and of the world whose uttermost ends the city brings to its doors."[1] Loyal but critical concern for the Church permeated the address. "With the churches so patently far from succeeding in their tasks, we are eager to turn out men of venturesome spirit, unfettered by tradition, willing to risk experiments and to lead their congregations in a serious attempt to leaven their communities with the mind of Christ."[2] Newspapers from coast to coast picked phrases or paragraphs out of the address and editorialized upon them. His assertion that "this Seminary has been

[1] *Alumni Bulletin* of Union Seminary, December 1926-January 1927, p. 53.
[2] *Op. cit.*, p. 58.

a protagonist for the freedom of the Christian mind"[3] provided the heading of an editorial in the *New York Times*. The stress on the need for a better educated ministry struck a responsive chord in the minds of newspaper editors throughout the country.

One hundred thirty-three universities and colleges in addition to thirty-three theological seminaries sent representatives to the inauguration, a testimony to the large place which Coffin had made for himself in academic circles. These visitors, together with a large number of leaders from alumni associations and church boards, as well as many friends of the Seminary were guests of the Board of Directors at a dinner that evening at the Hotel Biltmore. Whatever the assigned topic, each speaker devoted most of his time to hailing Coffin in some such words as those which Dr. Harry Emerson Fosdick used as he closed his remarks: "There are some of us who have known Dr. Coffin for a good many years who, when we think of Christianity, find his spirit coming across our vision as one of the best interpreters of it that we have ever known." Mr. William M. Kingsley, President of the Board of Directors, struck a prophetic as well as humorous note when in introducing Coffin he divulged the fact that when the Coffins had first looked over the President's house prior to occupying it, their only request was for a larger pantry —in fact they wanted one so large that an addition had to be built in the courtyard to accommodate it. "Dr. and Mrs. Coffin," he said, "are evidently given to hospitality and are prepared to distribute to the necessity of the saints."

They were "given to hospitality" in the President's house as they had been on Seventy-first Street. Perhaps the aspect of his new life which Coffin most thoroughly enjoyed was that of being pastor and friend to the students. They began by inviting two or three students to their home for lunch each day that they were not occupied elsewhere. When it became apparent that they would never get acquainted with all the men and women at

[3] *Op. cit.*, p. 34.

this rate, they began to invite students to breakfast also. Coffin was always accessible for consultation in his office to those who had problems. Let him hear of sickness in a dormitory or of a student being taken to the hospital, and he was at the bedside at once, inquiring, reassuring, making the practical arrangements that might be necessary, praying. "Will you walk with me this afternoon?" he would ask some surprised student as they moved up the aisle coming out of the morning Chapel service, and a brisk hour on Riverside Drive would provide a dual opportunity to admire the Hudson River and to discuss the student's hopes and fears and concerns. It was not long before he learned that in student conversation he was affectionately known as "Uncle Henry." This startled him at first. There was in him a blend of dignity and informality, but in personal relationships he liked to determine the boundaries of informality himself. Few even of his contemporaries addressed him except as "Dr. Coffin." But it warmed his heart to know that "the boys" had given him their accolade with a title which betokened affection. Especially during difficult years when certain groups of students were outspokenly critical of his administration, it was a comfort to him to know that behind his back he was "Uncle Henry" to the great majority.

Seminary lore abounds in anecdotes and legends of his humor which lightened many an awkward situation, of his devastating repartee which punctured many a pompous pretension, and of unexpected kindnesses in which he found delight. One hot September evening as the Seminary was about to reopen, a new student arrived from the South and rang the door-bell at the President's house thinking he was at an entrance to the Seminary. The door was opened by a man in shirt-sleeves, who instantly realized what had happened, seized the student's suitcase and, saying, "Oh, you belong in the dormitory office," led him across the quadrangle in that direction. "Are you the janitor?" the student asked as they walked. "No," the man replied, "but I try to be helpful to the janitor." The student's bewilderment turned to consternation when they arrived at the dormitory and the attendant's greeting revealed the fact that it was the President of the Seminary who had acted as his porter and guide.

A story went the rounds and subsequently appeared in *Newsweek* magazine regarding a meeting between Coffin and Bishop William T. Manning shortly after the bishop had preached in the Cathedral of St. John the Divine a sermon on the apostolic succession. The bishop had defined the doctrine in terms which made it plain that in his view Presbyterians were not included in that elect company. The meeting took place in a barbershop on Morningside Heights. The barber was just finishing his tonsorial job on the bishop when Coffin walked in. After a few words about the weather, the bishop rose to pay his bill and Coffin slipped into the chair which had just been vacated. As he did so he looked up with a puckish grin and said, "Well, bishop, I say to myself as I sit in your chair, still warm: 'Coffin, this is the closest you will ever get to the apostolic succession.'"

Two years after he became President, Coffin was largely responsible for a radical innovation in the Seminary's life in the founding of the School of Sacred Music. It came about in this way: Since 1837 there had been an Instructor of Music on the Seminary faculty. Since 1912 this position had been held by Dr. Clarence Dickinson, organist and choir director at the Brick Presbyterian Church in New York City. It would be more accurate to say that the post was held by Dr. and Mrs. Dickinson, for the Instructor was blessed with a gifted wife who cooperated with him in his work. A Ph.D. from Heidelberg where she had specialized in the Historic Liturgies and in Religious Art, Helen Adell Dickinson helped him plan an annual series of historical organ lecture-recitals which attracted a large public following and were greatly appreciated by the students of the Seminary. The Dickinsons had a long cherished dream of a School of Sacred Music at Union Seminary in which church musicians could receive the best possible professional training in organ playing and choir direction, at the same time learning something of church usages and the background of church music. No existing graduate schools of music provided courses in religion, and no theological seminaries admitted students preparing for leadership in church music. The Dickinsons believed that directors of church music should have some courses in church history and in theology which would enable them to share intelligently in the worship of the churches they served. They envisaged a school open only to college graduates, on a par academically with the theological school. In January, 1928, they asked Coffin if they could talk over their idea with him sometime soon. "Why not tonight?" he replied. They found him enthusiastically responsive to their proposal. Since leaving the Madison Avenue Church he had suffered acutely from the bad music in churches where he had been a visiting preacher. He had long deplored the practice of bringing into the leadership of worship through music people who were professionally qualified but religiously illiterate or unsympathetic. He knew that the average minister needed a better educated taste in music and greater familiarity with the Church's heritage of sacred music. He gave the Dickinsons' plan his immediate and hearty approval. "Never one to let the grass grow under his feet," as he would say in telling the story, he went immediately to Edward S. Harkness and Arthur Curtiss James, both of them members of the Seminary's Board of Directors, and found them willing to underwrite the expense of the School for one year. "The next thing to do is to write down the names of those whom you think would make up a faculty for a school of sacred music," Coffin then said to Dr. and Mrs. Dickinson. "We did that long ago," they replied, "and we have the list right here." Within a week the seventeen on the list had been interviewed and each had replied, "I would be proud to be a part of such a school." Coffin himself agreed to teach a course in Hymnology and throughout his presidency he communicated his own fine taste in hymns and his wide knowledge of the history of hymnody to class after class of delighted students. For some years the financial support of the School was precarious. The School had been in existence only a year when the Depression of 1929 compelled the Seminary Directors to order a twenty per cent reduction in all operating expenses and the Seminary faculty took a voluntary cut in salaries. Coffin made annual visits to various friends who were interested in the School and kept it solvent until it could become a regular part of the total Seminary budget. From the start the School attracted an enthusiastic body of students who went out to serve in churches from coast to coast. A series of notable choir festivals were held in Riverside Church, one of the greatest in 1945 in honor of Dr. Dickinson's retirement, when over fifteen hundred singers from seventy choirs directed by Union graduates filled the majestic nave with song which Dr. Harry Emerson Fosdick characterized as "one of my most worshipful experiences." Neither Coffin nor the Dickinsons foresaw the extent to which manses, parsonages and rectories would in the future be presided over by ministers' wives who combined personal charm with a musical education received at Union! Nor did they foresee that twenty-five years later alumni of the School of Sacred Music would be teaching in over fifty colleges, universities and conservatories. Even less did they anticipate the time when in scattered schools across the world, from Salonica to Pakistan to Thailand, graduates of the Union School of Sacred Music would be training Christian choirs to communicate through the universal language of song. Few achievements of his presidency gave Coffin such solid satisfaction as did the growing, creative influence of this School.

In the Autumn of 1928 Coffin introduced another innovation to the Seminary in the person of Reinhold Niebuhr. Niebuhr had been for thirteen years the minister of Bethel Evangelical Church in Detroit. He had become known to student groups as a stimulating speaker at conferences, had written for the *Christian Cen-*

tury and in 1927 had published a book *Does Civilization Need Religion?* To the theological world he was practically unknown. He was an ardent pacifist and *The World Tomorrow*, a paper backed by the Fellowship of Reconciliation, wished to bring him to New York as its editor. One of the generous supporters of the paper came to Coffin and asked if the Seminary would give Niebuhr an appointment on its faculty. The proposal was that Niebuhr should divide his time between the paper and the Seminary, the patrons of the journal bearing the entire cost. Coffin was not sure what Niebuhr could teach but felt that he would be a good influence upon the students, and, after all, the arrangement was to cost the Seminary nothing. So began a relationship which was to bring luster to the Seminary, was to introduce into the Seminary's life one of the most provocative and most enlightening teachers in its long history, and was to bring into Coffin's life one of his warmest and most deeply cherished friendships. He consulted the proper committees of the faculty and Board of Directors and Niebuhr was appointed Associate Professor of Christian Ethics. Coffin's intuition regarding Niebuhr's influence on the students was immediately vindicated. Soon, however, the students discovered that they had no stationary idol, but were trying to keep up with a mind on the move. It was not long before Niebuhr repudiated pacifism and became engrossed in relating love to justice and in trying to define the ethical uses of power. He also repudiated liberalism, traditionally the watchword of the Union Seminary community, and influenced by Continental theology, began to stress man's creaturehood and sin, the divine majesty and judgment, and the illusory character of nineteenth-century optimism. In 1932 he published his *Moral Man and Immoral Society* which burst like a bombshell upon naïve liberals and established its author as the central figure around whom theological argument was to revolve for two decades in the United States and round the world.

Coffin disagreed with many of Niebuhr's positions on theological and social questions but used to say that in a time when so many people were hazy or agnostic about the deity he was glad to have a man teaching his students who was so sure of God. He was sometimes obliged to listen to irate critics who objected to some of Niebuhr's pronouncements or activities which bore upon social questions. As always in such situations Coffin defended the teacher's right to have and to express his own views. The defense was often in the form of a quip. When some members of the Board of Directors were distressed because Niebuhr was running for Congress on the Socialist ticket, Coffin quieted their fears by telling them that "on that ticket his chance of winning an election is negligible."[4] When Niebuhr received the appointment to deliver the Gifford Lectures at Edinburgh University in Scotland, no one was more proud and pleased than Coffin. When the first series on *The Nature of Man* had been delivered, Coffin remarked that "Niebuhr has gotten man in so deep in the first series of lectures that it is a question whether or not he will be able to get him out in the second." He also had reservations about Niebuhr's use of the term "myth" when applied to Christian doctrines. But when he read the second series on *The Destiny of Man* which at Niebuhr's request he did in manuscript, chapter by chapter, he was all pride. Niebuhr on his part fully reciprocated the pride and affection in which he was held by the President. When Coffin retired in 1945 Niebuhr was editor of a little volume of tributes entitled *This Ministry* and wrote the glowing chapter on Coffin as "Theologian and Church Statesman" with which the volume concluded. When Niebuhr himself retired from the faculty of the Seminary in 1960 and wrote a brief review of his thirty-two years at Union, he said of the period between 1933 and 1945: "Religiously it meant the ascendancy of the 'liberal evangelicalism' of our revered chief, the late Henry Sloane Coffin, who had always claimed my personal loyalty and respect but whom I followed both religiously and politically more than ever

[4] *A Half Century of Union Seminary*, p. 149.

before. I think his thought and spirit dominated the whole Seminary." In some ways no two men could have been more unlike than Coffin and Niebuhr. Each recognized the other's greatness and loved the man behind the public figure whom the worldwide Church acclaimed.

Coffin was fond of saying that "Union Seminary lives by its brains." No aspect of his responsibilities as President concerned him more deeply than did the recruiting of new members of the faculty as retirements created vacancies in the ranks. New professors and instructors were elected by the Board of Directors on nomination by the incumbent full professors, but Coffin was continually "vigilant to detect theological luminaries rising on the horizon,"[5] as he once described the President's responsibility, and generally had a carefully considered suggestion to make when any appointment was under discussion. His initiative and influence were the determining factors in bringing to the Seminary distinguished scholars and Christian interpreters in whose work he found great satisfaction and in whose friendship he took great pleasure.

The first appointment to be made under the new regime was a successor to Dr. McGiffert as Washburn Professor of Church History, a post which he had held concurrently with the presidency. Coffin was ready with the name of James Moffatt, at the time occupying the history chair at the United Free Church College in Glasgow.[6] "Enormously learned," as Coffin called him, he was widely known to the general public for his translation of the New Testament into modern speech. Moffatt was one of the speakers at the Northfield General Conference in the summer of 1926, and at the conclusion of the meetings went with his wife for a visit with the Coffins at their summer home in the Adirondacks, and renewed the friendship which had been begun in Scotland. No doubt there was discussion of the church history chair at Union

[5] Charge to Henry P. Van Dusen at Inauguration, November 15, 1945.
[6] *A Half Century of Union Seminary*, p. 159.

and other serious matters but there was also much fun. One day it was proposed to make the journey to the Upper Ausable Lake and have lunch with friends who were camping there. Moffatt was not equipped with camping clothes, but was fitted out with a sweater and a pair of Coffin's knickerbockers, although the fit left much to be desired when the lanky Scotsman was in them. The four mile buckboard drive through the Reservation to the Lower Lake presented no problems, but when Moffatt was invited to get into a narrow and rather tippy skiff for the journey down the lake, he demurred. He was finally persuaded, but sat stiffly and unhappily silent while a guide rowed him to the lake's end. The plan had been that the party would make the trip down the Upper Lake in canoes. But when they had walked the trail between the two bodies of water and Moffatt saw what he considered to be the egg-shell in which it was planned to transport him to the camp, he refused absolutely to set foot in it, saying that it was no craft in which a human being ought to go out upon the water. For a few moments the expedition seemed to have reached an impasse. Then a guide produced a skiff from the bushes where he had it hidden, and it was agreed that Moffatt should be rowed down the lake while the rest of the party paddled canoes. Even then it was not all plain sailing; when Moffatt's skiff reached the middle of the lake smoke suddenly began to rise from the borrowed knickerbockers and the guide was seen to be frantically splashing water on the Glasgow professor. It seemed that in his nervousness Moffatt had stuffed the pipe which he was smoking in his pocket, forgetting that it was lighted. At lunch Coffin announced, "When we finish eating we will paddle Dr. and Mrs. Moffatt up the stream at the end of the lake and let them see a little American wild life." "Ye will not," replied Moffatt. So while the Coffins showed the wilderness to Mrs. Moffatt, the non-sea-going authority on the New Testament sat by the fire and discussed Canon Streeter's theory of Proto-Luke with his host. The next year Moffatt came to the church history chair at Union, where he added greatly to the distinction of its faculty, and along with his lifelong friend Ernest F. Scott, contributed a Scottish flavor to the Seminary's life which was a constant source of joy to the President.

Another Scotsman whom Coffin's eagle eye discovered was John Baillie, an Edinburgh graduate teaching Systematic Theology at Emmanuel College, Toronto, who in 1930 was brought to Union Seminary to succeed William Adams Brown in the Roosevelt professorship. After four years Baillie felt the pull of his native Scotland and became Professor of Divinity at Edinburgh University, later Principal of New College, Moderator of the Church of Scotland and one of the six Presidents of the World Council of Churches. Coffin found Baillie's mind and theological viewpoint most congenial, and the intellectual and spiritual bond between them was very close. In 1942, eight years after his return to Scotland, Baillie dedicated a spiritual autobiography entitled *Invitation to Pilgrimage* to "Six in New York—Reinhold and Ursula Niebuhr, Henry and Dorothy Coffin, Pitney and Betty Van Dusen." One hot July both Coffin and Baillie were giving courses of lectures at a Ministers' Conference conducted by a mid-Western theological school. The lectures were in the evening, the evenings were terribly hot, the ministers had been invited to bring their wives with them, and the hall was crowded with an audience which was not on tip-toe with eagerness for the truth in large consecutive portions. Baillie's first lecture was more suitable for an Edinburgh winter morning than for a mid-western summer night, and at the end his audience was fatigued. "John," said Coffin, "why don't you lighten it up a bit tomorrow night? Tell them some of your Scotch stories." "Coffin," replied the Scotsman, "when you are in Edinburgh you seem to be one of us, but over here you are terribly American!" Coffin regarded Baillie's return to Scotland "a great gain for Scotland and a sore impoverishment to the Seminary."[7]

[7] *A Half Century of Union Seminary*, p. 153.

In 1933 Coffin's instinctive compassion for a fellow human being in need had the unexpected result of bringing to Union Seminary one of the most illustrious theologians of the century. Coffin attended a meeting of a committee formed at Columbia for the aid of scholars who had been compelled to flee from Hitler's Germany.[8] A list of refugee professors was circulated, most of whom were Jewish, but toward the end of the roll appeared the name of Paulus Johannes Tillich, who had been removed from the chair of philosophy at Frankfort. Coffin immediately offered to provide a post for him at Union. Then he went back to the Seminary library and read Tillich's *Glaubensvoll Realismus* in German. Niebuhr was able to secure more information about Tillich, the faculty voted that each professor would contribute five per cent of his salary toward Tillich's stipend for the first year, some of the Directors made contributions toward the necessary fund, and a cable was sent to Tillich inviting him to come. Tillich learned English at a phenomenal speed after his arrival and within a few months was able to lecture in his adopted tongue. He became an Associate Professor four years later, and in 1940 was appointed Professor of Philosophical Theology. He quickly gained recognition throughout the United States, as he had previously in Germany, as a foremost thinker and scholar. By the wide range of his interests and knowledge, as well as by the simplicity of his character and gentle ways, he made a unique place for himself in the seminary life and won all hearts. Coffin's passion for concrete terminology in public speech made him somewhat wary of the abstract terms which came naturally to the German philosophical mind, and he was fond of repeating garbled remarks of students who had heard but not understood some of Tillich's lectures. He was never able to share completely Tillich's approach to theology, but he rated him "a massive theologian—perhaps the most outstanding thinker at the moment, whether one agrees or disagrees with his method and conclu-

[8] *Op. cit.*, pp. 134-140.

sions."[9] He was happy and proud to have him at Union as a colleague and warm friend.

Other distinguished scholars and able teachers were brought to the faculty during Coffin's presidency—Frank W. Herriott, Arthur Jeffrey, Frederick C. Grant, Walter Russell Bowie, John L. Casteel, Richard J. Kroner, John Knox, John T. McNeill, Charles W. Iglehart and others. All came under the spell of the magnetic President. He delighted in them all, and in none more than the younger men who had been his students in the Seminary before they came back as outstanding members of its faculty: Henry Pitney Van Dusen, Hugh Porter, Cyril C. Richardson, David E. Roberts, Samuel L. Terrien, and John C. Bennett.

Union Seminary prided itself on having a faculty which represented widely varying points of view. When these views were strenuously held by strong and able men, there were bound to be differences of opinion vehemently expressed. To the outside world, catching the echoes of some of these controversies, it sounded like a battleground. William Lyon Phelps wrote in a magazine that he would rather be an impresario at the opera or the lion-tamer at the circus than the President of Union Seminary. When this remark was called to Coffin's attention, he laughed and said that he liked it.

[9] *Op. cit.*, p. 137.

CHAPTER TWELVE

CRISES IN THE NATION

WHILE cherishing the independence of Union Seminary, Coffin was fully aware of the advantages which it enjoyed because of its location just across the street from Columbia University. There had always been reciprocity between the two schools, students from each institution taking courses for credit in the other. One of the first accomplishments in Coffin's administration was the negotiation of a new agreement in 1928 which made Union Seminary in effect one of the constituent faculties of Columbia University.[1] The President and two members of the Seminary faculty became members of the University Council. It was arranged that a number of advanced degrees were to be conferred by Columbia University on recommendation of the Seminary faculty for work done jointly in the two institutions. Other developments along this line followed during Coffin's presidency, making Morningside Heights increasingly one of the great centers for graduate study of religion in the world.

Another project which was close to Coffin's heart was the development in the Brown Memorial Tower at the Seminary of the Missionary Research Library.[2] For a number of years, such a library had been in existence, gathered together by cooperative

[1] From "Theological Educator" by Henry P. Van Dusen in *This Ministry*, Scribners, 1945, p. 30.
[2] *Op. cit.*, p. 32.

effort of the foreign mission boards of the churches. In 1929 Dr. John R. Mott on behalf of the Foreign Missions Conference of North America approached Coffin to ascertain if Union Seminary would provide a home for this outstanding library, its former quarters being no longer available. Coffin at once promised his enthusiastic support of the proposal. The Seminary already had extensive missionary book resources. When the two libraries were brought together under a committee jointly representing the Foreign Missions Conference and the Seminary, they constituted the largest and most useful collection of materials on the Christian mission to be found anywhere in the English-speaking world, numbering some eighty or ninety thousand volumes. This was always a source of great satisfaction to Coffin.

Three years after Coffin assumed the Presidency the economic depression of 1929 spread like a blight over the country and every educational institution faced the almost impossible task of maintaining standards of quality in its life and work on a steadily diminishing income. Interest on endowed funds fell off, students came from homes that felt the pinch acutely, potential donors were hard pressed by their personal and business obligations. By dint of heroic economies and the most careful management, Union Seminary was brought through the trying period without a deficit in any year. The Board of Directors requested a twenty per cent reduction in operating expenses. Heat was turned off at night in offices and hallways and night workers, as all theologians are, shivered. The lawn in the Seminary Quadrangle, for years the object of loving, albeit expensive, care and the delight of a Bursar's heart, was allowed to go to dandelions and plantain, a visible symbol of the cut-to-the-bone economy which was being practiced in every phase of the Seminary's life. Chief executioner of budget items was the President whose Scots background and habits of personal economy fitted him admirably for the role. At the same time, through the generous gifts of Mr. John D. Rockefeller, Jr. and others, McGiffert Hall was in 1931 added to the Seminary group of buildings to provide apartments for faculty and married students. A member of the Board of Directors who was on many business, educational and philanthropic boards said, when better days finally came, that he knew of no institution whose affairs had been so wisely handled through the depression years as had those of Union Seminary. For this achievement three men were jointly responsible: William M. Kingsley, President of the Board of Directors; Charles T. White, Comptroller; and Henry S. Coffin, President of the Seminary.

The depression years brought acute personal as well as official problems into Coffin's life. For the first time in his life he had to face financial stringency. He had always been abstemious to the point of parsimony in the use of money for the fulfillment of personal desires. One who knew him well once wrote of him that he "has always been an ascetic. That would surprise many who knew him, and know that all his life he has had more rather than less of the world's comforts. But born to wealth, he has deliberately refused to let it make him have any ease of life that others did not have. I have known him as a young man, weary from his strain of work, to walk a long cold distance rather than pay more than a carfare. I have known him to wear clothes until they shone with age, until they were patched, indeed until a providence in the shape of father or mother insisted on new garments. But while in his old clothes, working gaily but so unsparingly, his savings have gone all over the world in generous thousands, and many men have received education through his self-denial." When the depression struck, however, for the first time he was compelled to practice not voluntary but unavoidable rigid economy. Burdened with a huge President's House which could not be maintained and kept overflowing with guests in the customary Coffin manner on his President's salary, and with his personal income rapidly disappearing, he was confronted by problems which had never been his lot in earlier years. He reduced all personal expenditures to a minimum. His wife sold some of her belongings to realize ready money. Some business ventures in which he had an interest were in difficulties and their solvency became a matter of acute concern. Outwardly he was jovial, ready with humorous quips as he met students and faculty in the corridors, but inwardly he was disturbed, anxious, distressed.

In the midst of his financial troubles a major personal sorrow visited him. His brother, William Sloane Coffin, died suddenly. His father, Edmund Coffin, had died at the age of eighty-five in January, 1929, as the result of injuries sustained when an automobile had struck him on the street. At that time Henry Coffin wrote to a friend, "We wish Father had been spared the accident, but apart from that we have nothing but thankfulness for his rich and full and useful career through these long years." But William Coffin was in the prime of life at fifty-four. A dedicated Christian business man, he had gone into the firm of W. and J. Sloane which his grandfather had founded, but had many other business ventures in the fields of craftsmanship and housing which combined his philanthropic interests and executive abilities. An elder in the Brick Presbyterian Church, he was active in two mission churches, Christ Presbyterian Church on West 36th Street and the Spring Street Presbyterian Church on the East Side downtown. He was President of the New York City Mission Society. His artistic sensitivity led him into various positions of leadership in the Metropolitan Museum of Art of which he was President at the time of his death. He was coming out of the Museum on December 16, 1933, when he suffered a heart attack and died on the Museum steps. Henry Coffin wrote to a mutual friend who had expressed sympathy: "Will crowded several lives into one and the effort was straining and wore him out. But he enjoyed all his work and accomplished much. The business tension of these last years was severe for him. Many of his cherished projects—housing, schools, cooperative factories, etc., nearly went under. He kept them up but the cost to nerves and body was extreme. I am thankful that the press in its editorials was so appreciative." Through most of their mature years William had handled the business affairs in which the two brothers had joint interests, and his death added to Henry's responsibilities. After William's death, Henry regarded his brother's three children as in a sense his own. He kept in close touch with them and watched their development with affectionate pride.

The depression years brought Coffin painful experiences of quite a different nature because of difficulties which arose between him and certain elements in the student body who felt that he was unsympathetic with their social radicalism. They charged him with being inclined to deny students the liberty to express unpopular views on social matters that he claimed in theological controversy. A series of incidents in the Winter and Spring of 1934 lay behind this tension between the President and these particular students, in addition to the general discontent which the depression had engendered. One group of students felt that wages and working conditions for employees in the Refectory were inadequate, and even after a faculty committee had studied the matter and improvements had been made, wished to continue agitating for further increases. Some students joined a picket line with strikers at the Waldorf-Astoria Hotel, bearing a banner identifying them as from Union Theological Seminary. The Rector of the Church of the Heavenly Rest on Fifth Avenue got into the papers by sending a telegram of congratulations to Governor Rolph of California who was reported to have approved the lynching of two kidnappers. A group of Union students picketed the church on the next Sunday morning in protest, again bearing placards indicating the Seminary from which they came. A mild mêlée resulted and one student landed in jail. Coffin wrote a letter of reprimand to the student, objecting to the use which had been made of the Seminary's name, but beyond that he preferred to deal with the situation by the use of humor rather than the big stick. When a committee of indignant vestrymen from the church waited upon him and demanded the expulsion of the picketers he asked them how old their rector was. "Forty-eight," they replied. "Do you intend to ask him to resign?" he asked. "We do not," was their answer. "Well, if at forty-eight your rector does a foolish thing and you do not demand his resignation, I am not going to expel these boys who have done a foolish thing in their twenties." Then he called in those who had taken part in the picketing. "Why did you do this?" he asked. "Because we wanted to disassociate ourselves from Dr. Darlington," they answered. "Have you ever associated with Dr. Darlington?" he asked. "No," they replied. "Then," said he, "why do you feel that you must disassociate yourselves from someone with whom you have never associated?" With that unanswered question the incident was closed. A more serious incident occurred on May Day when police appeared at the Seminary saying that the red flag was flying from the Seminary tower and demanding its removal.[3] The Student Cabinet posted a notice asking the person or persons responsible to acknowledge it, but no one did so. A number of such incidents tried the patience of the President who was always called on to explain to the outside world that aggressive students, however conscientious in their attitudes on social questions, did not speak officially for the Seminary. His facility in epigrams did not always bring balm to the hurt feelings of humorless youth. They had a club organized for social action which they called the "Agenda Club."[4] Coffin dubbed it the "Leap-before-you-look Club." In a mild report on the year which he made to the alumni on Commencement Day, he facetiously remarked that they could not have the Seminary used as a guinea pig for a future Soviet. The newspapers picked up this phrase and published head-line articles about revolution and reaction at Union Seminary. Hubert Herring, Secretary of the Department of Social Relations of the Congregational Education Society, wrote a sensational article which was published in the *Christian Century* entitled "Union Seminary

[3] *A Half Century of Union Seminary*, p. 191.
[4] *Op. cit.*, p. 190.

Routs Its Reds." With it he published a letter stating that the threat to the historic freedom of the Seminary was a real one, that "President Coffin clearly plans for a purified seminary," and calling upon the alumni to write him in protest against his policy. The result of this appeal was not what its author intended. A few letters of protest came in Coffin's mail but a great volume of letters poured in from graduates of all epochs, affirming their confidence in him, insisting that the published article had misinterpreted his policies, and expressing their continued loyalty to the Seminary which in their judgment had not departed from its traditions of freedom. Coffin had already sent a letter to all students who planned to return to the Seminary the following autumn reminding them of the institution's history as a "comradely fellowship" of directors, faculty, employees and students, and adding, "There is room in such a fellowship for frank suggestions as to possible improvements in the methods by which the seminary operates; but there is no place for factions nor for organized criticism by one group of another. . . . Happily the seminary provides for the management of its business affairs executive officers in whose hands these matters necessarily remain, thus setting free most of the professors and all of the students for their academic tasks." All of the students did not want to be set free in this particular way, although most of them did. At the commencement Alumni Luncheon a year later, the Senior selected to speak for the graduating class took advantage of the occasion to criticize the administration of the Seminary and charge that he and his classmates had not enjoyed freedom of expression under Coffin's authoritative rule. Coffin made no rebuttal but asked for a show of hands indicating how many Seniors shared the views of their spokesman. Not a hand was raised. But a guest in the Coffin home that afternoon witnessed the unprecedented sight of the President sitting silent in the midst of a circle of friends, with a faraway look in his eyes, taking little part in the conversation. This exhibition of bad manners on the part of the young graduate marked the climax of the period of tension between Coffin and the left wing of the student body. For Coffin it had been a painful period.

He had planned to be away most of the academic year of 1934–1935 on his first sabbatical leave of absence. Late in May, immediately after the 1934 Commencement, he sailed with his family for Britain. On June 29 his steadily growing list of honorary degrees was augmented when St. Andrew's University in Scotland conferred upon him his third LL.D. This was an occasion of special pleasure for him, the Principal of St. Andrew's, Sir James Irvine, being an old and intimate friend. (Sir James had visited the Coffins at St. Hubert's in the Summer of 1925, when the Coffin children had greeted him at breakfast most politely, "Good morning, *Saint* James!" "The British Crown may make you a baronet," Coffin had laughed, "but it takes the Coffin children to give you an aureole!") The Dean of the Faculty of Arts in his citation referred to Coffin as "one of the first and finest figures and most kindly natures in American theological education." After a summer in England and Scotland, Coffin took his family across the Channel and saw them established for the winter at Vichy in France. He then returned to New York for the opening of the Seminary in late September. The New Year saw him back in Europe, and in early January he set out with Mrs. Coffin for a trip through the Near East. Their special objective was Roberts College in Istanbul, an institution in which both took deep interest and of whose Board of Trustees he was President. They spent nearly two weeks at the college, entertained at luncheons and dinners by officials and faculty members, Coffin preaching at various services, and seeing the fascinating old city when they could find spare moments. He spent long hours in conferences with college committees, bringing his own educational experience to bear upon the problems they faced. A hurried trip was made to Ankara, the capital, where the American Ambassador entertained them and arranged interviews for Coffin with the Minister of Education, the Under-Secretary for Foreign Affairs and with

Ismet Pasha, the Premier. With them all Coffin conversed in
French. One result of their visit was that no sooner had they
returned to Istanbul than the Minister of Education appeared to
make the first official visit he had ever paid Roberts College. Mid-
April found them back in New York, ready for another Commencement at the Seminary.

One day in the Spring of 1939, President Paul S. Heath of
Auburn Theological Seminary walked into Coffin's office. As he
has described the ensuing conversation, Coffin's first words to him
were, "What can Union Seminary do for Auburn?" Heath had in
mind a plan for a federation of the two institutions. Auburn
Seminary, located in the northern section of New York State, had
been founded in 1818 and was administered by a Board of Directors drawn from seventeen presbyteries in the Synod of New
York. Its student body was open to members of any denomination.
In its long and honorable history its associations with Union
Seminary had been cordial and close. Because of its remoteness
from other centers of higher education, however, it no longer
attracted students in sufficient numbers to justify or, in fact, to
make possible its continued independent existence. A committee
of the Presbyterian General Assembly had advised that it merge
with a Baptist institution, Colgate-Rochester Seminary, in Rochester, New York. This plan involved the erection of new buildings in Rochester, and the campaign to raise the funds necessary
for such a building project had failed. The Auburn directors now
proposed that they sell the campus and buildings where they had
been located and join forces with Union Seminary in New York.
Coffin enthusiastically endorsed the proposal and a plan was
worked out which was approved by the Boards of both institutions, met successfully the legal tests to which it was subjected,
and has had a happy and fruitful history in the subsequent years.[5]
Each Seminary retained its corporate identity, its Board of Directors, and its funds. Certain members of the Auburn Board were

[5] *Op. cit.*, pp. 165-167.

elected to membership on Union's Board. Two Auburn professors, Robert Hastings Nichols and Walter Seaman Davison were elected to the Union faculty. Auburn's scholarship funds were used to assist Presbyterian students in Union. Auburn's library was combined with Union's, and Auburn assumed responsibility for a circulating theological library for the use of alumni of both institutions. Through its extension program, Auburn has conducted conferences for ministers in New York City and also in presbyteries throughout New York State. In 1952 the Auburn directors raised funds for the erection of Auburn Hall, a valuable addition to the Union Quadrangle. Coffin was elected President of Auburn Seminary, which post he held concurrently with his Presidency of Union. At the time of Coffin's death, Dr. Heath reported to the Union Board that since the first day of the merger the Auburn group had never had a moment of dissatisfaction or unhappiness over any feature of the partnership, and that its extraordinary success had been primarily due to the fine spirit of fraternal cooperation manifested by President Coffin.

Although the decade of the Thirties was a period of growing anxiety and apprehension for the world, as the shadows of the depression deepened and then the menace of Hitlerism loomed on the horizon, Coffin went about his customary tasks with a heavy heart but nevertheless ready always with the gay word and the wise counsel for those who came across his path. The door between his office and the adjoining one of his secretary was generally open, and if a visitor asking to see him were known to him, a hearty welcome would often be called out before the secretary had time to give formal notice of the caller's presence. Seminary business was transacted with despatch. It was a rare faculty committee meeting which did not find him in attendance, feeling that it was better to be in on the early discussions of important matters and to have a part in shaping the preliminary formulation of policies than to be presented with decisions already agreed on by the professors. In the classrooms where he taught, his lectures sparkled with amusing anecdotes of pastoral experiences and his criticism of student sermons often brought laughter without tears. Halford Luccock, of the Yale Divinity School, a preacher famous for his pungent wit and telling illustrations, coming back to speak at an alumni dinner once struck a responsive chord in many of his hearers when he recalled that at the conclusion of a sermon which as a student he had preached in Coffin's classroom, his teacher had commented, "Well, now, Mr. Luccock has given us some fine illustrations, and if he can find some ideas to go with his stories, he will have a good sermon!" Every Sunday Coffin was off preaching in some college chapel or perhaps in the church of one of his former students whom he had recommended to a congregation seeking a minister. He was the person at the Seminary to whom churches came when they wanted ministers, either from the current graduating class or from among the alumni, and it was his word that they trusted in making selections. Consequently he was in great demand to preach installation sermons, as well as sermons at services in which young ministers were being ordained. Frequently he was asked to speak on religious topics before secular audiences. One night he debated with Clarence Darrow who defended atheism in a public meeting at Labor Temple. When Coffin finished his presentation of theistic belief, Darrow said that he did not know that there were ministers who could make such an intelligent case for their convictions. "Would to God there were more ministers like you," he said. "Would to what?" Coffin asked quietly, and the argument ended.

Coffin was a frequent lecturer at the Ministers' Conferences which brought hundreds of pastors back to Union Seminary for a week or two in the summer for theological reorientation and spiritual refreshment. His former students and others who had never sat in his classes were always grateful when he was one of the scheduled lecturers. One day in 1921 when the thermometer was creeping up into the nineties he startled his auditors by saying, "If fifty per cent of you will take your coats off, I will take mine off also." This was still the era when coats and respectability were synonymous in academic circles, but the crowded hall rose as one man and removed their jackets, the lecturer following suit, as the *New York Times* reported next day under the head-line, "Dr. Coffin Leads in Shirtsleeve Movement at Summer Conference."[6] At another Conference a dozen years later he was asked at the close of a lecture: "Should the Church put out a man who drinks?" "No," Coffin replied, "that would be an outrage. When a man joins a church, as I understand it, he promises loyalty to the Lord Jesus Christ as the Spirit of Christ shall enlighten a man's soul. A man must be safeguarded in his civil liberty." He had hardly paused when another man called out, "Do you drink?" "No, I am a total abstainer," replied Coffin. "I am a total abstainer for social reasons. I want my whole influence to count against the liquor traffic and for social sobriety. I don't believe, however, that the Church, as a Church, should legislate in regard to prohibition."[7]

Coffin had returned from Europe in 1935 profoundly disturbed by the rise of Hitler's power and impressed by the fear which he found everywhere among Germany's neighbors that the Nazi Fuehrer planned to extend his domain by force of arms. Student Christian groups in the United States were to a great extent committed to pacifism. Coffin felt that they were closing their eyes to the world's peril.[8] "At Student Christian Conferences there were frequent speeches upon the sinfulness of participation in War," he wrote in retrospect, "and it was assumed that the teaching of Jesus forbade such participation. There was no presentation of the complexity of international relations, whence wars arise; nor was anything said of loyalty to country as part of Christian duty. Pacifism, like Christian Science, was the refusal to employ approved means, and the substitution for them of love without

[6] *New York Times,* July 15, 1921.
[7] *New York Times,* July 21, 1933.
[8] *A Half Century of Union Seminary,* p. 194.

further discussion of possible methods of using it both for the oppressed and their oppressors. An entire generation of young people, and particularly Christian young people, was totally unprepared for the realities of the world." In the Seminary there were vigorous arguments between pacifists and those who believed that despotism must, if necessary, be checked by force. Reinhold Niebuhr had broken with the Fellowship of Reconciliation, a pacifist organization, and many students followed him out of pacifism. In April, 1936, however, a situation arose on which Coffin and the majority of his faculty took opposite sides. An annual demonstration for peace, called a student "Strike Against War," was held at Columbia University, and Union students requested a holiday in order to participate. Coffin objected, on the ground that classroom exercises should not be set aside. Over his protest, the faculty voted to grant the request. Coffin wrote out his dissent and posted it on a bulletin board, where it was signed by six other members of the faculty. He felt keenly the fact that the faculty had over-ruled him, as well as what he was sure was the unwisdom of their action. He even considered resigning the Presidency, but his love of the Seminary and his passion for healing breaches was too strong for such drastic action. No friendships were ruptured by the incident, and the faculty continued disagreeing on many things but united in spirit and purpose.

When the Selective Service Act was passed by Congress in 1940, the Seminary received much publicity from the refusal of eight students to register for the draft. The Act provided exemption from military service for theological students and also for conscientious objectors, but these particular men felt that registering for the draft would involve them in "the war system" in a way that violated their consciences and they refused to do so. They were arrested, tried and served short prison sentences. Coffin attempted without success to persuade them to register. Some of them were unusually gifted men who while students had been doing remarkable work in a slum district in Newark. Some

of them after the war went on into highly imaginative and constructive ministries like the East Harlem Protestant Parish in
New York City. In the crisis of 1940 they felt that Coffin was
urging them to conform to pagan mores. He felt that they were
opinionated and obstinate. He visited them in jail and was
shocked to see them in prison garb. After the war he publicly expressed pride in them, and when bewildered friends of the Seminary wondered how men who had served time in prison could
serve churches as ministers he would reply that Paul and Silas
had been in jail but the Lord seemed to have used them none the
less. But to the end of his days he referred to the episode as a
"heart-breaking incident."

Coffin's winter in Europe in 1934–5 had convinced him that
Nazi rule meant the extinction of the liberties which he had devoted much of his life to fostering. The presence of the German
refugee professors, Tillich and Kroner, at Union had brought him
first-hand knowledge of what had happened to the Universities
in Germany under Hitler's tyranny. The Fall of France and the
retreat of the British forces across the Channel from Dunkirk in
1940 made him painfully aware of the danger that all European
civilization might soon fall under this dreadful domination. He
came quickly to the conclusion that it was the duty of the United
States to aid Britain and her allies. When Clark Eichelberger,
who had been the executive of the American branch of the League
of Nations Association, wired him on June 5, 1940, asking for a
statement for a newspaper symposium on "Why America Should
Aid the Allies," he replied:

"The United States of America is partly responsible for present
conditions in Europe. We brought the last war to victory and then
withdrew from the peace to which our main contribution was the
League of Nations. Had we played our part in the League, subsequent history would have been very different.

"Now we are threatened with a far worse situation. Should the
Germans win, we shall be forced to conscription, to a huge arma-

ment consuming our wealth and to a long and bitter struggle. We have the chance at once to aid the Allies with every possible material and moral assistance. Should they prevent a German triumph, we can hope for a peace in which we could share and maintain justice and order in the earth. Already the Germans have cut our foreign trade and imposed on us a burdensome armament program. This is a faint foretaste of what is in store unless we act swiftly and save the Allies from a crushing defeat.

"The moral issue is between the triumph of unscrupulous and brutal tyranny and forces which promise an orderly world in which free men can breathe. I do not see how we can hesitate."

When the Committee to Defend America By Aiding the Allies was formed with William Allen White of Emporia, Kansas, as Chairman, Coffin became an active member. This Committee urged the President and Congress to make planes available to the Allies, and to provide funds for the purchase of food, clothing, and supplies for the millions of Dutch, Belgian, and French refugees in the war zone. Before long a group from the Committee was urging the United States government to turn over a substantial number of over-age destroyers to the British Navy. In August, 1940, when the German army was poised at the Channel ports, Coffin wrote from his summer home, "I am torn by the desire to do more to aid Britain ere the blow fall, and have been running about to New York, Washington and elsewhere for the William Allen White Committee. It seems madness not to send over the needed destroyers and do everything else to keep Britain going. With her in shape, we can be spared all but a brief militaristic period. If she falls we are in for full militarism for the rest of our lives. Strange how blind the country is!" When a large number of ministers in the United States issued a statement opposing any participation in the war effort, Coffin joined with another group which published a statement on "America's Responsibility in the Present Crisis." In it they said: "What has occurred in Finland, Denmark, Norway and Holland, as well as in Poland and Czechoslovakia, makes the issue transparent: It is the preservation of freedom for life, for worship, for thought and the basic essentials of humane living for tens of millions of citizens in progressive and peace-loving nations. . . . A German victory which would destroy the liberties of free peoples and subordinate all life under a rule of political totalitarianism would endanger every value embodied in western civilization by the Christian faith and by humanistic culture. . . . In the light of these facts, we urge that the United States immediately enlist its moral and material resources in support of the Allied Nations." On September 29, 1940, he took part in a Service of Prayer for Great Britain and All Civilization which was broadcast over the radio, and prayed, "Uphold rulers and people in the assurance that they contend on behalf of the spiritual heritage of Christian freemen, and that in their victory enthralled nations will be loosed from bondage and lovers of righteousness everywhere will rejoice. Forbid that we, their kinsmen in speech and heirs with them of a noble inheritance, should fail to render them all possible aid in this their hour of peril." In December, 1940, he became Chairman of the "Inter-Faith Committee for Aid to the Democracies" under the auspices of the Church Peace Union, which immediately passed a resolution urging that planes and ships, munitions and food be "freely given or lent" to Great Britain. In March, 1941, after a "Ministers' No War Committee" composed of outstanding clergymen such as Albert W. Palmer, Harold A. Bosley, Harry Emerson Fosdick, Ralph W. Sockman and others had issued a statement opposing the enactment of the so-called Lend-Lease Bill on the ground that it made "probable, if not certain, a swift entry into the war," Coffin and Bishop Henry K. Sherrill sent telegrams to a large number of clergymen and laymen of all denominations and secured signatures to a statement to the effect that "The undersigned citizens and ministers of the Christian Church urge the immediate enactment of Bill H.R. 1776 as the most effective assistance which the United States can render at this time to those who are struggling valiantly for the defense of the tradition of democratic liberties of which we are heirs." Churchmen in Britain urged him to come over to bring them a direct personal interpretation of the situation in America and to take counsel with them on matters of common concern, but he felt that such a trip at that time would be neither wise nor possible. He declined to join the "Fight for Freedom Committee" which advocated recognizing that the United States was already at war. He wrote to its Chairman, Bishop Henry W. Hobson, that he believed that this should be left to the authorities in Washington.

In April, 1941, he wrote an article at the request of the editor of *Life and Work*, the magazine of the Church of Scotland, which was published in that paper. Outlining some of the historical reasons for isolationism in America, and stating frankly that American public opinion had been critical of Britain's attitude toward the Spanish Republic and of her failure to support the United States in protesting Japan's course in China, he affirmed his conviction that "while war is an unholy thing, there are situations where it is much the lesser of two evils. To allow ruthless and brutal tyranny to violate justice and to enslave free nations cannot be the will of God." He concluded with a ringing pledge of solidarity, saying, "Your courage and endurance and steadfast faith compel our admiration and our hearts are with you in all that is being inflicted upon you. We are (in the words of Lincoln) highly resolving to stand by you to see that liberty shall not perish from the earth." In July, 1941, he joined with Reinhold Niebuhr and Henry P. Van Dusen in securing from eminent refugees from the conquered European countries a statement opposing a negotiated peace at that time when it was being advocated in some quarters. "To speak of a negotiated peace now," they wrote, "while Hitler holds Europe enthralled and imagines himself within sight of a complete triumph, is to serve his designs and to contribute to his purpose of breaking the resolute opposition which now prevents that victory." At the General Assembly of the

Presbyterian Church in May, 1941, he took the floor and persuaded the Assembly to amend a pronouncement that the United States could best serve the interests of the world and the cause of peace by staying out of the war. Coffin secured the addition of a statement that "it is the duty of the church to draw differences between enslaving dictatorships and those peoples valiantly defending their liberties and spiritual heritage" and that "our country should sustain them to the utmost in their brave struggle." "I claim," he said on the floor of the Assembly, "that in the present state of the world, standing for justice is as essential as standing for peace. All through the Scriptures, it is justice and peace, righteousness and peace, and in that order." Many of the students and faculty at the Seminary did not share Coffin's convictions about the war. He was subjected to severe criticism from them and from many ministers throughout the nation who had taken isolationist or pacifist positions. He was unshaken in his support for full aid to the nations struggling to avert conquest by Hitler.

On no other question did Coffin expose himself 'to such bitter criticism as he did in October, 1940, in connection with his opposition to ex-President Herbert Hoover's proposals for sending food to the civilian population of Poland, Belgium, Holland and Norway. Coffin and those who with him signed a statement opposing Mr. Hoover's plan were accused of being baby-killers, heartless advocates of the starvation of women and children. To all who wrote condemning him, Coffin replied that the statement he had signed had been misunderstood. He was thoroughly in favor of feeding the hungry in Europe if it could be done without aiding the enemy. He believed that Mr. Hoover's proposal was an attempt to arouse American public opinion to bring pressure upon the British government to lift their blockade. As such he thought it inappropriate and unfair on the part of private citizens and likely to arouse hostile feeling toward the British. In September Lord Lothian, the British Ambassador in Washington, had asked Coffin and a few others to dine with him. At that time he had told them that a representative of Mr. Hoover had approached the British government and had been told that the Hoover plan was unacceptable to the British. Coffin and his colleagues also had conferences with representatives of the Norwegians, Belgians and Dutch and found that none of them felt that the Hoover plan was a possible program. It was in the light of these facts, of which the public was largely unaware, that Coffin and those associated with him issued their statement opposing the Hoover proposals. The British position was made unmistakably clear on December 10, 1940, when the British Embassy issued a statement expressing appreciation of Mr. Hoover's services to the people of Belgium and other countries during and after the First World War, but, referring to his current plan, saying "His Majesty's Government has been unable to discover any scheme of distribution by neutral authorities in these countries which, in the light of the Nazi record, could provide guarantees against the strengthening of the German war potential by the importation of food stuffs." Coffin's group continued to meet occasionally with Lord Lothian and urged privately that ways be found to send milk, cod liver oil, and other vitamins for children into the subjugated countries. They offered to raise the money for the purchase and shipment of such supplies. When Lord Lothian died suddenly in 1941, they continued to press the matter with his successor, Lord Halifax. Two years later, in February, 1943, when the United States had been in the war for over a year and conditions had radically changed, the same group published a statement urging public support for a plan to send under proper safeguards dried milk and vitamins for children, nursing and expectant mothers, and for invalids into the occupied European countries, such aid having been now requested by the governments of the countries involved.

On January 4, 1942, four weeks after the United States had entered the war, an address by Coffin to the British people was broadcast overseas by the British Broadcasting Corporation. "A month ago," he began, "the Lord of history abruptly put an end to hesitation and debate in this country by confronting us inescapably with our national duty. . . . To many of us it is an unspeakable relief at long last to be in this conflict at your side. . . . We cannot be too grateful to you who single-handed, after the pitiable collapse of France, endured the full fury of the German and Italian onslaught. . . . Now, thank God, we are with you with our whole will and mind and might." He went on to speak of the "grim difficulty" of the task ahead in the annihilation of the forces of the predatory nations. "It is for us and our allies to loose the bonds of wickedness, to undo the heavy burdens, to let the oppressed go free, and to break every yoke. But this liberation, so eagerly awaited by millions brutally downtrodden and exploited, is only preliminary to the organization of a supra-national commonwealth to protect humanity against the horrors which twice in our lifetime Germany has brought upon the world, and to provide for the peaceful advance of the human race in one fellowship."

This was the aim which he continued to stress with voice and pen and influence throughout the years of the conflict. His son David went off to serve in the Navy in the Pacific area. Students from the Seminary went off into the armed services, into chaplaincies, and into conscientious objectors' camps. He would rise in the morning and turn on his radio, hoping for some news that would augur the return of peace to the world, and for weary months and years had to endure disappointment. In his broadcast to Britain he had quoted to them words which Abraham Lincoln had written in a private letter in the darkest month of America's Civil War: "The purposes of the Almighty are perfect, and must prevail, though we erring mortals may fail accurately to perceive them in advance. We must work earnestly in the best lights He gives us, trusting that so working conduces to the great end He ordains. Surely He intends some great good to follow this mighty convulsion, which no mortal could make, and no mortal could stay." So he saw the task of the English-speaking peoples, "following the best lights He has lit in our historic struggle for liberty, and letting them guide us through the present darkness towards the day of freedom in friendship for all nations." When the war finally ended he was one of the strongest advocates of the organization of the United Nations.

CHAPTER THIRTEEN

EDUCATOR AND MODERATOR

COFFIN was fond of saying that revision of the curriculum was "the favorite indoor sport of the faculty." Two or three times during his Presidency faculty committees were appointed to reconsider the course of study at the Seminary and changes were made in the offerings and requirements. Through all such discussions, however, he remained convinced of the basic principles which he enunciated in his Inaugural Address when he was inducted into the office of President.[1] He believed that Biblical studies, church history and systematic theology were the core of a theological education. Other studies and various forms of practical training were valuable. "But," he said, "let one who is being inducted to a chair of homiletics and pastoral theology, after a good many years both in the pastorate and in this same branch of teaching, bear witness that it is a mistake for students to devote a major part of their time to training in methods. A very modest number of hours in the classroom need be spent in such courses. Let the student apply himself to the basic studies which build up the content of his message; and let him spend several hours weekly under the sympathetic guidance of a skilled pastor leading younger and old folk into the Christian life. That is the theological education which equips ministers who last and remain fruitful their lifelong."

[1] *Alumni Bulletin*, December 1926-January 1927, p. 55.

Coffin's Presidency of Union Seminary coincided with a period of changing theological climate as influences from Continental Europe were increasingly felt in American intellectual circles. Karl Barth and Emil Brunner loomed on the European horizon. In the United States Reinhold Niebuhr rejected the liberalism of which he had been an exponent, and became the center around whom theological controversy was rife. Sören Kierkegaard, the lonely Danish thinker of the early Nineteenth Century, was translated into English and became a sort of patron saint for religious existentialists. A new movement popularly called "Neo-Orthodoxy" claimed adherents in large numbers, although there were wide variations of belief among those to whom the label was generally applied, and few theologians applied the label to themselves. What those most in the public eye had in common was their polemic against liberalism which they interpreted as belief in automatic progress, Utopian expectation of an inevitably rosy future, faith in the goodness of human nature, and the idea of God as immanent in the evolutionary process, hardly distinguishable from humanity's better nature and highest ideals. Union Seminary, always sensitive to new currents of thought, was divided between those who were now called "old-fashioned liberals" and the adherents of Neo-Orthodoxy. Arguments were heated in dormitories, classrooms and at refectory tables. Alumni who had been educated at Union in the heyday of liberalism sometimes felt that they were in a strange land when they returned for reunions. In the midst of this theological ferment, Coffin's liberalism remained basically unchanged. He was usually not attacked by the critics of liberalism, but was identified by them as one, like Dr. Fosdick, who had never succumbed to Utopian illusions but had consistently preached man's need for redemption if a more Christian society were ever to be a reality. In 1935 he published a defense of liberalism, defining liberalism as "that spirit which reveres truth supremely, and craves freedom to ascertain, to discuss, to publish and pursue that which is believed to be true, and seeks fellowship in its discovery."[2] At the same time he welcomed certain emphases in the new theological movements because of their stress upon the transcendent majesty of God. Although he did not specifically give up old beliefs or adopt new ones, a new accent came into his preaching and writing during the Thirties and Forties, which was not unrelated to the contemporary trend in theological thought. This was strikingly apparent in a sermon which gave its title, "God's Turn," to a volume of sermons published in 1934.[3] The initial sentence set the theme: "The outstanding spiritual fact of our day is the shattering of men's self-confidence." "By and large our religion has been the shallow confidence in ourselves of those who were floating comfortably on the flood tide of prosperity." "It is God's turn now." "When so many of our hopes have crashed, and so many of our designs have worked badly or not worked at all; when we realize how impotent we are to control the civilization we prided ourselves on creating, and when that civilization itself is so unsatisfactory that there is no room left for pride; perhaps we shall talk less of ourselves as creators, and begin again to know ourselves creatures." He returned to the same theme in lectures on *Religion Yesterday and Today* which he delivered at New York University in 1939 and at Emory University, in Atlanta, Georgia, in 1940.[4] "The shattering of faith in automatic progress, the realization that there is nothing in nature of itself which can save or help mankind and much that may destroy it, the appalling menace of the tribal gods of deified nation and race and class, is turning the thought of man wistfully to the God who is above and other than the cosmic forces or man-made divinities."[5] Coffin believed that Karl Barth and his disciples pushed the doctrine of the transcendence of God too far.[6] He thought that the modern emphasis upon the divine

[2] "Can Liberalism Survive?" *Religion in Life,* IV, 2 (Spring, 1935), p. 194.
[3] *God's Turn,* Harpers, p. 1.
[4] Cokesbury Press, 1940, p. 39.
[5] *Op. cit.,* pp. 64, 65.
[6] *Op. cit.,* p. 61.

immanence had brought enrichments to religion which should not be discarded. He never took much interest in Kierkegaard. However, there came into his public utterances a more dominant stress upon God's mighty acts which was in harmony with the prevailing theological trend of the era.

His own estimate of the changing emphasis in theology was expressed in lectures which he gave in the Far East in the winter of 1946–1947. He said: "Unquestionably the popular ideas of the last generation—evolution, progress, the immanence of God, the inherent divinity and limitless possibilities of man—became, when used by Christian thinkers, means of obscuring the historic Gospel. Man's religious experience, not God's self-revelation, was the main subject of investigation. The contemporary reaction, stressing decisive crises in history, the unbridgable difference between God and man, the necessity for His redemptive Self-revelation to close the chasm, His—rather than man's—part in their fellowship, is salutary."[7]

Reinhold Niebuhr, one of the most outspoken critics of liberalism in general, was like many others impressed by the consistency of Coffin's witness to the essential elements in the Christian gospel, whichever way the theological wind might be blowing. At the time of Coffin's retirement from the Seminary, Niebuhr wrote: "While Doctor Coffin consistently deprecated his competence as a theologian (just as he disavowed competence as an exegete even while subjecting a given text to the most searching exegetical scrutiny) he presented in his preaching and in his writings a consistent and profound account of the Christian gospel, expounding the great affirmations of our faith without abridgment or concessions to the prejudices of an age. In his memorable book, *The Meaning of the Cross*, he gives as adequate an account as can be found in the homiletical literature of our age of the centrality of the Cross in the faith of the Christian. . . . The gospel which he preached was the gospel of the mercy of God, as

[7] *God Confronts Man in History*, Scribners, 1947, p. 122.

revealed in Christ, overcoming the sin of man and reclaiming the sinner. He was consistently evangelical in his exposition of that gospel. . . . In a day in which the Church was threatened with degeneration into an association of likeminded idealists, he insisted upon its profounder character as a community of grace."[8]

Although no longer responsible for a parish, Coffin continued to be an active churchman throughout the years of his leadership of the Seminary. In his classes he taught his students to be faithful to their responsibilities as members of the ecclesiastical bodies with which they were affiliated. He would refer to one of his predecessors in the Presidency, Dr. Francis Brown, as an example of a great scholar who was not too busy or too remote to be present regularly at the meetings of the Presbytery to which he belonged. Coffin followed this practice himself, and for a man with so many responsibilities had a remarkable record for regularity at Presbytery meetings. He kept himself informed on questions which came before that body, took vigorous part in discussions, and was heard always with respect and generally with agreement. His particular interest was the work of the Committee on Church Extension, under which he had begun his ministry in the Bronx while still a student in the Seminary. He continued to give much time and thought to the planning and building of new churches in growing sections of the city and to the aiding and strengthening of Presbyterian churches in impoverished neighborhoods.

Coffin had been elected a member of the Presbyterian Board of Home Missions in 1905, and had been one of its most useful members. He had given his strong support to Charles Stelzle when he founded Labor Temple, an unconventional but for many years very effective institution on the corner of Fourteenth Street and Second Avenue, where night after night crowds of men were gathered together for open forums on religion, economics, social

[8] From "Theologian and Church Statesman" by Reinhold Niebuhr in *This Ministry*, Scribners, 1945, pp. 123 ff.

problems and whatever interested them. When Labor Temple came under attack from people who thought it not sufficiently evangelical, Coffin was one of its staunchest defenders. He was also spokesman for the Board of Home Missions when Warren Wilson, a highly respected pioneer in rural missions, was similarly criticized and his work temporarily discontinued. Coffin fought his battles before the General Assembly of the Presbyterian Church in the U.S.A., meeting in Atlanta in 1913, and then pulled the opposing factions together into a harmony which disappointed some of his own followers who were ready for a decisive show-down with the fundamentalist leaders who were responsible for the attack on one of the Church's noblest servants. (Some years later the Presbyterian Church named its best known missionary school near Asheville, North Carolina, after Wilson and it is now Warren Wilson College.) In 1923 the Board of Home Missions was combined with several other boards to constitute the Presbyterian Board of National Missions. Each of the dozen boards involved had loyal members and supporters who thought its work the most important feature of the entire program of the denomination. The combination of them all into one new board involved many adjustments of programs and personalities. Some of the personalities were more conspicuous for aggressive leadership than for the gift of applying the oil of tact or humor to friction spots. One who was in close touch with all the board's work in the difficult period of the new adjustments says: "Dr. Coffin was liked, respected and trusted by everyone on the Board and was constantly exerting his influence to keep the ship on even keel. He was a very important factor in developing a growing sense of unity in the Board." Toward the end of the decade of the Thirties, when it looked as though the depression years would at last come to an end, Coffin was chosen Chairman of a Special Committee to make plans for the future work of the board. Members of the committee found what promised to be a tedious, monotonous task turned into a delightful experience by the humor and understanding of the chairman. Coffin sometimes found it difficult to sit patiently through the regular meetings of the board which inevitably involved a considerable amount of routine business and verbose discussion. When important matters were up for decision, he was there. He believed that the primary function of the board was the planting of new churches, and was mildly satirical when he thought the board was holding in reserve funds which ought to be at work in church extension. "The committee has been sitting on the funds for quite a while," he would say. "It is time they hatched something." He was remarkably persuasive with board members of very different theological and geographical background. "As I look back on it now," wrote Dr. Hermann N. Morse, for many years General Secretary of the Board, "I can't recall a single important issue in which his general point of view failed to prevail. . . . It would be difficult to over-estimate his value to the Board." In 1953 the General Assembly elected Coffin Member Emeritus of the Board for life. He was the first member to whom that honorary title had been given.

On May 27, 1943, Coffin was elected Moderator of the General Assembly of the Presbyterian Church in the U.S.A. Thus the highest honor in the gift of his Church and its post of greatest influence came to him. He had not expected that after being so frequently spokesman for the liberals in the Church he would ever be called to this office. Dr. William P. Merrill once recalled that at a General Assembly meeting he and Coffin found themselves about to enter a hotel elevator simultaneously with William Jennings Bryan. There was a bit of good-natured deference to one another as to who should take precedence in entering the elevator. Coffin bowed to Bryan, saying, "Mr. Bryan should precede, for he at least has been a candidate for the Moderatorship. Neither Merrill nor I will ever by any chance have that honor." There was, however, a growing feeling that the Presbyterian Church needed his leadership. In 1941 he was nominated for the Moderatorship but was defeated. The combination of those who feared his liberalism and those with pacifist tendencies who disagreed with his outspoken advocacy of aid to the Allies in the war then raging in Europe was enough to prevent his election. In 1943 the situation had completely changed. In January a letter[9] had appeared in church papers signed by five well-known ministers from the Middle West asserting that the year ahead would be one of unparalleled opportunities and demands for American Presbyterianism, and urging the election of Coffin as Moderator. When the Assembly met in Detroit, Coffin was nominated by Dr. George A. Buttrick, his successor in the pulpit of the Madison Avenue Church, who said, "Some of us have tried to succeed him at Madison Avenue but no one really succeeds him." The nomination was seconded by Dr. Harrison Ray Anderson, minister of the Fourth Presbyterian Church of Chicago, and Coffin was overwhelmingly elected. In accepting the election Coffin announced that the first task before the Church was to seek unity with the Southern Presbyterian Church, officially known as the "Presbyterian Church in the United States," separated from the Northern Church since before the Civil War. "Every word which we utter here must be seriously considered," he said. "Anything trivial or petty would be quite incongruous to the hour. The Christian Church must at this time have a clear word for a world which is torn in pieces."

The Moderator presides over the General Assembly at which he is elected, which Coffin did brilliantly. The business of the Assembly was transacted with despatch. Decisions as to parliamentary procedure were made with a fairness which left everyone satisfied. There was a light touch combined with deep earnestness in the presiding officer which made long business sessions both interesting and profitable. Between the adjournment of the Assembly over which he presides and the opening sermon which he preaches at the next Assembly a year later, the Moderator is

[9] Letter of J. Harry Cotton, George A. Frantz, P. Park Johnson, Thomas R. Niven, and Harrison Ray Anderson, January 13, 1943.

expected to devote a considerable amount of his time to visiting the churches in various parts of the country, bringing to them the message of the Assembly and stimulating them in their work. When Coffin returned to New York from Detroit his first task was to make arrangements for the carrying on of his work at the Seminary during the long absences which the Moderatorship would entail. One of his first letters after his return was from the veteran Stated Clerk-Emeritus, Dr. Lewis S. Mudge, who wrote: "No Moderator, within my memory, has made a finer beginning for his year of service than have you." Referring to "the miracle of reconciliation" which had taken place, he added: "It prophesies a glorious future for our church—now united as it has not been within my memory of almost fifty years."

In late November Coffin crossed the Atlantic to make a fraternal visit to the churches in Great Britain. A Moderator of the Church of Scotland, Dr. James Hutchison Cockburn, had recently visited the American Presbyterian churches during his term of office and on the invitation of the Church of Scotland and of the British Council of Churches, Coffin returned the visit. Transatlantic travel in war-time was uncomfortable and of course hazardous. Coffin arrived in Edinburgh quite exhausted from the voyage on which he had little sleep or opportunity to rest. He went to rest up at the home of the John Baillies. Baillie had been elected Moderator of the Church of Scotland, and the two friends had the common experience of moderators to add to their other mutual interests. His old friends, Principal Alexander Martin, now eighty-seven years of age, and Dr. David Cairns, eighty-two, were overjoyed to see him again, and he them. Food was scarce because of war conditions, and he came to the homes of his friends bearing gifts of lump sugar, bottles of lemon extract, noodle soup packets, etc., as well as stockings for the ladies. Soon he was caught up in the heavy schedule which had been arranged for him, preaching in St. Giles' Cathedral in Edinburgh, in the Glasgow Cathedral and in the Cathedral at Dunblane (in Scotland the pre-Reformation cathedrals are now Presbyterian Church of Scotland centers) and in other churches, and addressing the students of New College and the Presbytery in Edinburgh. On Christmas Eve he spoke over the radio at the request of the British Broadcasting Corporation. In London he preached in the Anglican church of St. Martin's-in-the-Fields on Trafalgar Square and at a service of St. Columba's Church, a Church of Scotland congregation whose building on Pont Street had been destroyed by bombs. He was invited by the Queen to have tea at Buckingham Palace, an engagement which had to be cancelled because of the Queen's illness. He had a conference at Lambeth Palace with Dr. William Temple, Archbishop of Canterbury, and discussed Christian unity with him. Every spare moment was taken up by conferences and receptions with groups of ministers and Christian lay leaders. Everywhere he interpreted the task of the churches in the United States as an obligation to "sensitize and stimulate and stretch the conscience of America," especially with regard to the problems of isolationism, economic justice and racial tensions. Everywhere he was cordially received and met with enthusiastic response. After preaching in St. Giles' Cathedral, he wrote home: "I wish you might have been present yesterday. After the sermon and offering, the minister stood at the Communion Table and said, 'God save the President and people of the United States of America' and while everyone stood the 'Star Spangled Banner' was sung, then followed 'God Save the King.' They took me about with a mace-bearer and all the formalities used for the Moderator here." Coffin returned to the United States deeply moved by what he had seen. "Beneath surface indications of weariness and of strain one is impressed with the massive qualities of the British soul," he said. "Courage, conscientiousness, determination to discover and do that which is right and faith that right must eventually triumph in God's world— these superb virtues abound in the British character. Britons went trustfully through the crucial months when their land stood alone against the foes of Western civilization. That experience has fortified their faith, deepened their characters and unified the nation. This confidence in Providence, one visitor thinks, is the underlying faith by which contemporary Britons, like their forefathers through many generations, live and bravely carry on."

On his return to New York a dinner was given in Coffin's honor by a large number of citizens of the city, eager to welcome him safely home and to bear witness to their respect and affection for him. The ball-room of the Hotel Roosevelt was crowded. The list of one hundred and forty-four sponsors read like a directory of the distinguished in all walks of life—clergymen of all denominations, bishops and rabbis, college and university presidents, lawyers and judges, physicians, bankers, leaders in industry and commerce. Dr. John Sutherland Bonnell, minister of the Fifth Avenue Presbyterian Church presided. The Right Reverend Henry St. George Tucker, Presiding Bishop of the Protestant Episcopal Church and President of the Federal Council of Churches, spoke for the Churches. Dr. James Rowland Angell, President emeritus of Yale University, voiced the gratitude of all for Coffin's leadership of the Churches in so critical a period, at the same time referring humorously to the fact that on an impending Moderatorial tour Coffin was about to eat his way across the country at the expense of the Presbyterians, keeping one eye on the Episcopalians as he went. Coffin responded with warm thanks to his many friends, and then after a brief description of conditions in Britain devoted himself to what was most on his heart—the spiritual problems which the nation would face upon the conclusion of the war.

A few days later, on January 20, 1944, Coffin and his wife left New York for the great swing around the circle, visiting Presbyterian churches in some forty cities, beginning in Cincinnati, moving down into Texas and out to the West Coast, then back through the Northwest and finishing up in Detroit. It was a strenuous expedition, with almost every minute crowded with meetings and conferences, offering few opportunities for rest, but one which he and the churches visited enjoyed hugely. He was impressed by the vitality of the churches and by the fine character of the ministers leading them, but often disturbed by the ugliness of their houses of worship and more than disturbed by the banal church music to which too often he had to listen. Interested as he was in the possibility of organic union between the Presbyterian and Protestant Episcopal Churches he was delighted by the large number of Episcopal clergymen and lay people who came to luncheons given in his honor, and by the frequency with which Episcopal bishops were among those gathered in Presbyterian churches to welcome him. In the Northwest, where fundamentalism had been strong during the days of controversy, he was given a courteous but guarded welcome which turned into enthusiastic applause when he finished speaking on the challenge of the times to the Church. Wherever he went he laid on the consciences of his hearers their responsibility for creating better race relations, for economic justice to returning soldiers when the war should end, for Christian unity, and for international arrangements to guarantee peace after the conflict. The emphasis upon social righteousness which had become somewhat muted under the pressure of administrative responsibilities again became the dominant note of his message. At the University of California, where President Robert Gordon Sproul introduced him to an audience of six thousand students, Coffin told them that "we are today fighting two wars—the external war against our foes, and the internal war against injustices and prejudices in the minds of both our foes and some amongst us."

Often there were ministers' conferences in the morning or afternoon. Sometimes he would be driven miles to address the students in some near-by college in between church gatherings. Frequently Mrs. Coffin was asked to speak at luncheons and women's meetings which she did charmingly and effectively, taking "The Ecumenical Church" as her topic. (In one city the

local newspaper reported that she had spoken on "The Eco-
nomical Church.") In Oakland, California, they spent a Sunday
evening in the First Presbyterian Church where Mrs. Coffin's
grandfather, Dr. James Eells, had been pastor from 1873 to 1879.
When the last sermon was preached in Detroit on March 5, they
were weary but pleased with the enthusiasm with which they had
been everywhere received and proud of the work which they
found the Presbyterian churches doing.

The climax of Coffin's Moderatorship came in May, 1944, when
the General Assembly met again, this time in the Fourth Presbyterian Church in Chicago. As the retiring Moderator he presided over the election of his successor, and then preached the
opening sermon,[10] in which he stressed again the themes which
had been the burden of his message to the churches throughout
the year—the Church's responsibility for a ministry of reconciliation in international, inter-racial, economic, intra-Church and
inter-Church affairs. A congregation of four hundred and fifty
commissioners and three thousand others heard him reverently.
As an ex-Moderator he was for the next two years a member of
the General Council of the Church to which he contributed his
wisdom and experience.

Although carrying such heavy responsiblities in the Seminary
and the Church, Coffin continued to be active in the affairs of
three educational institutions. He was a President of the Board
of Trustees of Atlanta University, an institution for the higher
education of Negroes, of which his friend, Edward T. Ware, was
the president. Although the meetings of the Board were for his
convenience held in New York City he visited Atlanta when he
could, kept in close touch with its affairs, and made Negro education one of his major concerns. For thirty years he was President
of the Board of Trustees of The Masters School at Dobbs Ferry,
New York. Two distant cousins of his father, Miss Eliza B.

[10] "The Kingdom of God Presses In" in *Religion and Life,* Vol. XIII, p. 516
(Autumn, 1944).

Masters and Miss Sarah Masters, had founded a school for girls in 1877. When it was decided in 1916 to incorporate the school and transfer the ownership to a Board of Trustees, Coffin became president of the Board and continued in that capacity until 1946. After his death a Henry Sloane Coffin Chair in the school's Bible Department was established in his memory.

Next to the Church and the Seminary, however, it was Yale University that was dearest to his heart. Throughout the entire duration of his Presidency at Union he journeyed to New Haven for monthly Corporation meetings, to say nothing of the frequent meetings of special committees, personal interviews, telephone calls and correspondence which his unique place in the Yale family entailed. His frequent appearance as a preacher in Battell Chapel had made him known personally to members of the faculty and of the student body so that the lines of communication were open between him and the varied phases of university life. He brought to the Corporation meetings an intimate knowledge of the people and the problems behind the formal decisions which the governing body was called on to make which made him invaluable. In discussions about the Corporation table he was forthright and decisive, quick to formulate policies and to defend them, persuasive in presenting his point of view, not less so because of his facility in relieving movements of tension with a penetrating witticism or a humorous thrust at the adherents of opposing views. Yet on two major matters on which he felt deeply he was unable to carry the Corporation with him. In 1926 Yale discontinued the requirement of compulsory attendance at daily and Sunday Chapel. Coffin had for years been foremost in the defense of the requirement. He was appointed Chairman of a special committee of Corporation members, faculty and students to study the matter and make recommendations when the undergraduate revolt against the old tradition became vocal and almost universal. He was unable to stem the tide running heavily against compulsion in matters having to do with religious worship, and both faculty and Corporation voted to abolish required attendance. Coffin never ceased to regret the action. He was equally unsuccessful in efforts to preserve the requirement of Latin for the Bachelor of Arts degree. Certain local conditions resulting from the reorganization of departments brought the question to the fore in 1923. The Permanent Officers of Yale College voted to abolish the requirement. When it came to the Corporation, William Howard Taft roared, "Over my dead body!" and Coffin, a convinced classicist, strongly supported the ex-President. The matter was dropped for the time being. Walking with Angell over the open fields at Hurricane Lodge in the Adirondacks in the summer, Coffin argued for the essential place of the classics as "mind-filling subjects." Angell argued that the field of education had become so broad that no one subject could any longer be regarded as essential for everyone. The proposal came up again in 1931 as the result of a faculty vote to do away with the requirement. Coffin was put on a committee of the Corporation to recommend what action should be taken on the faculty's request. Again he fought for the classics but to no avail. Yale joined the great number of American universities where neither Latin nor Greek is required for graduation.

A glance at the long list of committees on which he served indicates how consistently his counsel was sought when important decisions had to be made. Among other responsibilities placed on his shoulders he served as Chairman of the Educational Policy Committee, as Chairman of the Honorary Degrees Committee, as a member of a Committee on Student Affairs, and on several committees having to do with the religious life of the University and with the teaching of religion. When President Angell was about to retire, Coffin was made Chairman of a Corporation Committee to canvass the field and to recommend a choice of a successor. He early concluded that Charles Seymour was the right man and the Corporation agreed. Two years after his retirement from the Corporation he was elected President of the Yale-in-

China Association, through which Yale graduates and under-graduates were still aiding higher education in China.

One other great service Coffin rendered to Yale several years after his retirement from the Corporation. In 1951 during the first year of A. Whitney Griswold's Presidency of the University a furore was created by the appearance of a book, *God and Man at Yale* by William F. Buckley, Jr., which charged that students at Yale were being indoctrinated with radical views and with irreligion. The writer appealed to alumni to cease making contributions to the University until the faculty had been purged of undesirable elements. A flood of letters from puzzled or irate graduates poured in upon the young President asking about the truth of Buckley's charges, or in some cases protesting on the assumption that they must be true. Griswold turned to Coffin as the University's elder statesman and asked him to be chairman of a committee "to survey the intellectual and spiritual welfare of the university, its students and faculty." Coffin immediately agreed to serve. A committee was formed containing among others Irving S. Olds, Chairman of the Board of the United States Steel Corporation; George L. Harrison, Chairman of the Board of the New York Life Insurance Company; Judge Thomas W. Swan, of the United States Circuit Court of Appeals, and other distin-guished Yale graduates. They worked together for four months. They found no basis for the charges which had been made. "The administration of the university . . . knows of no member of the faculty who is trying to undermine or destroy our society, or our democratic form of government, or to indoctrinate students at Yale with subversive theories. Our inquiries confirm the accu-racy of the judgment of the administration, and of the University Council," they said. "The committee believes that religious life at Yale is deeper and richer than it has been in many years and stronger than in most places outside the university. The charge that Yale is encouraging irreligion or atheism is without founda-tion. That religious life at Yale may become even stronger is the hope of the Corporation, the university officers and this committee." The report included a ringing defense of academic freedom and of faith in Yale's purpose to supply light and truth to an age needing religion to give wholeness of outlook and direction to life. So great was public confidence in the committee that the report was trusted. The alumni who had been urged to stop their gifts to the University gave more than ever before, and for the first time in the history of any university, the Yale annual giving program realized more than one million dollars that year.

The problems of academic freedom at Yale with which Coffin's committee dealt were familiar problems to him. He had been obliged to deal with them frequently as President of Union Seminary. Several members of the Union faculty were frequently signing papers or making speeches on controversial questions which would appear in the public press and would arouse the indignation of some conservative citizens. Coffin's telephone would begin to ring and his mail would be full of angry letters asking why he did not dismiss the professors. Through it all he stood staunchly by the right of faculty members to express views with which he did not agree, much as he sometimes wished that they would exercise more restraint in doing so. On Commencement Day in 1940, when there had been an unusual number of protests about the activities of one particular professor, Coffin made a statement on the subject to the alumni. In it he said: "Obviously there are requirements which the professors of a theological seminary like this must meet. They must be loyal to the basic convictions of the Christian faith and loyal ministers or members of the Christian Church or they could not fittingly train its leaders. They must be competent scholars in the field in which they are appointed to teach and they must be men of Christian character. If charges are brought against any of us that we do not meet these requirements, it would be the duty of the Board of Directors to take them up. But the Seminary has never assumed responsibility for the political or economic or other social views of its professors. They are at liberty to join whatever organizations they wish. One hopes that men in responsible positions will act with Christian discretion but there will be inevitable differences of opinion as to what is and what is not Christian discretion. In a day when freedom in so many lands is in jeopardy, it must certainly be maintained in this country, above all in an institution with so honorable a record of liberty as this Seminary." A faculty which differed among themselves on many matters were united in loyalty to their President, knowing they could count on him to stand squarely behind their liberty to differ in private and in public.

Coffin unconsciously described himself as a teacher in some remarks which he made in a Convocation Address at a Summer Session of Columbia University in July, 1929. "Enthusiasm is not good form at the moment among our self-styled intelligentsia," he said. "But those of us who are, or who intend to be, teachers cannot succeed without it. We must not only have delight in our subject, but a contagious delight. Whether it be sociology or domestic science or dentistry or metaphysics, we must be infectiously devoted to it.

> 'What we have loved
> Others will love, and we will teach them how.' "

An even deeper insight into his own mind was revealed in the same address in his definition of education: "To be voraciously inquisitive, so curious that we demand accurate information on any subject we treat, that we savor what we discover with zest, and that we press boldly on to find out the meaning of the whole and our consequent duty to mankind and to God Whom we discern over all, however we name Him—that is to be educated and to be on the way to yet further education."

CHAPTER FOURTEEN

ECUMENICAL CHURCHMAN

THROUGHOUT his career Coffin was a convinced advocate of Christian unity. Not only did he advocate the uniting of the Churches but he labored heroically to bring it about. It was not merely a unity of spirit which he felt was desirable. He believed that institutional unity was God's will for his Church.[1] He did not base his conviction primarily upon the wastefulness of denominationalism, although he felt that keenly. He believed that while there was variety of organization and forms of worship and even of doctrine in the New Testament Church, it was essentially one body of Christ, bearing a united witness to him, and that competitive denominationalism was a denial of Christ's Lordship over all. "To me the continued maintenance of our denominations in their separatedness is a sin against Christ, a denial of our obedience to him," he wrote in 1950. "Everything else one may allege against it—its wastefulness of men and financial resources, its impoverishment of the sundered churches who hold back from adopting helpful and enriching modes of worship or methods of work because they are 'Methodist' or 'Episcopalian' or whatnot else, its erection of barriers between fellow-Christians and stimulation of them to competitive efforts for the growth of their par-

---

[1] "Are Denominations Justified?" by Henry Sloane Coffin, in *Presbyterian Life*, January, 1950, p. 19.

ticular congregation—all these are subordinate to this appalling disloyalty to him whom we acknowledge 'Head over all things to the Church, which is his Body.'" "In our country today I am persuaded that denominationalism among Protestants should be outgrown and abolished. It prevents our giving the world a cogent, because wanted, witness to Christ. It hinders our worshipping at one communion table as followers of one Lord. It frustrates our attempts to devise a unified strategy to win our land and all lands to the obedience of Christ. Above all it is, unless one is to scrap the plain teaching of the New Testament, a flat denial of the will of Christ for his people. No Protestant Christian need give up anything of worth in his particular denominational tradition; all can be conserved and combined in a united Church which fulfils Christ's wish for 'one flock, one Shepherd' (John 10:16)."[2]

All of Coffin's experience had combined to foster this passionate devotion to the cause of Christian unity. From his Scottish forbears he had inherited a loyalty to the Presbyterian tradition which never became diluted in his ecumenical interests. He believed that each of the denominations had made distinctive contributions, and was interested in the possibility of an inclusive organization which might embrace them all without sacrificing any part of their distinctive inheritances or impairing their freedom in Christ. "No one," he said, "is eager for some lowest common denominator upon which all can agree, but for some comprehensive arrangement which shall afford each liberty to believe his utmost, to worship at his fullest, and to work to the peak of his capacity." In his student days he had been active in the inter-denominational church and Christian Association at Yale. He had studied with and taught prospective ministers of all denominations at Union Seminary. His work on the Church Extension Committee of New York Presbytery and on the Presbyterian Board of National Missions had convinced him of the in-

[2] *Op. cit.*

adequacy of the denominational approach to urban problems. In China, Japan, Korea, the Philippines, and the Near East he had seen at first hand how the Christian Church was handicapped by its divisions in confronting the non-Christian world. As a young minister at the Edinburgh Conference in 1910 he had been thrilled by the prospect of growing unity in the missionary work of the churches. The formation of the United Church of Canada in 1925, made up out of what had been the Congregational, Methodist and Presbyterian Churches, brought about, he believed, by the necessities of the missionary task of the churches as they confronted newly settled areas, seemed to him a harbinger of what ought to happen on a much larger scale. There were many influences which had conspired to make him a convinced advocate of a united Church.

It was therefore a great satisfaction to him when in 1929 he was appointed to represent the Presbyterian Church in the U.S.A. at the ceremonies in Edinburgh uniting the Church of Scotland and the United Free Church of Scotland, bringing to an end a division which, it was said, "had embittered and impoverished the religious life of Scotland." In 1909 conversations looking toward reunion had been begun between the Church of Scotland and the United Free Church. It took twenty years to bring them to fruition, but by 1929 the committees had labored, the reports had been debated, revised and accepted. A Plan of Union had been agreed upon which maintained the position of the Church of Scotland as the Established Church, at the same time "maintaining the liberty of judgment and action heretofore recognised in either of the Churches united."[3] This satisfied all but a very small minority in the United Free Church, and the churches were now ready for the Act of Union. In company with Dr. John H. Finley, editor of the *New York Times*, his fellow-delegate, Coffin sailed for Scotland with a high heart. To those who had all their lives been familiar with the stories of the sacrifices made by those

[3] *The Uniting Act*, Paragraph III, Section 5, *London Times*, 1927.

who "went out" in the Disruption, it seemed like "something of a miracle," as it was frequently described.

On the first of October Coffin and Finley were present at the final meeting of the Assembly of the United Free Church. Coffin's former teacher and long-time friend, Principal Alexander Martin of New College, was in the Chair as Moderator, apparelled in lace stock and cuffs, silk knee-breeches and silver buckled shoes, as Scottish Moderators traditionally are. That night a terrific storm of wind and rain beat upon Edinburgh, but the next morning it cleared long enough for the Assemblies of both Churches to march in procession, 1800 strong, to St. Giles' Cathedral for a Service of Thanksgiving. Coffin met with the United Free Church delegates in the Assembly Hall on The Mound. They marched two abreast from the Hall into Bank Street and up to the High Street where they met the double line of Commissioners of the Church of Scotland Assembly. Four abreast they marched down High Street to St. Giles'. As the two processions met and became one, a little group in the great crowd that lined the street began to sing the metrical version of Psalm 133:

> "Behold, how good a thing it is,
> and how becoming well,
> Together such as brethren
> in unity to dwell!"

The marching ministers took up the psalm, and with its solemn cadences filling the air entered the Cathedral to give thanks to God.

The Act of Union took place in the afternoon in the huge Industrial Hall on Annandale Street, off Leith Walk, which had been transformed into a temporary Assembly Hall capable of seating 1200 people. Coffin sat on the platform with the civic representatives of Edinburgh, Glasgow and other cities in full regalia, the Lords of Session, the Archbishops of Canterbury and Wales, the Primus of the Scottish Episcopal Church and other dignitaries. Both Moderators signed the Act of Union with the actual quill pen which had been used in the signing of the Deed of Separation eighty-six years before. The throng which filled the hall rose and from full hearts sang Psalm 72:18:

> *"Now blessed be the Lord our God,*
> *the God of Israel,*
> *For he alone doth wondrous things*
> *in glory that excel."*

The Duke of York, as Lord High Commissioner representing the King, George V, brought the royal greetings and expressions of regret that illness had prevented His Majesty from carrying out his intention of visiting the Assembly in person. "We have indeed come a long way since the days of King James the Sixth, whose intrusions called forth the just indignation of Andrew Melville," wrote the correspondent for *The Record of the Church of Scotland.*

Coffin addressed the Assembly at its closing session on the evening of October 3. His topic was "The Church in the World of Today." *The Record of the Church of Scotland* reported the occasion as follows: "When the Assembly resumed in the evening, the scene was almost as brilliant and impressive as it had been at the first session. The Hall was completely filled, and the platform was occupied by a large and distinguished company. Very appropriate was the paraphrase with which the proceedings opened:

> *'How glorious Sion's courts appear,*
> *The City of our God!*
> *His throne He hath established here,*
> *Here fixed His loved abode.'*

With business-like promptitude the Moderator, who had changed into his LL.D. gown, introduced the first speaker, Dr. Henry Sloane Coffin, President of the Union Theological Seminary, New York, as one whose name was known in all the churches, and who had received part of his training at New College. Dr. Coffin was dressed as a layman; his clear-cut features were pale; and he spoke with only a slight American accent. Once more the Assembly was given a picture of a new and strange world. With deadly earnestness he described the passing of the old ideas about God and the universe, and the growing tendency to believe that religion does not give a rational interpretation of existence. The Christendom which once was, he declared, is now gone for worse or for better. Against this dark background was sketched a suggestion of wistful, longing humanity, seeking to find certainty and live a satisfied life. In this attitude of soul lay the hope of the Church, which would have to appeal to it by being a worshipping Church, a teaching Church, setting forth clearly and persuasively the Christian message—a witnessing Church, and a Church whose fellowship bound the whole of humanity in one.

"The gathering had been listening too intently to interrupt, but when the speaker concluded it broke out into a storm of applause. 'I was about to convey your thanks to Dr. Coffin,' remarked the Moderator, smiling, 'but you have anticipated me.'"

Coffin returned to New York, deeply moved by the spirit of unity which he had found at high tide in Scotland, only to become involved within a month in an inter-church difficulty which resulted in one of the most unpleasant experiences of his life. The Christian Unity League, an unofficial organization made up mostly of clergymen of various denominations who were working for a united Church, were to hold their annual conference in St. George's Protestant Episcopal Church on Stuyvesant Square from November 13 to 15. It was proposed to conclude the conference with a communion service and to invite Coffin to officiate. Dr. Karl Reiland, the rector of St. George's Church, who was active in the affairs of the League, extended the invitation to Coffin. Coffin demurred. He inquired as to the legality of such a service from the standpoint of Episcopal canon law and concerning the attitude of the officers of St. George's Church toward it. Reiland assured him that the matter had been thoroughly discussed, and that it was the earnest desire of his vestry that Coffin should accept the invitation. The officers, one of them a former Attorney General of the United States, had gone into the legal aspects of the proposal and were thoroughly convinced that St. George's Church could with perfect legality lend its edifice to the Christian Unity League for a communion service at which the officiating minister would be one who had not been episcopally ordained. With this assurance, Coffin accepted. He was therefore taken aback when on November 12 he received a message from Dr. Reiland stating that Bishop William T. Manning of the Diocese of New York had prohibited the communion service in St. George's Church as planned. Coffin promptly offered the Chapel of Union Theological Seminary for the service. It was held there on the evening of November 15, with Coffin officiating, assisted by Dr. Reiland and Dr. Robert Norwood, rector of St. Bartholomew's Episcopal Church.

Coffin was not a member of the Christian Unity League and thought the approach of its President, Dr. Peter Ainslie, of Baltimore, a rather naïve attempt to by-pass the basic problems involved in achieving a unity of the Churches. Still, on the assurance of the officers of St. George's Church that the way was clear, he had accepted the invitation believing that such a communion service would be a step forward toward the goal which all desired. He was surprised to find himself caught in the middle between two groups in the Episcopal Church who held quite different views on matters of church polity. A letter had appeared on October 19 in *The Churchman,* an Episcopal weekly paper, signed by a vestryman of St. George's, arguing that the parish authorities of an Episcopal Church had an undoubted right to lend their church building "for sacred purposes" and pointing out that in December a service had been held in the Cathedral of St. John the Divine in which clergy of the Russian Orthodox Church had officiated. This was taken up and discussed in headlined articles in the secular press when the plans for the service in St. George's were announced and Coffin was embarrassed to find himself the center of controversy in a denomination to which he did not belong. The Anglo-Catholics pointed out that the Russian Orthodox Church was in fellowship with the Episcopal Church since its priests were episcopally ordained, which was not true of Presbyterian and other Non-Conformist clergymen. Critics of Bishop Manning's action charged him with overlooking serious violations of the laws of their Church with regard to the reservation of the sacraments on the part of the Anglo-Catholics. Bishop Manning gave to the press his letter to the officers of St. George's in which he based his decision upon the advice given him by Mr. George Zabriskie, the Chancellor of the Diocese of New York. To Coffin who was not personally involved in any of the issues which had been raised, it was all most distressing. But he was a proud Presbyterian. Personal slights he could brush aside with a laugh, but to have been put in a position where he seemed to have exposed his Church to disrespect wounded him deeply. He said so frankly in his letter replying to Dr. Reiland and since the matter was already the subject of public discussion, he too gave his letter to the press. After inviting the Conference to hold its communion service in the Union Seminary Chapel, he added: "May I say that, of course, I should not have accepted the invitation of the conference had I not been assured by you that you and your vestry had thoroughly thought through your ecclesiastical right to offer the use of St. George's Church to the conference for this service and had you not said that it was your and their wish that I should officiate.

"The ministry of the church in which I serve has as unbroken a tradition, reaching back to the earliest age, as the ministry of any church in Christendom—if one cares to boast of these carnal things. I would not willingly expose this ministry to such disparagement as appears to be put upon it by Bishop Manning." Thirteen Episcopal clergymen attending the conference, only two of

whom were members of the Diocese of New York, issued a statement to the press taking issue with the Bishop's action, terming
it "a usurpation of authority under the guise of interpreting the
canon."

In 1937 Coffin was one of the leaders in the Conference called
by the Universal Christian Council for Life and Work and held
at Oxford, England, from July 12 to 26. Temperamentally he was
not addicted to conferences. As a rule he was too impatient to
get things done to sit through day after day of speeches and discussions which to his quick mind sometimes seemed to wander
needlessly about before arriving at conclusions. He recognized
the strategic importance of this gathering, however, an intuition
which was vindicated when the World Council of Churches
emerged from its deliberations and those of the Conference on
Faith and Order which immediately followed it at Edinburgh.
When he was asked to be Chairman of the Oxford Conference's
Section on Church, Community and State in Relation to Education, he accepted. At Oxford he found himself one of four hundred
and twenty-five delegates from forty different countries representing the principal non-Roman Churches of the world. The streets
and halls of Oxford were made picturesque by the presence of dignitaries of the Eastern Orthodox Churches in their flowing robes
and towering head-gear. A cosmopolitan flavor was added by the
delegates from the younger churches in Japan, China, India,
Africa and South America. There was a tenseness in the atmosphere occasioned by the rising power in the world of two totalitarian, anti-Christian systems—Communism and Nazism.
Delegates had been appointed by the German Evangelical Church
but had been forbidden to come. In the light of what was known
about the training of children and youth in regions ruled by Stalin
and Hitler, discussions of "Christian Education in a non-Christian
Environment" were far from being academic. Before leaving New
York Coffin had written the pre-conference report for his section.
At Oxford he presided over its daily meetings (with such courtesy

toward the European and Asian delegates that some of the Americans thought they found it difficult to do the much speaking to which they were accustomed) but he also labored far into the nights with the drafting committee which prepared the Report which the conference as a whole received and "commended to the serious and favorable consideration of the churches." While the Report was a composite product, Coffin's hand is visible behind some of the simple statements which, under the circumstances of the time, were actually calls for heroic faith. "For any education worthy of the name truth is supreme, and there must be freedom to seek and to teach it." (This freedom was denied in totalitarian countries.) "In all cases we should claim for the church and for all Christian parents the right to instruct their children in what they believe to be the truth." (In Germany and Italy this right was restricted.) "The Christian may and should give a respect to past or present political leaders, but he must withhold worship." (Emperor worship was a burning issue for Japanese Christians.) "The church must beware of a syncretism which loses the distinctive significance of her message, while at the same time she must welcome everything in the background of each nation which is close to the mind of Christ." "The church must regard excellence as in accordance with the mind of Christ. She must not accept a tinge of added piety as an excuse for inefficiency. . . . She must see that the education which she offers is of the best." "Where the church is allowed to retain her institutions of learning, these should be conserved even if opportunities for Christian influence are restricted. She must think not in decades but in generations." "The church's largest contribution to education, like her supreme ministry to human life, is her gospel, with its interpretation of existence and its inspiration to live worthily." "In considering her task we discover that frequently an impediment more serious than any restriction from without is the disunion of the church's own forces." Coffin returned from Oxford an enthusiastic supporter of the ecumenical movement. He left further attendance at ecumenical conferences, however, to his younger colleagues.

In 1940 Coffin was made a member of the Department of Church Cooperation and Union of the Presbyterian Church in the U.S.A. There were two important matters before the Department at the time. One was the proposal for reunion with the Presbyterian Church in the United States, commonly referred to as the Southern Presbyterian Church. This had been under discussion ever since the division between the two branches of the Presbyterian Church took place before the Civil War. Coffin felt keenly the urgency of this reconciliation within the Presbyterian family. The major responsibility assigned him, however, was in connection with another proposal which had been brought forward. In 1937 the General Convention of the Protestant Episcopal Church had taken the initiative in a Declaration of Purpose looking toward union with the Presbyterian Church. There were many Episcopal clergymen who had been students in Coffin's classroom at Union Seminary. He had many other friends in the Episcopal Church and was highly regarded by a large number who did not know him personally. He was obviously the man to take the lead on the Presbyterian committee appointed to negotiate with the Episcopalians.

As the conversations developed he became very hopeful about the results which he believed would ensue. In the summer of 1941 he wrote to a friend: "You will be glad to know that we had an astonishingly helpful meeting of our Department of Cooperation and Union with the Episcopal Commission at Princeton last week. We agreed with utter unanimity on a plan for Joint Ordination of future ministers, and the plan is being sent down with our endorsement to the Dioceses and Presbyteries in the hope of favorable consideration and with the request for comments. . . . Most bold and startling was their offering us a sketchy blueprint for the constitution of the reunited church. They give us bishops and we give them elders. We have the four councils—

vestry, presbytery, synod and Assembly. They plead for Confirmation. . . . It is still too tentative and vague for public discussion. We shall have a joint committee at work on it for a year, and then perhaps it will be in shape for general study."

During the next two years a set of "Basic Principles" was drawn up which was satisfactory to the committees of the two churches.[4] It began by recognizing the need for diversity of organization and worship in any organic unity which might be acceptable, and also the need for more or less gradual growth into a more perfect union. "The union of the Episcopate and the Presbytery, which in the two traditions have respectively represented the church universal," said the document, "assures an administrative direction and leadership under which, without sacrifice of inherited principle the members of the two Churches may work and worship together and grow into one fellowship."[5] It recognized that the life, ministry, ordinances and Sacraments of the Holy Catholic Church would be transmitted to the United Church through both the Episcopate and the Presbytery. It looked forward to the ordaining of presbyters or priests "by the Bishop and the Presbyters of the presbytery of jurisdiction, who shall join in the laying on of hands."[6]

Soon, however, difficulties began to appear on the horizon. Certain Episcopal bishops, not on the negotiating committee, made public statements in opposition to what was proposed. Certain Presbyterian leaders were so disturbed by these statements that when the General Assembly met in 1943 two requests for the termination of the negotiations were presented to it. Bishop Frank W. Creighton, of Michigan, was appointed to address the Presbyterian General Assembly, and he did so with such fine spirit and such obvious dedication to the cause of Christian unity that

[4] *Basic Principles Proposed for the Union of the Presbyterian Church in the United States of America and the Protestant Episcopal Church in the U.S.A.*, paragraph 1.
[5] *Op. cit.*, section III, paragraph 6.
[6] *Op. cit.*, section IV, paragraph 1.

those who were calling upon the Presbyterian Church to break off negotiations voluntarily withdrew their requests. This was the Assembly over which Coffin presided as Moderator. He wrote to Bishop Creighton, "I am more grateful to you than I can say. Men like you, in the language of Richard Baxter, 'sweeten churches.'"

When the General Convention of the Protestant Episcopal Church met in Cleveland the following October, Coffin was invited to address a Joint Session of the House of Bishops and the House of Deputies. He stirred the Convention in what a seasoned newspaper correspondent described as "the most powerful address he had ever heard in any church assembly." Bishop Henry K. Sherrill, warm friend and a strong supporter of the union, wrote to Coffin, "Your address at Cleveland was *perfect*, made a deep impression, and furthered the cause *immeasurably.* In fact I heard no word but of gratitude and praise. I almost burst with pride!" In his remarks Coffin spoke with complete frankness. After expressing appreciation of the action of the Episcopal Church in initiating the negotiations, he said bluntly that there had been misgivings among the Presbyterians as to whether or not the Episcopalians really meant what they said in their Declaration of Purpose. "You have still to convince us that you mean business."[7] He thanked the Episcopal Commission for expressing in its report to the Convention the mind of the Presbyterian Church "as if we had written it ourselves," when it said, "The Presbyterian Church has always maintained that it is part of the Holy Catholic Church and is unwilling to negotiate on any other basis. To say that the Presbyterian Church in the U.S.A. is part of the Holy Catholic Church is to say that its ministry is a real ministry of the Word and Sacraments, and that its Sacraments are genuine means of grace." He spoke with great admiration of the historic Episcopate and of the lack which it

[7] Address of H.S.C. before 54th Triennial Convention of the Protestant Episcopal Church, Cleveland, Ohio, October 8, 1943, pp. 2-5.

could supply in the Presbyterian system. He rose to the greatest heights, however, when he asked and answered the question, "Why are we interested in Church unity?" His answer was, "First, because we believe with you that it is the will of God, and if it is the will of God we dare not say it is premature. The Christian Church has many sins against its account, but haste in doing the will of God is not one of them. We cannot declare a moratorium on the will of God. We are not interested merely in federation, although I especially honor the Federal Council of Churches of which your Presiding Bishop is now president; but we are concerned with organic union—a united Church in which the ministers shall everywhere be recognized and in which there shall be complete communion so effectual and absolute that, 'We, being many, are one bread and one body; for we are all partakers of that one body.' "[8] He closed his address by quoting an Anglican Archbishop, Robert Leighton, who in the Seventeenth Century had pleaded for the union of Episcopacy and Presbytery (and was rejected equally by the Anglicans in England and the Presbyterians in Scotland). The Archbishop had lamented that "the body of religion is torn, the soul of it expires, and we are fighting over the hem of the garment."[9] The General Convention voted to continue the negotiations.

In 1944 Coffin was Chairman of a Joint Drafting Committee, representing the Commissions of the two Churches, which prepared "A Proposed Basis of Union" and unanimously agreed to submit it to the bodies which it represented. It was drawn up in an atmosphere of the utmost cordiality and good feeling. Its signers appended to their report the statement that "we cannot forbear adding that our meetings together were so harmonious and so heartening that we are persuaded that the Spirit of God was present with us."[10] One of the salient features of the Pro-

[8] *Op. cit.*, p. 7.
[9] *Op. cit.*, p. 9.
[10] Statement of H.S.C. and Alexander C. Zabriskie, January 22, 1945.

posed Basis of Union was that it envisaged three liturgical usages continuing side by side in a United Church: One according to the Episcopal *Book of Common Prayer*, a second according to the forms associated with the Presbyterian *Book of Common Worship*, and a third for congregations which desired to use a combination of both or to make liturgical innovations. Coffin felt that the document was a milestone on the road toward ultimate unity.

During the entire period of the negotiations Coffin devoted a great deal of time to speaking on the subject of the union before gatherings of Presbyterians and Episcopalians and often before community meetings made up of people from both communions. Always he won his hearers by his fervor and delighted them by his forthright answers to embarrassing questions put to him. At one such meeting a very young curate asked, "Dr. Coffin, isn't it true that the educational qualifications for the Episcopal ministry are higher than the Presbyterian and that this union would mean a lowering of the educational standards of the Episcopal Church?" Like a flash came the answer, "Just try to get into the Presbyterian ministry and see," and a sedate church full of people rocked with laughter, unfortunately at the expense of the unhappy curate. Coffin frequently referred to Presbyterian doubts as to Episcopalian willingness to carry the negotiations through to a favorable conclusion. In one meeting he said, "We Presbyterians feel like a woman who has been proposed to several times by the same man, and still doesn't know whether the man wants to marry her." As the differences of opinion within the Episcopal Church became audible outside the bounds of that Church, Coffin sometimes said that the Presbyterians were like a couple who had been invited to dinner by some neighbors. As they approached the house of their prospective hosts, they could hear a violent quarrel going on within its walls, the head of the house shouting at his wife, "I don't see why in thunder you wanted to invite those people anyway." Behind the humor, however, lay a deadly seriousness. His concern for the unity of Christ's church was one of the great passions of his life, and he wore himself out in arduous labor for the cause.

The outcome of the years of toil and negotiation was to Coffin a bitter disappointment. The Presbyterian General Assembly approved the plan of union. In the Episcopal General Convention, however, the proposal was voted down in the House of Deputies. It therefore never came before the House of Bishops. It was now clear that the division in the Episcopal Church over the validity of the Presbyterian ministry was too deep to make possible any further steps toward union with anything approaching unanimity. For all practical purposes the action of the Episcopal General Convention in 1946 marked the end of what had been one of Coffin's great hopes. A few weeks before the 1946 General Convention, Canon Theodore O. Wedel of the Washington Cathedral, one of the most valiant of the Episcopal workers for the union, wrote to Coffin, "I receive evidence in every mail of the storm which the *Basis* has raised in our Church. It illustrates the meaning of the New Testament parable about the leaven. When once the ferment of the Kingdom gets started in three measure of meal, nothing can stop it. Whatever the immediate political outcome in General Convention, a *ferment* has started. God will surely see to it that the leaven does its work." Coffin continued to cherish that faith.

In 1951 Coffin was invited to deliver four lectures on Preaching at the Seabury-Western Theological Seminary, an Episcopal school at Evanston, Illinois. He gave his lectures the title *Communion through Preaching*. Some of his friends in the Protestant Episcopal Church had lamented to him a waning interest in preaching among the younger ministers, accompanied by an increased emphasis upon the Holy Communion and the frequency of its celebration.[11] Beginning with the charge in the Ordination Service in the Episcopal *Book of Common Prayer*, "Be thou a

[11] Scribners, 1952, p. VII.

faithful Dispenser of the Word of God and of His holy Sacraments,"[12] he pointed out that in all Churches which were heirs of the Sixteenth Century Reformation, sermons and sacraments had both been regarded as means of grace and media through which God offered himself in personal fellowship. The main point of the four lectures was a plea for "sacramental sermons—sermons which enable God to have face to face Communion with His people."[13] These lectures stressing the common tradition of emphasis upon the Word and the Sacraments as the marks of a true Church, were attended not only by the Episcopal students of Seabury-Western Seminary, but also by visitors from the seminaries of other denominations around Chicago, and became in themselves an experience in ecumenical worship.

Coffin hailed the organization of the National Council of Churches in 1951 and was deeply moved by the gathering at which it was launched one snowy day in Cleveland. In *Christianity and Crisis*,[14] a journal of which he had been one of the founders ten years before, he wrote that the formation of the new fellowship embracing so much of the inter-denominational activity of the time had given the work of the Churches "a push ahead in our bewildered world." He had been a member of the Executive Committee of the Federal Council of Churches, and from 1945 through 1950 had been Chairman of its Research Department. Now he gave even more enthusiastic allegiance to the larger body of which the old Federal Council had become one of the constituent parts. But he was concerned that the National Council seemed so far removed from the local churches. "We still lack enough things which the churches combine in doing to bring the unity expressed in the National Council down into the hearts and minds of the people," he said. He hoped that the Churches in the Council could pool their educational materials and issue a cur-

[12] *Op. cit.*, p. 1.
[13] *Op. cit.*, p. VIII.
[14] *Christianity and Crisis*, March 19, 1951.

riculum for Church Schools which would bear the name of the National Council rather than that of some particular denomination. He suggested that conferences on preaching and evangelism and missions be planned together by Churches represented in the National Council. He recognized the difficulties, but, he said, "pooling resources, learning the work together, discovering the similarity of our problems and the identity of our faith and hope and love, above all the augmented response to our needs in God who opens Himself to His children in proportion to their community in waiting upon Him, will more than repay the requisite effort and will bring our common leadership into the consciousness of all our churches."

CHAPTER FIFTEEN

CLOSE OF DAY

COFFIN retired from the Presidency of Union Seminary after the Commencement Exercises in May, 1945. He was at the height of his powers and gave no sign of any falling off in capacity for intellectual and spiritual leadership. Some members of the Board of Directors wanted in his case to set aside the regulation making retirement from the faculty mandatory at the age of sixty-eight. Coffin would have none of it, but insisted that the rule which applied to other professors be applied to him also. The approaching end of the academic year saw a series of farewell gatherings at which different groups voiced their affection and gratitude. The faculty came together on May 3 for a Farewell Dinner at the Columbia Faculty Club, and sang

> *"President Coffin, our hats are off to you,*
> *We like your laugh,*
> *We like your chaff,*
> *We like you through and through."*

Friends of the Seminary contributed more than $550,000 to a Henry Sloane Coffin Fund to augment the Seminary's endowment. $175,000 was designated to establish a Henry Sloane Coffin Professorship of Homiletics and $100,000 as the Clarence and Helen Dickinson Endowment for the School of Sacred Music, which had throughout its existence been dependent upon Coffin's annual efforts to raise its budget. On May 15 the Refectory was filled with two hundred and twenty-five friends who had contributed to the Fund and came to a dinner in honor of the man in whose leadership they believed. Coffin told them that in giving money to Union Seminary they had made a good investment. Admiration for Coffin's services as a theological educator, as a pastor, and as an ecumenical churchman was expressed by Dr. Nicholas Murray Butler, President of Columbia University, by Dr. George A. Buttrick, Coffin's successor in the pastorate of the Madison Avenue Presbyterian Church, and by Bishop G. K. A. Bell of Chichester, England, one of the pioneers in the formation of the World Council of Churches. The Board of Directors announced that the Administration Building, which had never had any other name, would henceforth be known as the Henry Sloane Coffin Administration Building. At the Alumni Luncheon on May 16, after glowing tributes by representatives of the reunion classes, Reinhold Niebuhr presented to Coffin a volume of essays, entitled *This Ministry: The Contribution of Henry Sloane Coffin*. The book consisted of ten chapters dealing with various aspects of Coffin's work as minister and educator, written by colleagues and friends. Dr. Willard L. Sperry, Dean of the Harvard Divinity School, in reviewing the book, later made the comment on what the essays revealed: "It is Henry Coffin's distinction to have been able to manifest in his own person during one professional lifetime a diversity of gifts, to have compassed a diversity of operations, to have insisted upon the synoptic view of things, and yet to have won and kept the respect of specialists." At each graduation during Coffin's Presidency, his Farewell Words to the outgoing class had been memorable. This year he included himself among those about to depart, and characteristically based his remarks on a line in the Psalms: "Thou makest the outgoings of the morning and of the evening to rejoice." "Ours," he said, and all knew that he spoke autobiographically, "is a calling in which we share the joy of our Lord."

The Coffins moved to a home in Lakeville, Connecticut, which they had purchased in 1937. At that time they had wanted to find a house where they could spend their summer vacations in less strenuous activities than the mountain-climbing which they had enjoyed in the Adirondacks. They also wanted it to be a place where they could live the year round when the time for retirement came. They had found what they wanted in a commodious Victorian house in Lakeville. It was set back from the road in a wooded section on the outskirts of the village, with an open stretch of lawn and rocky banks where some of the beloved wild flowers from St. Hubert's could be transplanted. Here they had spent seven summers. They named it "Coombe-Pine" after the Coffin ancestral home in Devonshire. The house had been placed on a knoll, with a long, winding flight of steps leading down to the driveway. Visitors, and as usual there was a steady stream of guests who came to enjoy the Coffin hospitality, would hear a shout of welcome from the veranda, would see a white-haired, slender figure come bounding down the stairs, and before they realized what had happened would have their bags seized and carried up to a guest room to the accompaniment of a running fire of inquiries as to their well-being and of jocose comments on whatever cropped up in the conversation. Unexpected callers would often find Coffin in working clothes lovingly tending his flowers. When the time came for retirement from the Seminary, therefore, it did not involve migration to a strange place, but settling in for permanent residence in what had come to be the familiar surroundings of a part-time home.

On November 15, 1945, Coffin had the great pleasure of returning to the Seminary to give the Charge to his successor in the presidency, Henry Pitney Van Dusen, who was being inaugurated. Appropriately he began by addressing the incoming president as "My dear son in the Church of God." He had become acquainted with Van Dusen when the latter was an undergraduate at Princeton University. When Van Dusen entered Union Seminary in

1922, Coffin had enlisted him as one of the student assistants at
the Madison Avenue Presbyterian Church. The first appointment
which Coffin made as president in 1926 was to name Van Dusen
a member of the faculty with the rank of Instructor in the Departments of Systematic Theology and Philosophy of Religion. Later
he had appointed him Dean of Students. He had commended Van
Dusen to his friends on the Faculty of New College, Edinburgh,
when the younger man had taken a leave of absence to study
there for his doctorate, and they had regarded Van Dusen as the
ablest man to come to them from America during their teaching
careers. There was a strong bond, personal and vocational, between the two men, and it was a great satisfaction to Coffin to
turn over his responsibilities for the institution to one in whom
he had such confidence and for whom he cherished such affection.

Stressing the necessity of maintaining the intellectual standards
of the Seminary and its faculty, and of keeping strong the cordial
and confident relations between the institution and the churches
from which its students came, Coffin in his remarks made a final
plea for "the kindling and rekindling here of the fire of piety (to
employ the fine old word of our godly founders).[1] It is easy for
faculty and students to fall into a professional attitude toward
religion. Theology has not always been taught or studied de-
voutly. Thinking and talking *about* God may take the place of life
with Him, of speech *to* Him, of thought *in His presence*. The
things of God must be examined fearlessly. But they disclose
themselves only to humble, reverent and obedient souls." Then,
becoming autobiographical, he went on, "The chapel with its
daily worship, is the most sorely missed part of the Seminary by
those of us who no longer serve here. It has been a place of re-
newal in God, a place where conscience has been searched by His
light, a place where He has spoken with us face to face."[2] A further autobiographical note appeared as he neared the end and

[1] Inaugural Address, p. 3.
[2] *Op. cit.*, pp. 4-5.

pleaded for the maintenance of liberty and harmony in the Seminary which he loved. "In this Seminary, if one may speak from past experience, you will find yourself on the bridge of a ship, frequently careening on stormy seas, and with a crew on board, in students, faculty, alumni, directors, of sharply different opinions. There may seem as much storm inside as outside the ship. Thank God there is here in both Auburn and Union a noble tradition of mutual forbearance, even when feelings run high. It is yours to maintain the glorious heritage of liberty under Christ for all to think and to speak their minds, and yours also to maintain unbroken the fellowship of them all in Christ." Here were the familiar themes of liberty and unity which had been central in his life and utterance through the years.

As might have been expected with so vital a person, retirement for Coffin did not mean idleness. It meant the transfer of his gifted abilities from one field of constructive activity to others. No sooner had he moved to Lakeville than he started writing a new book. The Westminster Press, the publication department of the Presbyterian Church in the U.S.A., had asked him for a book for the guidance of ministers in the conduct of public worship. This he had been unable to undertake in the midst of all the other obligations which crowded into his final months at the Seminary, but he turned out the chapters with astonishing rapidity as soon as he was a Lakeville resident. *The Public Worship of God*[3] was a summary of what he had been teaching his students for over forty years, but it was also his personal testimony to the reality which he had found in the experience of worship. Worship, he said, "is the awed and glad spontaneous response of the spirit of man confronted by the God of Christian revelation—the God of creation and of redemption. This response is itself God-initiated." "We worship for sheer delight. . . . To stand before God, viewing his glory in the face of Jesus Christ, with our faculties raised to their height of acute perception by a company of fellow devotees,

[3] Westminster Press, 1946.

is the acme of bliss—the beatific vision."[4] He wrote particularly
for those in the tradition of the Reformed Churches, although he
refused to attempt too strict a definition of that tradition, pointing
out that it had been a living and growing thing. The liturgical
opinions and standards of Zwingli, Calvin, Knox and their associates deserved careful study, he thought, but it was a mistake to
regard them as finally authoritative. An essential part of the Reformed tradition in worship was its emphasis upon the "overwhelming greatness and mystery" of the Sovereign Father, along
with His graciousness. "If there be one characteristic more than
others that contemporary public worship needs to recapture," he
wrote, "it is this of awe before the surpassingly great and gracious
God."[5] "The contribution of the Reformed tradition is the ideal
of a reverent and orderly freedom in common worship, which
exalts and is dominated and pervaded by the Word of God."[6]
The volume concluded with a plea for Christian unity in worship.[7] Pointing out that differences in forms of public worship
had often been divisive forces, still, he maintained, "it is the universal Church which offers its sacrifice of thanksgiving to God in
every service of public worship. Could this be kept in the thought
of congregations, the act of common worship would become to
them, as it *is*, a symbol of the unity of the Church, a protest against
the divisions which break the spiritual fellowship of its people and
mar their witness to Christ, in whom 'all things hold together'
(Col. 1:17), and an aspiration by God's grace to end them."[8]
The book has been used as a text-book in theological seminaries
and has been a boon to many ministers.

The idea that he might be permitted to settle down to a life of
quiet scholarship in Lakeville was soon proved to be an illusion.
The Presbyterian Board of Foreign Missions asked him to go

[4] *Op. cit.,* pp. 7-9.
[5] *Op. cit.,* p. 17.
[6] *Op. cit.,* p. 185.
[7] *Op. cit.,* p. 180.
[8] *Op. cit.,* pp. 192-193.

around the world on the Joseph Cook Lectureship which had been established in 1901 by a bequest stipulating that the lectures should be given by Christian scholars for the defense of Christianity.[9] When told that he might be an encouragement to Christians who had undergone unspeakable hardships during the War he accepted the appointment, not without misgivings as to whether the chaotic conditions in the countries to be visited might not make it impossible to get a hearing. His apprehensions on that score were unfounded, for he spoke to crowded halls in most of the cities on his itinerary, although the political and economic chaos was in most places greater rather than less than he had anticipated. When Mrs. Coffin and he arrived in the Philippines in September, 1946, they found Manila a wreck from the bombing but the new Republic full of hope. Gratitude to the United States, initially unrestrained, had been tempered by the passage of the "Tydings War Damage Act."[10] This made the payment of an American loan for the rehabilitation of the Islands contingent upon the repeal of a clause in the Filipino Constitution safeguarding local ownership of sixty per cent of the stock of any corporation operating in the Islands and guaranteeing to United States citizens equal rights of "exploitation." Coffin was outspoken both in the Islands and after his return home in denouncing this as "a major blunder in foreign policy as well as a shameful moral lapse."

In China, where he lectured in seven cities, they found a land which after eight years of foreign invasion, was torn by even more destructive civil strife.[11] Two-thirds of the country was controlled by the Kuomintang government while the rest was in the hands of the Communists. Thoughtful Chinese seemed to be utterly frustrated, trusting neither the government nor the Communists. Inflation was ruining everyone who had money. Coffin lectured on the campus of Yenching University, ten miles outside of Pei-

[9] *God Confronts Man in History*, Scribners, 1947, pp. 1-2.
[10] *Op. cit.*, p. 3.
[11] *Op. cit.*, pp. 5-12.

ping and in the Y.M.C.A. within the city. He was flown over hostile lines to Tsinanfu, completely surrounded by Communist forces, and lectured at Chee Loo University, at the Y.M.C.A., and early one Sunday morning spoke to six hundred soldiers at the headquarters of General Wang, the governor of Shantung Province. His message to the soldiers was based on the stories of the centurions in the Gospels and on John the Baptist's counsel to the soldiers in Luke 3:14. In Nanking the Coffins were the guests of the United States Ambassador, Dr. Leighton Stuart, their friend from the days when he had been President of Yenching University. General George Marshall was also staying at the Embassy on a special mission for the United States government. The Coffins found it an exciting experience to watch the two American statesmen attempting to end the civil chaos—trying to persuade Chiang-Kai-shek to clean house in the Kuomintang Party, and trying without success to persuade him and Chou-en-lai, the Communist negotiator, to enter a coalition government. General Marshall presided at Coffin's final lecture in Nanking and gave to the twelve hundred students present a simple, sincere testimony to his belief in the supreme importance of Christian loyalty. In the middle of a lecture in Shanghai, Coffin became faint and had to discontinue speaking. It developed that he was a victim of a form of influenza which was prevalent at the time and his condition was not serious, but the incident created consternation among his friends when it was reported in the New York papers the next day. He had to omit Hua Chung University at Wuchang and Yali at Changsha from his schedule, but was able to fulfil his engagements as the Christmas season approached at Canton. As he met church and student groups in the cities which he visited, Coffin naturally contrasted them with those whom he had known during his previous visit to China thirty years before. There was a striking change, he felt, in the caliber of the men and women filling posts of responsibility. They were no longer under foreign leadership. The missionaries and Western teachers were now colleagues of the Chinese, not superiors. The Chinese Christian leaders were

— living on the most meager resources but were carrying on their work with heroic courage. Coffin left China with his faith in the future of the Church reinforced, feeling that although the political and economic situation seemed desperate, "one cannot despair of China."[12]

In Thailand he was surprised by the extent to which Christmas was celebrated, and was thrilled by the Christmas services in churches and schools, and by Christmas pageants in the streets. The American minister, Mr. Stanton (later raised to the rank of Ambassador) invited some of the parents of young people attending Christian schools to meet him. He found the Thai people charming and was convinced that Christianity should be presented to them through beauty, especially in music, as well as through the intellectual and ethical aspects of the Gospel. He hoped that Thailand could conserve the fruits of its Buddhist culture and let them become richer with the redemptive power and spiritual energy of evangelical Christianity.

Coffin was in India when the British Cabinet announced that it would withdraw from the country by June, 1948.[13] Political, educational and religious leaders whom he met were convinced that bloody strife between Muslim and Hindu could not be avoided. He was in Lahore when the coalition cabinet of the Punjab fell and serious rioting broke out. Everywhere he found intense feeling on the question of racial discrimination in America and elsewhere, of which much had been heard. This was brought to his attention so frequently that he became convinced that racial prejudice in the United States was one of the major obstacles to the advance of the Christian faith. In spite of these burning issues which were raised in speeches whenever the floor was thrown open for questions, he succeeded in giving his lectures in seven cities and spoke to student groups in several other places. Among Muslims especially there was the added complication of

[12] *Op. cit.*, pp. 14-16.
[13] *Op. cit.*, pp. 17-24.

hostility toward the United States which had been engendered
by American advocacy of the immigration of Jewish refugees into
Palestine, Muslims in India strongly taking the side of their Arab
co-religionists in the Middle East. A bright interlude for Coffin
was the privilege of being in Madras when the Anglican Synod
brought five dioceses into the new Church of South India, taking
their places on equal footing with the Congregationalists, Methodists, Presbyterians and members of the Reformed Church. This,
Coffin believed, was "the most significant ecclesiastical development among the heirs of the Reformation since that disintegrating
event."

A brief visit to Egypt,[14] where he lectured at the American
University in Cairo and spoke in a number of churches and
schools, finding again that the Palestine issue was foremost in the
minds of many of his hearers, and then home. It had been a
gruelling journey, with many hazards to health and to personal
safety, heart-warming in the hospitality of missionaries and friends
but sometimes rather grim when makeshift accommodations had
to be endured, disconcerting when plans were interrupted by the
uncertainties of airplanes and weather, but finally accomplished,
leaving grateful groups of listeners around the world. "There is
no more devoted company of men and women than these servants
of the Church far from their homes and on battlefields where the
forces of Christ are at grips with antagonists," he subsequently
wrote. "The impression of the world's present plight is disheart-
ening. But the impression of the Christian Church fills one with
confidence."[15]

After the hectic days and months of travel in a turbulent world,
moving from crisis to crisis, Coffin enjoyed the novel experience of
being a citizen of a quiet New England community. As was to be
expected, he was a good citizen. He found himself surrounded by
interesting neighbors, and there was much coming and going be-

[14] *Op. cit.*, pp. 24-25.
[15] *Op. cit.*, p. 26.

tween their homes and his. When not preaching elsewhere he attended the village churches on Sundays. As a pastor and president he had kept aloof from partisan politics, although never hesitating to express himself on particular issues which became centers of controversy in political campaigns. Now he identified himself with the local Democratic organization. He attended town meetings and took an active part in the discussion of town affairs. He was immensely respected and his views carried great weight. On one occasion a public meeting was being held to discuss some improvements in the village school. There was, as always in such cases, strong opposition on the part of some who felt that the town could not afford any improvements which would necessitate an increase in taxes. When the opposition had been fully expressed Coffin's voice was heard in the rear of the hall, "Mr. Moderator." A silence fell upon the meeting as he walked forward. As he reached the platform, before he began to speak, the assembly burst into applause. Very simply but earnestly he argued that the one thing on which the town could not afford to skimp was the education of its children. An educated citizenry was the foundation of democracy, and the best possible education was a prime essential in an American community. The meeting voted overwhelmingly in favor of the program which Coffin advocated.

"You are a very old man," a Chinese general had said to Coffin when he was in the Far East. "Go home and lie down now." Nothing could have been further from Coffin's mind or more out of character for him. The Presbyterian Church was engaged in raising a large Restoration Fund for the rehabilitation of overseas churches which had suffered damage during the war. With the plight of the churches in Asia fresh in his memory, Coffin threw himself into the campaign to raise the necessary funds, living in sleeping-cars, airplanes and hotels for days on end while on speaking tours in its behalf. He also pleaded for more adequate support of the regular work of the missionaries, pointing out that inflation was eating away the budgets so that it now cost three dollars to do what one dollar had done before. Thousands of dol-

lars which he received in fees and from other sources he sent to
the Bangkok Christian College in Thailand for its building projects. A new electronic organ for that institution was his gift. In
1948 he became President of the Yale-in-China Association. His
calendars for the years 1947 to 1954 reveal a staggering schedule
which would have exhausted a much younger man, as he criss-
crossed the continent speaking at dinners and mass meetings, lecturing and preaching in churches, schools, colleges and theological
seminaries of all denominations. Now he had opportunity to
preach in small churches as well as in the great ones, and to lend
a hand to ministers in struggling parishes, an opportunity which
he especially enjoyed and of which he made full use. In 1948 he
conducted a week of meetings at Beloit College in Wisconsin and
gave the Earl Lectures in Berkeley, California. In 1950 he spent
three days lecturing at Drew Seminary, a Methodist school at
Madison, New Jersey, and a week at the Colgate-Rochester Seminary, Baptist, at Rochester, New York. In 1951 he gave the lectures on *Communion through Preaching* to the Episcopalians at
Seabury-Western Seminary, Evanston, Illinois. In three different
years he gave lecture series at the College for Preachers conducted
by the Episcopal Cathedral in Washington, D.C. In 1952 he delivered the Remsen Bird Lecture at Occidental College in Los An-
geles, California, speaking on "The Spiritual Foundations of
American Democracy." In 1953 he and his wife visited the west
coast of South America. Wherever there were Protestant Churches
—in Colombia, Peru, Chile—he was met by their representatives,
eager to know him and to discuss their problems with him. In
cities like Lima, Peru, and Santiago, Chile, where there were
Union Churches with services in English, his coming had been
heralded and promises secured in advance that he would preach.
In the sense of ceasing to be a preacher and a leader of men, he
never retired.

Even when well past seventy he was enthusiastically received
and heard by schoolboys and schoolgirls, as well as by college men
and women, and the names of Hotchkiss, Exeter, Mt. Hermon,

Williston, Millbrook, Milton, Gunnery, Salisbury, Shipley, Northfield, Dobbs Ferry, Chatham Hall, keep appearing on his list of
engagements along with the colleges and universities where he
was an old friend. Early in January, 1954, he spent three days at
the Groton School in Massachusetts, carrying out a schedule of
talks and conferences which, as the Head Master wrote, "would
give pause to a man in his thirties." He added, "Your final sermon
was in my opinion the finest we have ever heard in the chapel."
Coffin had caused consternation by fainting in the service that
evening, revealing the fact that he was fatigued, but he had recov-
ered his usual vigor after a night's rest. A boy representing the
Upper School wrote to thank him for his talks and added for Coffin's comfort an account of how he himself had once fainted in
church when singing in a boys' choir at the age of ten! The entire
Fifth Form signed a letter which read: "The Fifth Form will remember with deepest gratitude your most beneficial visit to the
school. Not only did you enlighten us with your answers to questions raised in our Sacred Studies class, but also your inspiring
sermons gave us a more vivid understanding of the Christian
faith. We were very glad to hear that you were feeling fine on
Wednesday morning, and hope that the future will bring you
many years of health and happiness."

That was not to be. Immediately after the Groton visit the Coffins flew to Puerto Rico for two months of travel in the Caribbean
Islands. He took advantage of opportunities to swim and to bask
in the sun when they presented themselves. More frequently than
ever before he rested during part of the day. In the Virgin Islands,
Haiti and Jamaica, the trip was in the nature of a holiday. But in
Puerto Rico, the Dominican Republic and Cuba the Presbyterian
Board of National Missions had for fifty years carried on a vigorous and thriving work planting and aiding churches, schools, hospitals and theological seminaries. As a long time member of that
Board, Coffin was keenly interested in these enterprises and their
leaders, many of whom he knew. Word had been sent in advance
by the Board of his coming, and wherever he went he was met,

cordially welcomed, hospitably entertained—and called on to preach, lecture and lead discussions. He enjoyed it all hugely, and was very favorably impressed by what the churches were accomplishing. There were times, however—never when on his feet before a group—when the fatigue showed in the lines on his face and in the added stoop to his shoulders. It was necessary to make some slight changes in a schedule which had been planned for a man of unlimited strength. It may have been when weariness drove home to him the realization that his strength was not unlimited that he had a copy made of George A. Birmingham's verses to his wife. They began:

> "We shall go adventuring, out, away adventuring.
> Not for us the meadowland, the sleek and sleepy kine,
> Not for us the homestead, with drowsy, smoking chimney stacks.
> Ours the singling breeze and the spindrift from the brine."

They concluded:

> "End of our adventuring? Is there any end to it?
> We are but beginning when upon us comes the night.
> We shall lift our hearts up bravely, oh, beloved one,
> To meet the great adventure in the country out of sight."

He met that great adventure on November 25, 1954. He had spoken at Amherst College where a group of undergraduates had asked him to talk with them about the ministry. Some sixty or seventy of them had gathered for dinner with him on Wednesday, November 17, and after his presentation they had put questions to him until a late hour. He was ill through the night afterwards and cancelled an engagement to go to New Haven the next day. However, after a brief rest at Lakeville he felt better and insisted on being driven down to Yale after all. He had promised to speak at a service in memory of Robert D. French who had been the Master of Jonathan Edwards College until his death which had occurred not long before. Coffin had been an Associate Fellow of the College and had always stayed as a guest in the Master's House on his trips to New Haven for meetings of the Yale Corporation.

In the midst of his tribute to his friend, for whom he had great admiration and affection, he had a heart attack. He concealed it as best he could but was compelled to curtail his speech and sit down. He was taken to his Lakeville home, where he lingered for a week. "Rest, perturbed spirit" he said to a busy nurse who was over-solicitous for his comfort. He died in his sleep on the morning of Thanksgiving Day.

"It is not hard to be a pioneer if one is without responsibility for a company of others," he had said to a graduating class at Union Seminary in 1931.[16] "Nor is it difficult to be a churchman if one settles into the grooves of existing situations. But to be both on the frontier in thought and life, in work and faith, and maintain the confidence and sympathy of a group, so that one can share one's heart and mind with them—that is another matter. That is our task. To lead one must both be in advance of his company and carrying them with him. This requires a combination of courage and tact, of boldness and understanding, of devotion to the Most High and devotion to the most lowly—sometimes cranky, sometimes absurd—among His sons and daughters." Then he had unconsciously summed up his own ministry in the stirring conclusion which he threw out to his younger brethren: "Be frontiersmen, be churchmen, be companions of Christ. And of the three the last is the only one you need bear in mind. Be sure that the frontier where you take your stand is His frontier—a spot where you must be to share His conscience, His purpose, His faith. Be sure that the Church to which you are loyal is His Church, and that your loyalty is not some self-protective loyalty, but His devotion to God's children. Keep in His company. So shall it be yours to move forward the boundaries of God's Kingdom, to add to the heritage of His Church, and

> At the end of your day
> As faithful shepherds to come
> Bringing your sheep in your hand."

[16] *Union Seminary Alumni Bulletin,* June, 1931, pp. 155-156.

INDEX

271